Dictionary of International Economics Terms

Series Editor: John O E Clark

LES50NS
PROFESSIONAL
PUBLISHING

LES50NS PROFESSIONAL PUBLISHING Limited
A Division of LES50NS (PUBLISHING) Limited
Fitzroy House
11 Chenies Street
London WC1E 7EY
United Kingdom

Email: info@fiftylessons.com

Typeset by Kevin O'Connor

Printed by Loupe Solutions

ISBN 0-85297-685-2

Preface

This book is intended to provide access to the terms of general
economics for students and professionals in the growing world of
international finance, and especially its interaction with banking and the
stock exchange. It should also assist private investors and people who
read financial journals and the financial pages of daily newspapers. Like
its companion volumes it does not limit itself merely to well-established
terms. It also includes definitions of the everyday jargon, acronyms and
newly adopted words (many from the United States) that are now
common in national and international financial dealings.

The Dictionary of International Economics Terms is one of a series of
publications compiled from Lessons Financial Publishing's unique
database of dictionary definitions that relate to various aspects of
finance and their applications. As a result, some definitions appear in
more than one book – as they should to maintain a comprehensive
coverage of the subject within a single self-contained volume. The
dictionaries in the series published **to date** include:

Dictionary of International Accounting Terms
0-85297-575-9
Dictionary of International Banking and Finance Terms
0-85297-632-1
Dictionary of International Business Terms
0-85297-574-0
Dictionary of International Insurance and Finance Terms
0-85297-631-3
Dictionary of International Investment and Finance Terms
0-85297-577-5
Dictionary of International Trade Finance
0-85297-576-7

John O E Clark

John O E Clark is a writer and editor who regularly contributes to dictionaries, encyclopedias and other types of information books for publication in Britain and abroad. He specializes in explaining technical subjects to students and other non-experts, and to people whose first language is not necessarily English.

A

ability-to-pay taxation A theory of taxation whereby those who are able to pay more are taxed at a higher rate. Ability-to-pay taxation may be applied to luxury goods, which thereby attract a high rate of tax.

above normal profit Also called excess profit, a profit that is in somebody's opinion larger than normal. Impossible to quantify absolutely, it is usually cited with respect to past profits, or the rate of return in comparable industries that involve a similar risk.

absenteeism Absence from work for no valid reason.

absolute advantage An argument in favour of international trade, put forward by Adam Smith (1723-90). Absolute advantage applies where, for example, two countries can both produce two commodities they need, but country A is more efficient at producing commodity X and country B is more efficient at producing commodity Y. They would therefore both profit by concentrating on the particular commodity each produces best, and trading them.

absolute purchasing power parity The theory that the currency exchange rate between two countries equalizes the price of a basket of goods in the two countries. But as the composition of the goods and the price indices can vary substantially and because some goods may not be traded or are subject to tariffs, it is unlikely that the theory will apply in reality.

absorption The use of absorption rates to allocate a company's overhead to its production. It is a method used in absorption costing, in which a product is assigned a fixed manufacturing overhead as well as material and labour costs as a product cost to the units being produced.

ACAS Abbreviation of *Advisory, Conciliation and Arbitration Service.*

accelerated depreciation The practice of depreciating an asset at a rate greater than the actual decline in its value in order to obtain tax concessions. It need not occur throughout the life of an asset; a substantial proportion of its total value is often written off in the first year, and reduced allowances for depreciation are made thereafter.

accelerated tariff elimination The speeding up of the reduction in tariffs, usually resulting from trade agreements between nations. The total elimination of tariffs results in a free-trade situation.

accelerator coefficient A factor that indicates how a change in output affects investment, which depends on such things as the price of labour, the amount of spare capacity (if any), and the rate of interest.

accelerator model *See accelerator principle.*

accelerator-multiplier model Also called multiplier-accelerator model, a model that uses the interaction of the accelerator (which increases investment when output increases) and the multiplier (which increases output when investment increases) to deduce economic variations. It can predict a series of alternating booms and slumps, creating the normal *trade cycle.*

accelerator principle The theory that growth in production is directly related to the level of investment. If consumer demand increases, for example, a company is likely to invest in more equipment, thereby accelerating the current economic growth.

acceptance A written irrevocable promise to pay, thus equivalent to a *promissory note.* A bank-endorsed bill of exchange, for example, is guaranteed.

acceptance credit A type of short-term borrowing for companies (generally for work capital).

accepting house Also known as an accepting bank or, in the USA, as an acceptance house, a financial institution whose business is concerned mainly with negotiation of exchange, by either guaranteeing them or accepting them. It usually operates in much the same way as a commercial bank.

accommodating transactions In international trade, below-the-line items employed to offset any imbalances (such as those caused by a country's trade deficit).

account (a/c, acc or acct.) In general terms, any note kept of a financial transaction, often also referred to as *accounts.* There are two more specific meanings: 1. In banking, it designates an arrangement made to deposit money with a bank, building society or other financial institution. There are various types of such accounts, with different conditions of withdrawal, rates of interest, minimum deposits, and so on. 2. On the London Stock Exchange, it is a period of two weeks (usually extended to three weeks when bank holidays occur) in which trading is carried out. Broadly, transactions are made in the two weeks of the account and the relevant paperwork is carried out during the following week, followed by payments (settlements) made on the sixth business day after the end of the account. This method of working allows transactions to be made with deferred payment, enabling speculation to take place.

account day The Monday ten days or six business days after the end of each stock exchange *account*, on which all settlements must be made. It is also known as settlement date or day.

accounting period The time for which accounts are prepared, such as a year for a company's financial accounts or a month for internal management accounts.

accounting rate of return (ARR) The anticipated net profit from an investment, calculated as a percentage of the amount invested.

accounts payable The accounts on which a company owes money and for which it has been invoiced. They are also sometimes referred to as trade creditors and are a *current liability* on the balance sheet.

accounts receivable The accounts on which money is owed to a company and for which it has issued invoices. They are also sometimes referred to as trade debtors and are a *current asset* on the balance sheet.

accrual A gradual increase in something by addition over a period of time (and not resulting from a specific transaction). For example, an accrued charge or liability is a charge that has not been accounted for or paid, such as a demand for rent made in arrears which must appear on the accounts as an accrued charge, because the service had already been used but not paid for.

ACT Abbreviation of *Advance Corporation Tax*.

active labour-market policy A method of reducing unemployment (by increasing the prospects of employment) without causing demands for increased wages. As opposed to passively paying unemployment benefit, it actively pursues such measures as job creation, subsidies, job training and offering employment in the public sector.

activity rate Also called participation rate, a fraction found by dividing the actual number of workers in a particular group by the total population of that group.

ACTPN Abbreviation of *Advisory Committee on Trade Policy and Negotiations.*

actual gross national product A country's current real level of output, which depends on the way that *aggregate demand* interacts with *potential gross national product.*

actuary A statistician employed by an insurance company to calculate the likelihood of risk and advise insurers on the amount of premium to be charged for each type of risk and how much to set aside to cover it.

adaptive expectations The principle that the future value (expectation) of a variable such as inflation can be determined by its recent value and trend (up or down).

adjustable peg A system that allows exchange rates to vary between certain narrowly defined limits.

adjustment cost The expense of changing economic variables under one's control (such as production output, staffing and prices).

adjustment mechanism A way of adjusting the balance of payments to bring it back into equilibrium by altering internal incomes and prices, altering external prices, or altering any restrictions to foreign exchange and trade.

adjustment programme A programme of measures to solve problems with the balance of payments, including such things as increasing taxes, reducing government spending, increasing production and, *in extremis,* devaluation.

adjustment speed The speed with which markets change as a result of changes in economic factors (such as the effect of excess demand or supply in commodity markets and money markets).

administered price A price set and partly controlled by the seller, based on his or her knowledge of the costs of production and estimates of demand and competition. An administered price lies between monopoly and free market prices, and characterizes a state of imperfect competition.

administration Broadly, the sum of actions involved in the organization or management of a company. In law, however, it is either the winding-up of the estate of a deceased person in the absence of an executor or in the event of intestacy, or it is the *winding-up* of a company. Both cases involve the court appointment of somebody to act as administrator.

ad valorem tax A tax that is calculated as a percentage of the value of the transaction it applies to, rather than charged at a fixed rate. For example, value-added tax (VAT) is paid as a percentage of the price of the goods or services sold, whereas car road tax in the UK is mainly paid at a fixed rate.

advance A part-payment for goods or services made ahead of total payment and usually before the goods or services are made available.

Advance Corporation Tax (ACT) In the UK, corporation tax is levied in two parts. The first part is levied on the distribution of profits and is known as advance corporation tax. The second half of the tax is estimated on the company's earnings. *See also* **Corporation Tax**.

adverse selection The likelihood that poorer-quality dealers will outnumber good ones in a market because of the difficulty, in a trade, for one dealer to assess the quality of the other.

advertising A range of activities that surround the practice of informing the public of the existence and desirability of a product. The main purpose of advertising is to boost sales or, in the case of charities and national bodies, to provide information or solicit contributions.

Advertising Standards Authority (ASA) A UK organization that regulates advertising, making sure that advertisements are even-handed, truthful and unambiguous.

Advisory Committee on Trade Policy and Negotiations (ACTPN) A committee appointed by the US president to advise on trade policy and related matters, such as trade agreements.

Advisory, Conciliation and Arbitration Service (ACAS) An organization established in the UK in 1975 to prevent or settle industrial disputes. It is an independent body used by companies, individual people and trade unions.

after-sales service Acts performed by a manufacturer or supplier after the goods have been sold, such as repair, maintenance work or perhaps training. After-sales service packages are frequently put together as inducements to buy, especially in the sale of branded capital goods.

after-tax income A person's or company's income that remains after the payment of direct taxes.

after-tax profit The profit calculated after all tax deductions have been made.

age-earnings profile A graph that shows how workers' average earnings vary with age.

agency cost The expense of employing an *agent* rather than doing the job for yourself.

agent A person or company that has entered into an agreement with another party and acts as its representative, usually in buying and selling goods and services. Legally, an agency is a contractual arrangement by which one party agrees to represent another, the agent's word becoming binding in the affairs of the other as if the latter had acted on his or her own behalf.

agglomeration economy An economy that can arise in large centres of population where there is much economic activity, in fact it is one factor in the formation of such population centres. Markets are larger, choice is wider and specialist facilities are available.

aggregate demand In any economy, the total level of demand (ie, consumer spending, company investment spending, government spending and net foreign revenue).

aggregate demand schedule A graph of total domestic spending (*aggregate demand*) versus national income (**gross domestic product**).

aggregate rebate A method of calculating *discounts* in terms of a customer's total purchases over a period of time rather than in terms of individual orders (to encourage buyer loyalty).

aggregate supply In any economy, the total amount of domestic goods (ie, consumer products and capital goods) and services supplied by businesses and the state.

aggregate supply schedule A graph of total amount of domestic goods and services supplied (*aggregate supply*) versus total expenditure.

AGM Abbreviation of *annual general meeting*.

Agricultural Adjustment Act 1933 US legislation that helped to maintain farm incomes by giving price support for agricultural products.

Agricultural Marketing Service (AMS) A service that the US Department of Agriculture provides by guaranteeing contract specifications of products exported to overseas buyers.

agricultural policy A policy designed to support the agriculture industry by means of subsidies (for farm incomes and prices) and encouraging farms to consolidate and mechanize.

agricultural protection A method of raising farmers' incomes by imposing tariffs and trade controls to increase farm prices.

aid *See foreign aid.*

aids to trade Various activities (often services) that assist other businesses, such as advertising, banking, insurance and transport.

AIM Abbreviation of *Alternative Investment Market.*

allocative efficiency A principle that, in a given market, a consumer's welfare is at a maximum when market prices equal the minimum real resource cost of supply (while allowing the supplier a normal profit). It has implications in the allocation of scare resources for the best interests of consumers.

alpha A broad stock exchange categorization of the most actively traded shares with a large capitalization value.

Alternative Investment Market (AIM) A replacement for the UK's Unlisted Securities Market, which closed at the end of 1996, aimed at helping smaller companies to raise capital.

American Stock Exchange (AMEX) One of New York's two stock exchanges, which deals mainly in the shares of younger and smaller companies. It is also known as the Little Board or the Curb Exchange. Larger companies are listed on the *New York Stock Exchange.*

AMEX Abbreviation of *American Stock Exchange.*

AMH Abbreviation of *automatic materials handling.*

amortization The spreading of the cost of a fixed asset over a period of time, rather than writing the total cost into the profit and loss account when it is first bought. Debt repayment can also be amortized in this way. The term is sometimes used to mean *depreciation* in the USA.

AMS Abbreviation of *Agricultural Marketing Service.*

analysis of variance (ANOVA) A breakdown of the variance in a company's total profit into fractions assigned to various activities or departments. It attempts to determine why actual profit differed from budgeted profit.

Andean Pact A free-trade customs union formed between Bolivia, Chile, Colombia, Ecuador and Peru at Cartagena in 1969; Venezuela joined in 1973 (and Chile left in 1976). A common external tariff was established in 1994 and the member states committed to the formation of a Economic Community (similar to the EU) by 2001.

announcement effect The principle that a policy change (such as a future tax reduction) has an effect as soon as it is announced and even before it is implemented.

annual general meeting (AGM) A shareholders' meeting, required by law to be held yearly by every public company. An AGM is normally used to discuss the annual report and accounts, to announce dividends and to elect auditors and directors. This is often the only opportunity that shareholders have to air their views.

annualized percentage rate (APR) Also known as annual percentage rate, the rate of interest charged on a monthly basis (eg for credit) shown as a yearly compound rate (*see compound interest*).

annual report A document required under company law to be released every year by public companies, describing the company's activities during the previous year. It usually includes the company's balance sheet for that year, and may be combined with the annual accounts as the annual report and accounts.

annuity A contract whereby a person pays a certain amount of money to an insurance company, either as a lump sum or in instalments, and receives in return periodic payments for life or a specified period.

ANOVA Abbreviation of *analysis of variance.*

anticipated inflation The expected rate of inflation, which affects current prices, wage demands and decisions whether or not to save.

anticompetitive practice Any practice that restricts competition, often illegal under the terms of the UK *Competition Act 1980.*

anti-dumping duty A tariff designed to protect domestic producers against the *dumping* of imports (and the unfair competition it causes).

antitrust laws US legislation that was enacted to prevent the formation of monopolies. It is similar to the *Monopolies and Mergers Act 1965* in the UK.

APC Abbreviation of *average propensity to consume.*

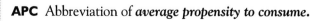

APM Abbreviation of *average propensity to import.*

applied economics The use of economic theory in the analysis of real situations, such as the development of an economic policy.

appreciation An increase in the value of an asset resulting from a rise in market price (often due to inflation).

appropriation In general, the putting aside of funds for a special purpose. In company accounting, it is the division of pre-tax profits between corporation tax, company reserves and dividends to shareholders (*see also* next entry). In another application, if a debtor makes a payment to a creditor and does not specify which debt the payment is in settlement of, the creditor may appropriate it to any of the debts outstanding on the debtor's account. This latter procedure is often known as appropriation of payments. In the USA, appropriation also describes an authorization to spend up to a certain amount.

appropriation account An account that shows a company's net profits (current and carried forward) and how they are split between dividends and reserves. In the USA, it may be an account set aside to accommodate funds that have been authorized for a particular purpose.

APR Abbreviation of *annualized percentage rate.*

a priori Determined by deductive reason alone (from first principles) rather form empirical evidence to hand.

APS Abbreviation of *average propensity to save.*

APT Abbreviation of *average propensity to tax.*

arbitrage The practice of dealing on two markets almost simultaneously in order to profit from differing prices or exchange rates. Arbitrage may take place when dealing in commodities, bills of exchange or currencies. It also occurs in situations in which prices and returns are fixed and in this sense arbitrage may be contrasted with speculation, in that there is little risk involved.

arbitrager (or arbitrageur) A person who practises *arbitrage*. In the USA, the term is sometimes shortened to arb.

arbitration In disputes arising out of a contract, the parties involved may either go to court or appoint somebody (an arbitrator) to settle the dispute. The agreement to go to arbitration does not preclude either of the parties taking legal proceedings if it desires.

A

arc elasticity The proportional change in one variable divided by the proportional change in another over the same discrete range (along an arc on a graph), as frequently applied to changes in price and demand and other pairs of related economic factors. *See also* **point elasticity**.

arithmetic mean An average; the total of a series of values divided by the number of values.

arithmetic progression A numerical series in which consecutive terms have a common difference. If the nth term of such a progression is given by $[a + (n - 1)d]$, the sum of n terms is $n[2a + (n - 1)d]/2$ (where a is the first term and d is the common difference).

ARR Abbreviation of *accounting rate of return* and *average rate of return*.

Arrow's impossibility theorem In a multi-person economy under majority voting, there does not *have* to exist a situation in which equilibrium occurs (although it might).

ASA Abbreviation of *Advertising Standards Authority.*

A-share A share with rights that are different from those legally attached to ordinary shares. There are also B shares, C shares, and so on. The term is frequently used for a *non-voting share.*

assembly line A method of manufacture in which components or sub-assemblies are joined to make the final product. Generally the workers remain in one place, repeatedly performing the same tasks, alongside a moving conveyor belt.

assessable profit That part of a company's profit that is taxable (after allowable deductions).

asset Something that belongs to a person or company and which has value, an economic resource (for example buildings, plant, stock and accounts receivable). There are several types of assets for business purposes, and they are usually classified in terms of their availability for exchange. Examples include *tangible* and *intangible assets*, and long-term (US long-lived or noncurrent) and short-term (or current) assets.

asset-growth maximization In the *theory of the firm*, an alterative to profit maximization, often favoured by company executives whose salaries are based on the growth rate of assets and as a discouragement to possible takeover bidders.

asset motive A reason for storing value in the form of money, a sensible policy only in a situation of falling prices.

asset specificity The property of a (fixed) asset that has little or no other use (such as an oil refinery) and results in a *sunk cost*.

asset-stripping The practice (which is normally frowned upon) whereby a company is bought merely so that the buyer may sell off its assets for immediate gain. It is also known colloquially as unbundling.

asset value The value of a company's assets less its liabilities. It is often divided by the number of issued ordinary shares and expressed as the asset value per share, theoretically payable to shareholders if the company were to be wound up. In economics, asset-value theory predicts that speculation (in currency) can cause fluctuations in exchange rates

associated company Also termed an associate company, a company that is partly owned by another, which has a stake of more than 10% but less than 50%.

asymmetric information Data about a (potential) transaction that is not shared equally between the two parties, a factor to be taken into account when they come to decide on their respective strategies.

atomistic competition A market in which *perfect competition* can safely be assumed because there are so many buyers and sellers.

auction A method of selling goods, property or land in public. The auctioneer acts as an agent for the seller, offers the goods and normally sells to the highest bidder (for which service the auctioneer charges a commission). After the item is knocked down, the auctioneer is also an agent of the buyer. An advertisement for an auction is not legally an offer for sale but an invitation to attend.

auction system An order-driven stock exchange system in which brokers and dealers bid for stock using open outcry (or an auction), as on the New York Stock Exchange.

audit A formal examination of a company's accounts. It is a legal requirement in the UK that the accounts of limited companies over a certain size (and certain other organizations) be scrutinized annually by an independent auditor. This is termed a statutory audit, from which small companies (with a turnover of not more than £90,000 and not more than £1.4 million on the balance sheet) are exempt.

auditor A person appointed by a company or other organization to carry out an *audit*. In the UK, in order to act as an external auditor he or she must be registered or a member of a recognized supervisory body.

Austrian school A group of 19th-century economists based at the University of Vienna under Carl Menger (1840-1921). They became known for the development of the *marginal utility* theory of value, which proposed that the value of a good comes from its utility rather than its cost.

autarky A self-contained economy, with little or no external trade resulting from the imposition of exchange controls, quotas and tariffs.

authorized capital The amount of a company's capital, as stated in its memorandum of association. It is thus the limit of what the company can issue as shares.

autocorrelation Also called serial correlation, a correlation between successive values of a single variable (as opposed to a correlation between two different variables).

automatic materials handling (AMH) A computerized system designed to move materials and components from one location to another in a warehouse or factory.

automatic stabilizer Also called a built-in stabilizer, a factor of monetary policy that automatically reduces the effects of variations in economic activity. For example, increasing unemployment leads to a need for increased benefit payments and a reduction in the government's receipts from taxation. This in turn increases the budget deficit which then replaces some of the lost income.

automation A repetitive production process that uses usually computer-controlled electrical or mechanical machines ('robots'), with no human contribution.

autonomous consumption The part of *consumption* that does not vary with changes in income. It is the lowest consumption commensurable with a basic standard of living and therefore exists even for people with no income.

autonomous investment The part of *investment* that does not vary with changes in output, such as government-determined investment in public services and the infrastructure.

average *See arithmetic mean; geometric mean; median; mode.*

average cost For a unit of output, the total costs (fixed and variable) divided by the number of units produced.

average cost pricing The determination of a selling price in accordance with the *average cost* of producing a good. The manufacturer makes neither a profit nor a loss.

average physical product In the short-run theory of supply, the total amount of output divided by the number of units of input employed. It is thus the average output produced by each extra unit of input.

average propensity to consume (APC) A fraction given by total consumption (on goods and services but not investment) divided by national income. The sum of the average propensity to consume and the *average propensity to save* is 1.

average propensity to import (APM) A fraction given by the value of imports divided by national income.

average propensity to save (APS) A fraction given by the value of savings (including investment) divided by national income. The sum of the average propensity to save and the *average propensity to consume* is 1.

average propensity to tax (APT) A fraction given by the amount paid in taxes divided by national income.

average rate of return (ARR) The average annual profit (on an investment) expressed as a percentage of the sum invested. It is equal to 100 times the profit per annum divided by the capital outlay.

average rate of taxation The total amount of tax a person pays in a year as a fraction of his or her annual taxable income.

average revenue For a production company, the total amount of money received divided by the number of units of product sold.

average revenue product For a production company, the total amount of money received from using a given amount of input to produce and sell a product divided by the number of units produced.

Averch-Johnson effect For a company whose rate of return is regulated, a tendency to accumulate excessive capital to increase the amount of profit (the limited rate of return being applied to a larger capital base).

avoidable cost A cost that does not have to be met if an alternative course of action is taken. For example, if production of an item ceases, its associated material and labour costs are avoided.

B

back door The system by which the Bank of England purchases Treasury bills at the market rate, rather than assist discount houses by lending cash to them directly, in order to inject funds into the money market.

back-to-back credit A form of credit by which a finance house acts as an intermediary between a foreign seller and a foreign buyer, concealing the identity of the seller. The seller passes to the finance house the documents relevant to the sale and the house reissues them to the buyer in its own name.

back-to-back loan A loan in one currency matched by another loan in another currency, usually to get round exchange controls or high interest rates.

backwardation In a commodity market, the situation in which the future price is lower than the spot price, because of excessive present demand, which is expected to fall with the passage of time. It is opposite, in commodity terms, to *contango*. In stock markets, backwardation is the situation in which the highest bid price is higher than the lowest offer price, making it theoretically possible to buy from one market-maker and sell to another immediately, at a profit.

backward-bending supply curve An anomalous *supply curve* which shows that the amount of a good supplied decreases as the price rises.

backward integration The amalgamation of a company that operates at one stage of production with another that is located farther back in the chain. For example, it occurs when a manufacturing company amalgamates with a company that provides raw materials.

bad debt A debt that has not been, and is not expected to be, paid. Such losses are practically unavoidable in business (and allowances are almost always made for such instances), although some bad debts may be sold to a factoring company, which attempts to recover the debt on its own account.

balanced budget A situation in which a government's expenditure exactly equals its receipts, not necessarily desirable in a varying economy.

B

balanced budget multiplier A rise in the amount a government spends on goods and services accompanied by a similar rise in taxes (thus leaving a budget deficit or surplus unaffected) increases the national product by the amount of spend. This theory of Keynesian economics rarely applies in practice.

balanced growth The situation in an economy whose sectors all grow proportionately at the same rate (eg national income grows at the same rate as consumption, employment and investment), a rare (and not necessarily desirable) occurrence. *See also* **steady-state growth.**

balance of payments (BOP) An account of all recorded financial exchanges made between the residents of a country and those of other countries. The balance of payments is divided into the current and capital accounts. The current account takes stock of all visible and invisible trade (the *balance of trade* is part of the balance of payments current account), and the capital account includes all movements of capital in or out of the country.

balance-of-payments crisis A situation in which the balance of payments cannot be sustained (eg because of a rapid decline in foreign exchange reserves), often leading to a domestic recession or devaluation and the imposition of tariffs, quotas and exchange controls.

balance-of-payments equilibrium The situation of a country whose overseas investments and spending do not exceed the amount other countries invest and spend in the home market. In the long term, the country's international reserves remain static.

balance of trade (BOT) Also known as the visible balance, the difference in value between a country's visible imports and visible exports. When the value of visible imports total is more than the value of visible exports, it is known as an adverse balance of trade. *See **balance of payments.***

balance sheet A statement that shows the financial position of a company in respect of its assets and liabilities at a certain time, often the last day of its accounting period, which must be included in the company's financial accounts. It must also give a true and fair view of the company's affairs. After listing the fixed and current assets, and the liabilities (part 1), the statement indicates how they were financed (part 2). The totals of parts 1 and 2 should be equal – they must balance. The balance sheet should also show the corresponding figures

B

for the previous accounting period. In the USA, a balance sheet is sometimes known as a statement of financial condition or position.

balancing figure Also called a balancing item, a figure included (in an account) in order to make two totals equal.

bank An organization that carries on the business of banking and is so authorized by the *central bank* (in the UK the Bank of England).

bank deposit Money paid into a bank account, usually either a sight deposit in a current account or a time deposit in a deposit account (often with a commercial bank or savings bank).

bank-deposit creation The way that the activity of commercial banks leads to new bank deposits. Of the money deposited with a bank, some is retained and some invested or used to make loans. The loans become new deposits elsewhere, and so on. It is also called credit creation.

banker's draft Also called a bank draft, a cheque drawn on a bank by itself. A banker's draft must be honoured, because it is drawn on the bank itself rather than on the debtor's account. The debtor must pay the bank the sum drawn in advance.

Bank for International Settlements (BIS) An international bank that acts as agent and trustee for various international organizations. It is also a clearing house for interbank transactions using European currency. The Bank of England is the agent of BIS in London. BIS was originally established in Basle, Switzerland, for dealing with German war reparations after World War I.

Banking Acts 1979, 1987 Acts of Parliament that define banks (as takers of deposits), authorize their supervision (by the Bank of England) and specify their minimum paid-up capital reserves (£1 million).

Banking Directives Directives of the EU that are aimed at streamlining banking practice across European borders. For example, the Second Directive of 1989 allows banks to operate in any country as long as they are authorized in their own. In 1993 this facility was extended to companies dealing in investment products.

bank loan A loan made by a bank for specified term and at a specified rate of interest, usually against some form of security. It is also called a bank advance. *See also* **personal loan**.

B

bank multiplier The reciprocal of the *reserve asset ratio*; eg, if the reserve asset ratio is 12½%, the bank multiplier is 8.

banknote A piece of paper currency produced by a bank of issue that carries a promise to pay the bearer on demand the sum specified on the note. Often called simply a note, it is also known as a *bill* in the USA.

Bank of England The central bank of the UK. Founded in 1694, it now has various functions including the supervision of other banks, managing monetary policy, and acting as a banker's bank and lender of the last resort. It also issues banknotes in the UK.

bank rate The official rate of interest charged by the central banks as lender of the last resort. The term has fallen out of use in the UK, to be replaced by *minimum lending rate*.

bankruptcy The state of an individual or unincorporated body that is unable to pay debts, as determined by the court. A similar situation involving a limited company is termed *insolvency*.

bargaining The act of negotiating a price or other terms.

barrier to entry An economic or other condition that makes it difficult to set up a business, ie for a newcomer to enter the market. Such barriers include existing monopolies, the threat of price wars and overcomplicated licensing systems.

barrier to exit An economic or other condition that makes it difficult to leave a market. Such barriers include the difficulty of capitalizing assets (perhaps because they are one-use or because they have little second-hand value) and the difficulty of selling products elsewhere.

barter A way of obtaining goods or services without using money, by exchanging them for other goods or services. It obviously limits the possibilities of trade, which is why money was introduced and continues to be the principal means of exchange.

base currency A currency that forms the basis of an exchange rate. For example, a foreign currency may be quoted in terms of the pound sterling or the US dollar, which are base currencies.

baseline Assuming existing economic policies and trends continue unaltered, a projection of how the economy is expected to develop. This is then used to investigate the likely result of changes in specific aspects of the economy.

B

base period A time period selected as the base for an index number series. The index for a base period is usually 100, and changes in prior or subsequent periods are expressed relative to it.

base rate The minimum amount of interest a bank charges on a loan. The base rate is normally augmented in actual circumstances, according to current market pressures and the risk involved in the loan.

base year Sometimes known as the base date, the time from which an index (eg, the Financial Times All Share Index) is calculated.

basing point price system A method of pricing which charges different prices to customers in different places, those located near the base point (source of supply) paying less than those farther away. It is used mainly for bulky products that are expensive to transport.

basis point A unit used to measure the rate of change of interest rates or investment payments for bonds or notes. Each basis point is equal to 0.01 per cent.

batch production The use of labour-intensive methods to produce small quantities of a (often non-standard) product at the same time.

Baumol effect An effect identified by W. Baumol in 1967, that as an economy develops some services become relatively dearer whereas some manufactured goods become relatively cheaper—mechanization and new technology increase productivity in the manufacturing industries.

Bayesian statistics A statistical system that takes into account how we update previously held 'beliefs' as a result of experience. It assumes that we regularly revise beliefs about measurable quantities using a weighted average of the previous belief and the most recent result.

Baye's theorem A method of finding the probability of a previous unknown event from knowledge of a later related event, of dubious validity to some statisticians. It was formulated in 1763 by the British mathematician Thomas Baye.

BEA Abbreviation of *Bureau of Economic Analysis.*

bear A stock exchange dealer or analyst who believes that prices or investment values will go down.

B

bearer Somebody who holds a bill, cheque or certificate.

bearer bill Also called a bearer note, a bill of exchange, cheque or other negotiable instrument that is payable to the bearer (or is endorsed in blank).

bearer bond A bond that is payable to the bearer, rather than to a specific, named person.

bear market A market situation in which share prices are falling.

before-tax income A person's or company's income before deduction of direct taxes.

beggar-my-neighbour policy An economic policy based on self-interest that seeks to benefit one country at the expense of others. For example, depression and unemployment at home can be tackled by shifting demand away from imports to home-produced goods by means of tariffs, import quotas and possibly devaluation.

behavioural assumption The aspects of human behaviour included in an economic theory, such as the belief that suppliers inevitably react to previous market prices or that all entrepreneurs seek the maximum profit.

behavioural theory of the firm The theory that the behaviour of a firm depends on the objectives of the people within it, rather than the usual theory based solely on a profit motive. For example, managerial ambition may lead to a desire to maximize turnover (not profit) or complacency may make managers reluctant to introduce change when change is needed.

below-the-line Describing items, included in a company's accounts, that refer to the distribution of profits (and financing of losses). For example, dividends are included in below-the-line accounts. Capital account transactions in national accounts are also described as below-the-line.

benefit principle The idea that people who benefit from public expenditure should pay for it (as opposed to taking into account the ability to pay).

benefit-in-kind income A benefit that an employee receives instead of or in addition to wages. Examples include company cars, mobile telephones and medical insurance. Most of such benefits can be assigned a value and therefore be assessed for income tax.

B

benefits-received principle of taxation A theory of taxation by which taxes to cover public services are paid by those who use them, rather than by the general public at large.

Benelux A customs union formed in 1948 by Belgium, the Netherlands and Luxembourg. It joined the European Economic Community (now the EU) on its foundation in 1958.

Bernoulli's hypothesis An idea proposed by Swiss mathematician Daniel Bernoulli (1700-82) that deciding to accept a risk depends on utility as well as money—risking your last pound on a long shot is unattractive if you have nothing to eat.

Bertrand competition A form of competition between two firms in a *duopoly* in which each assumes the other will not change prices (ie they behave as if there were perfect competition). The eventual result is usually drastic price competition.

beta factor Also called the beta coefficient, a measurement of the volatility of a company's shares, ie how sensitive the stock is to market fluctuations. The beta is denoted in figures, eg 1.5, which means that the share price will rise by 15% in a market that has risen 10%. Shares that underperform are rated below 1.

beta stocks Second-line shares, as opposed to the less numerous highly-capitalized alpha (first-line) or the more numerous gamma (third-line).

Beveridge curve A graph that plots unemployment against job vacancies. It confirms that unemployment tends to be high when job vacancies are few—not enough jobs to go around. It was named after the British economist William (Lord) Beveridge (1879-1963).

bid An offer to buy something (eg shares) at a certain price. A seller may make a certain offer and a prospective buyer may make a bid. The bid cancels out the offer. More especially, a bid is an offer by one company to buy the shares of another; a *takeover bid*.

bid price The price a market-maker is prepared to pay to buy securities.

Big Bang The popular term for the deregulation of the London Stock Exchange on 27 October 1986. Among the changes implemented were the admission of foreign institutions as members of the exchange, the abandonment of rigid distinctions between stockbrokers, jobbers and bankers, and the abolition of fixed commissions.

B

big push A theory to account for balanced economic growth. It postulates that, in the absence of external trade, overall growth can take place only if each sector of the economy grows at the same time (because each needs the others for its markets).

bilateral flow A concept that allows the movement of money in an economy to be studied independently of the matching and opposite movements of goods and services between the various sectors.

bilateralism A situation in which two trading nations agree on mutual but exclusive special privileges, such as favourable import duties and quotas that are not extended to other nations.

bilateral monopoly A market that has a single seller and a single buyer (ie a combination of a monopoly and a monopsony). Prices are arrived at by bargaining.

bilateral oligopoly A market in which there are only a few large sellers and a few large buyers (ie a combination of an oligopoly and an oligopsony).

bilateral trade A balanced trade between two nations. *See also bilateralism.*

bill 1. A list of charges to be paid for goods or services. In this sense the usual US term is *check*. 2. A document, issued by a bank, promising to pay somebody a certain amount of money. It is in this sense that the US meaning of the term is *banknote*. 3. A document describing goods, most often used in dealings with customs. 4. Short for bill of exchange.

bill broker A person or company that buys or sells bills of exchange, either on their own account or as an intermediary.

bill-discounting interest rate The interest rate that a central bank charges for loans to discount houses.

bill of exchange A document that indicates that one party (the drawee) agrees to pay a certain sum of money on demand or on a specified date to another party (the drawer). Two familiar bills of exchange are cheques and banknotes.

bill of lading A document that details the transfer of goods from a (foreign) supplier to a buyer. It may be used as a document of title (establishing ownership).

B

bill of sale A document that certifies the transfer of goods (but not real estate) to another person. Goods transferred in this way may not become the property of the receiving party but may be redeemed when the bill is paid.

bimodal distribution A type of distribution that has two major peaks with a valley between them.

binomial distribution For a random event of constant known probability, the distribution of the expected number of occurrences resulting from a number of independent trials.

birth rate The average number of live births per year per 1,000 population.

BIS Abbreviation of *Bank for International Settlements.*

black economy The illegal economic activity conducted largely for cash by companies and people who pay no taxes on the proceeds.

black market An illegal market that usually deals in scarce or stolen goods. Such markets frequently come into existence in wartime because the goods concerned are rationed or in very short supply, or because the market is exceptionally high – in which case counterfeit or imitation goods often appear. Trading is often in kind, one valued commodity being exchanged for another. *See also* **grey market.**

Black-Scholes formula A complicated expression for working out a fair price for financial options. It was devised in 1973 by US economists Fischer Black (*d.*1995) and Myron Scholes (1941-).

Blair House Agreement An agreement made in 1992 between the European Economic Community (now the EU) and the USA on relaxing regulations about international trade in agricultural products.

Blue Book A popular name for a UK government publication entitled *National Income and Expenditure*, best described as the national annual report and accounts.

blue chip Describing an investment that is regarded as extremely safe, without being gilt-edged. It also describes a company whose shares are regarded as an extremely safe investment.

board of directors A decision-making group consisting of all the directors of a company, who are legally responsible for their actions. The board of directors is specifically charged with the management of the company, and in the case of a public limited company (plc) is elected by the shareholders at the company's annual general meeting (AGM). In the USA, the board of directors draws up company policy and appoints executives to run the company. It is sometimes known simply as 'the board'.

Board of Trade   A UK committee whose main responsibilities included commercial relations with other countries, supervision of shipping, publication of statistics about UK industry, and acting as a go-between for the government with UK industry. In 1972 it was incorporated into the new *Department of Trade and Industry*.

BOP   Abbreviation of *balance of payments.*

bond   1. A security issued at a fixed rate by central government, local authorities occasionally by private companies. It is essentially a contract to repay money borrowed, and as such represents a debt. Normally, bonds are issued in series with the same denominations and conditions of repayment. It is also known as a fixed-interest security. 2. If dutiable goods are imported and duty is not paid immediately, the goods are placed in a bonded warehouse (ie they are held in bond) until all customs formalities are concluded. 3. A from of tie or agreement between individuals. 'My word is my bond' is the motto of the London Stock Exchange.

bond-rating agency   An agency, such as *Standard and Poor*, that rates the creditworthiness of organizations that issue bonds.

bonus   An additional payment, as usually applied to a premium paid in addition to normal salary or wages.

bonus issue   An issue of shares made by a company wishing to reduce the average price of its shares. Shareholders receive a number of extra shares in proportion to the number they already hold. It is also known as a capitalization issue.

bonus scheme   A type of pay scheme in which workers are incentivized through payments of a *bonus*.

book value   Also called written-down value, the value shown in a company's books for an asset or liability (or owner's equity), taking due account of any depreciation. Of a company as a whole, it is the amount by which total assets exceed total liabilities (ie, the net assets).

B

boom A popular term for a period when employment, prices and general business activity are at a high level and resources are being used to the full.

borrowing A term most widely used in the sense of accepting money that is not one's own on the understanding that it will be repaid, usually with interest, at a later date. On the London Metal Exchange, borrowing is the process of buying a metals contract due to be completed on a near date, and at the same time selling forward a contract for a date farther in the future.

Boston matrix A 2 by 2 matrix that classifies a company's products in terms of market share and growth rate, identifying those that generate income (high-share, high-growth 'stars') and those that consume it (low-share, low-growth 'dogs'). High-share, low-growth products are referred to as 'cash cows', and low-share, high-growth products are 'problem children'.

BOT Abbreviation of *balance of trade.*

BOTB Abbreviation of *British Overseas Trade Board.*

bottleneck A hold-up of anything from traffic or a factory's production line to the whole of a nation's economy. Most bottlenecks are caused by bad planning.

bottom line The last line of an account, showing either a profit or a loss. From this sense the term has come into general usage to mean the 'brutal truth'.

bounded rationality The idea that there is a limit to how much data an economist (or anyone else) can take in and manipulate mentally. As a result, the first acceptable course of action is often the one chosen (without consideration of further alternatives). The idea was first proposed by the US economist Herbert Simon (1916-). *See also satisficing.*

boycott A refusal to trade with a certain company or nation or in certain goods.

BP curve An upward-sloping straight-line graph of gross domestic product (national income) against interest rate joining all points at which the balance of payments is in equilibrium. *See also* **IS-LM model.**

B

brand To put a name (the brand name) on something or to design and package a product so that it is easily recognizable by a consumer. A brand name can be protected by law against misuse by competitors hoping to benefit from the reputation associated with a particular branded product.

brand loyalty A marketing concept by which customers continually purchase certain goods which they identify by brand name (and associate with quality and value for money).

brand proliferation A rise in a product's number of brands, each of which is very similar to the others. It is usually stimulated by competitive rivalry in an oligopoly.

brand switching A consumer's change to a brand that is different from the one normally purchased.

brand transference A producer's use of an existing brand name for a new or modified product.

brand value The monetary value assigned to a company's brand name, classified as an intangible asset.

break even To exactly cover one's costs, making neither a profit or loss.

break-up value Of an asset, its value assuming the company holding it will cease trading and that the asset will have to be sold in a hurry (perhaps following a successful takeover of the company).

Bretton Woods Agreement An international agreement between the USA, Canada and the UK formulated at a conference held at Bretton Woods, New Hampshire, in 1944 (formal name United Nations Monetary and Financial Conference). It defined a new system of international monetary control that resulted in the setting up of the International Monetary Fund and the International Bank for Reconstruction and Development (World Bank).

bridging loan A short-term loan in anticipated arrival of funds, whether for a venture company on the verge of raising new capital or a home buyer who needs to pay for a house before receiving the proceeds on the sale of the former property.

British Overseas Trade Board (BOTB) An organization that promotes UK exports and advises exporters on the complexities of overseas marketing. It is sponsored by the government and its head is the Secretary of State for Trade and Industry.

B

British Technology Group An organization established in 1981 by merging the National Enterprise Board and the National Research and Development Corporation. It finances industrial investment to encourage efficiency and innovation.

British Venture Capital Association (BVCA) A trade association of companies that deal in venture capital.

broad money An alternative name for M3. *See* **money supply**.

broker Broadly, an intermediary between a buyer and a seller; a mercantile agent. There are several forms of broker, the job title referring to what it is that a particular broker deals in; eg a stockbroker deals in stocks and shares. Most brokers' earnings take the form of commission. In the USA, a broker is more often known as a brokerage house.

brokerage A payment made to a broker for services rendered, also known as a broker's commission.

bubble A company, industry or trend with no substance to it. A bubble usually bursts with more-or-less disastrous consequences for those involved.

budget A plan that details expected future income and outgoings from an activity, normally over the span of a year. It is often referred to in controlling the activity. A budget is also the sum of money set aside for a given activity or project.

budgetary control The management of a the activities of an organization with regular reference to an approved budget (so that spending is not allowed to exceed the budgeted amount).

budgetary policy An alternative term for *fiscal policy*.

budget constraint A spending limit imposed on a person, company or government. In general, only by borrowing can spending exceed income (and present wealth).

budget deficit A budgetary imbalance, caused by excess of expenditure over revenue. In the case of the British government budgets, the deficit is generally funded by the authorization of an increase in the National Debt.

B

budget line A diagram that shows the various combinations of two goods that can be bought with a particular (fixed) amount of money.

budget surplus A situation that arises when revenue (including a government's revenue) is larger than its expenditure.

budget year The US fiscal year, which runs from 1 October to the following 30 September.

buffer stock On the commodities markets, stocks that are held for release at certain strategic times in order to stabilize prices and markets.

building and loan association A US organization roughly equivalent to a building society in the UK. It is also known as a savings and loan association.

building society A financial institution in the UK that accepts deposits, on which it pays interest, and lends money, originally only in the form a mortgage to enable people to purchase property. Many building societies now issue cheque books and plastic cards, and so operate in much the same way as a bank.

built-in stabilizer An alternative term for *automatic stabilizer*.

bulk buying Purchasing in sufficient quantities to obtain a discount on the normal retail price (although capital is thereby locked up in stock that has to be held for a comparatively long time).

bull A stock exchange dealer or analyst who believes that prices or investment values will increase. On this conviction, the dealer buys now and profits later by selling at a higher price.

bullet The final payment of a loan usually consisting of the whole of the principal (previous payments being of interest only). Or it is a security that pays a guaranteed (fixed) interest at a specific date.

bullion Bars or ingots of a precious metal (such as gold or silver), as opposed to coins.

bull market A market situation in which share prices are rising.

Bundesbank Full name *Deutsche Bundesbank*, the central bank of Germany, with headquarters in Frankfurt. It was established in 1957, when it replaced the Bank Deutscher Länder, founded in 1948.

bundle of goods A particular collection of various goods and services, often used for constructing a *price index*.

B

burden of debt The cost of servicing a debt, ie the interest payments on the accumulated debt.

burden of dependency The part of a country's population that is not economically active, such as dependents (young, old, sick and disabled) and the unemployed, which (in the final analysis) has to be supported by the working population.

Bureau of Economic Analysis (BEA) A US organization, part of the Department of Commerce, that publishes the national income accounts.

business cycle The fairly regular swings in economic activity (demand and output) that tend to repeat every few years.

business saving The part of a company's net revenue that is retained (ie not paid as dividends, interest or tax). *See also* ***reserve***.

business strategy A company's long-term plans, particularly those concerned with production and marketing.

business rates A tax levied on business premises by UK local authorities (although the rate is determined nationally as the uniform business rate). A local District Valuer values the premises for rates.

buy back A company that is originally financed by venture capital may pay back the capital invested either by seeking a quotation or by being taken over. In either case, it will be buying itself back from the venture capitalist.

buyer concentration The number of buyers in a market, which may vary from many (perfect competition) to a few (oligopsony) to only one (monopsony).

buyer credit A system in which a seller makes a cash contract with an overseas buyer, who pays up to 20% of the price and funds the rest through a long-term loan with a UK bank. The repayment of the loan to the bank is guaranteed by the Export Credits Guarantee Department (ECGD).

buyer's market A market in which there are too many sellers and not enough buyers, so that buyers are in a position to influence prices or conditions of purchase.

buy-in 1. The purchase of more than 50% of a company's shares, in order

B

to gain financial and managerial control. 2. A situation in which a seller of shares and so on fails to deliver on the agreed date, which sometimes happens if the seller is selling short. In this case the buyer is entitled to buy shares from another source and to charge the seller with any expenses incurred. This process is known as buying in.

buy-out The purchase of a major holding of a company's shares by its existing management.

BVCA Abbreviation of *British Venture Capital Association.*

by-product A secondary product from a process which, although not the main purpose of the operation, is capable of yielding revenue.

B

C

cabotage 1. A law that restricts coastal traffic to vessels of the country that owns the coast. 2. Permission for an air transport company to operate in a country other than the one in which it is registered. 3. The exclusive right of an air transport company to operate all routes within its own country.

CACM Abbreviation of *Central American Common Market.*

Cairns Group A non-official organization established in 1986 (at Cairns, Australia), consisting of agricultural exporting countries (mainly from eastern Asia, Austalasia, Oceania and South America). They seek to reduce subsidies and other measures of support for agriculture.

calibration With a model of an economy, giving numerical values to its parameters to make predicted quantities in line with actuality.

call The act of demanding payment for stocks or shares, or repayment of a debt. A lender may advance money on condition that it is repayable on call (ie without notice).

called-up capital The face value of a company's shares that the shareholders have agreed to pay for. See also *paid-up capital.*

call money A type of loan made by a bank, which must be repaid on demand. It is also known as money at call.

call option An option to buy shares, commodities or financial futures at an agreed price on or before a future agreed date.

calls in arrears The difference between a company's *called-up capital* and *paid-up capital* resulting when shareholders' phased payments fall into arrears.

Cambridge equation In the *quantity theory of money,* a formula that equates the demand for money balances to general price level times real national income times a ratio determined by monetary habits and economic structure.

Cambridge school A school of economic thought based on Cambridge University, England. At first economists Alfred Marshall (1842-1924) and his pupil Arthur Pigou (1877-1959) championed late classical economics but later the school eschewed neoclassicism in favour of the theories of John Maynard Keynes (1883-1946), proceeding to an emphasis on macroeconomics.

CAP Abbreviation of *Common Agricultural Policy.*

capacity A measure of the ability of a company to produce goods or provide services. For a manufacturing business it is the amount produced in unit time, which may be expressed in direct labour hours, machine hours or standard hours.

capacity utilization The extent to which a company uses its maximum capacity, expressed as a percentage and equal to 100 times the actual output in a given period divided by the full output capacity during the same period.

capital An imprecise term that, unqualified, generally refers to the resources of an organization or person (such as cash, equipment or skills), as contributed by the owners (ie the owners' equity). More precisely it is the total value of assets less liabilities—financial assets that can be employed to produce income.

capital account A part of the *balance of payments*, which refers to international movements of capital, including government loans.

capital accumulation Also called capital formation, the additions to an economy's real capital stock; ie investment in means of production to try to attain greater total output in the short and medium term.

capital adequacy A legal requirement that a financial institution should have enough capital to meet all its obligations and fund the services it offers.

capital allowance An amount deducted from a company's profits before tax is calculated, to take into account depreciation of capital assets (such as vehicles, plant and machinery, and industrial buildings).

capital appreciation An increase in the value of a company's assets, most often as a result of inflation.

capital asset pricing model (CAPM) A method of weighing risk and return to achieve the best equity value of a company in planning its financial policy.

capital assets Another term for *fixed assets.*

C

capital budget A budget that details proposed outgoings to obtain long-term assets, ie a company's capital expenditure. It involves longer timescales than a cash budget. It is also known as a capital expenditure budget or capital investment budget.

capital charge A company expense attributable to interest payments (on borrowed capital), loan repayments or depreciation of assets.

capital consumption 1. A reduction in the value of a company's assets through wear and tear, ageing or obsolescence. 2. A reduction in the value of a country's capital stock consumed in producing a year's gross national product. Both types require new investment.

capital deepening A situation that arises when an economy's capital increases faster that the labour input (and as a result the national output uses a greater ratio of capital to labour).

capital employed The capital that a company uses to finance its assets. It is taken to be the sum of the shareholders' funds, loans and deferred taxation.

capital expenditure Alternative term for *capital costs*.

capital flight Also called flight capital, capital removed from a country that seems to be politically (or economically) unstable, and taken to a more stable environment.

capital formation An alternative term for *capital accumulation.*

capital gain Any gain made from a capital transaction, such as the buying and selling of assets. It is the amount by which the proceeds exceed the cost.

capital gains tax (CGT) A tax paid on a *capital gain*. In the UK the rate of tax, which was introduced on 6 April 1965, depends on when the asset was acquired (before or after 31 March 1982 or after 6 April 1988). Rates of tax vary between 10% and 40%, depending on other income. Under US tax laws, a lower rate of capital gains tax is levied if the asset was held for more than nine months before resale.

capital gearing Also called leverage, especially in the USA, the relationship between a company's funds derived from ordinary shares and long-term, fixed-interest rate funds such as preference shares and debentures. It is the ratio of the company's debts to total capital or shareholders' funds. High gearing, ie a high proportion of debt, generally represents a speculative investment.

C

capital goods Goods (such as machines) that are used for the production of other goods. Ships are also sometimes regarded as capital goods.

capital inflow A flow of foreign funds into the domestic economy. It results from overseas purchases of domestic assets and securities or from borrowing overseas by the government or domestic residents.

capital-intensive Describing a business in which capital is the most important and costly factor of production. Thus, an industry in which the major cost is the purchase and maintenance of machinery (fixed assets) is capital-intensive.

capitalism An economic and political system in which people are entitled to trade for profit on their own account. It is also known as free or private enterprise.

capital issue An issue of shares to raise capital. *See new issue.*

capitalization The conversion of a company's reserves into share capital by issuing more shares (a bonus or scrip issue); or the total amount of capital available to a company in the long term; or the process of providing such capital.

capitalization issue Alternative term for *bonus issue*, also called a scrip issue.

capitalized ratios The proportions of each kind of security issued by a company, which give a picture of its capital structure.

capitalized value At current interest rates, the capital sum needed to yield an asset's current earnings. It equals the ratio of the asset's annual income to the annual interest rate, multiplied by 100.

capital-labour ratio The capital required to produce a good divided by the cost of labour involved. A capital-intensive product has a high capital/labour ratio.

capital levy An alternative term for *capital tax*.

capital loss A negative *capital gain*, also called allowable capital loss.

capital market A market made up of the various sources of capital for (medium- or long-term) investment in new and already existing companies. In the UK it is centred on the London Stock Exchange and the Alternative Investment Market.

capital mobility The ease with which capital can be moved between

C

different countries (often limited by government controls) or different applications (often limited when the capital is invested in a fixed asset). *See also* **liquidity**.

capital movements The movements of foreign currency between countries, mainly through purchases of assets and securities or through making loans.

capital outflow A flow of foreign funds out of the domestic economy. It results from purchases of overseas assets and securities or from lending overseas by the government or domestic residents.

capital-output ratio For a process, company or whole industry, the capital employed divided by the output obtained in a given period (usually a year). It is thus the cost of producing each additional unit of output.

capital reserve The profits from a company's trading that are set aside as part of its capital and so may not be repaid to shareholders until the company is wound up.

capital stock The value of all capital goods owned by a company (or an industry or even a whole nation), after depreciation has been taken into account.

capital stock adjustment A method of explaining investment in terms of a company's target capital-output ratio. The company invests to reduce the gap whenever capital stock falls below that implied by the ratio.

capital structure The make-up of a company's borrowings in terms of the proportions of owners' equity, short-term debt and long-term debt. The complete financial structure includes also its assets and any other liabilities.

capital tax Also called capital levy, a tax levied according to the value of a person's or company's capital.

capital theory The inputs to production have usually themselves been produced and an analysis of the economic results of this is the major function of capital theory.

capital transfer The use of a gift or bequest to transfer assets from one person to another, who regards them as additions to capital (not income).

capital transfer tax (CTT) A tax paid on the transfer of capital over a certain value, eg in the form of a gift or bequest. In the UK it covers the former inheritance tax.

capital widening A situation that arises when an economy's capital increases at the same rate as the labour input (and as a result the national output uses the same ratio of capital to labour).

CAPM Abbreviation of *capital asset pricing model.*

CAR Abbreviation of *compound annual return.*

cardinal utility The satisfaction (utility) obtained by consuming a product, which involves the controversial idea that personal welfare can be measured.

Caribbean Common Market (CARICOM) An organization established in 1973, with headquarters in Georgetown, Guyana, by 13 English-speaking Caribbean countries for purposes of mutual trade.

Caribbean Community and Common Market An organization that set up a free trade area in the Caribbean, superseded in 1973 by the *Caribbean Common Market.*

Caribbean Development Bank An organization founded in 1970 as a regional development bank for making low-interest loans and grants to finance projects in agriculture and industry. There are 20 Caribbean members in addition to Canada, France, Germany, Italy and the UK.

Caribbean Free Trade Association (CARIFTA) An organization that set up a free trade area in the Caribbean, superseded in 1973 by the *Caribbean Common Market.*

CARICOM Abbreviation of *Caribbean Common Market.*

CARIFTA Abbreviation of *Caribbean Free Trade Association.*

carry forward losses Past company losses that may be deducted from present profits before establishing the liability to pay tax, as an encouragement to investment.

carry-over To postpone payment on a deal (bargain) traded on a stock exchange from one settlement day to the next.

cartel A group of companies that come together to monopolize a market, agreeing between them which company presides over which area of operation. Cartels are illegal in the UK and USA.

C

cash Ready money (legal tender such as coins and notes), or to convert something (such as a cheque) into ready money.

cash discount A reduction in the price of goods or services in return for (prompt) payment in cash. Discounts allowed in this way are classified as expenditure. To the receiver of the discounts, they are regarded as revenue.

cash drain A shortfall in *bank deposit creation* caused when people keep more than usual amounts of money as cash, thereby also slowing down the expansion of the money supply.

cashflow The movement of money through a company from when it is received as income (or borrowing), to the time it leaves the company as payments (for example, for raw materials, wages, and so on). A negative cashflow occurs when there is too little money coming in to pay for all the outgoings. Conversely, a positive cash flow occurs when a company receives more income than its outgoings (or receives income before it is due to pay the associated outgoings).

cash limit 1. The maximum amount a business can spend in a specified time. 2. The maximum amount provided by a loan or overdraft. 3. The maximum amount stated on a cheque guarantee card. 4. The maximum amount that can be withdrawn from a cash dispenser (automated teller machine).

cash ratio The amount of reserves a bank considers it necessary to maintain, calculated with reference to the bank's turnover.

cash reserve ratio The fraction of a bank's total assets that it retains in the form of cash or other highly liquid asset to meet its day-to-day financial commitments.

cash-rich Describing a person or company that has surplus liquid funds.

catch-up The benefit to a country's economy derived by copying techniques from other higher-productivity countries.

caveat emptor Latin for 'buyer beware'. In legal terms this maxim means that a buyer of goods should use his or her own common sense, and that the law is not prepared to aid someone who buys goods foolishly.

caveat subscriptor Latin for 'signer beware', meaning that anyone who signs a document is bound by its contents, regardless of whether or not he or she has read it, or understands its legal implications.

C

caveat vendor Latin for 'seller beware', meaning that a seller of goods or services is legally required to tell buyers of any inherent defects.

CBI Abbreviation of *Confederation of British Industry.*

CCA Abbreviation of *current cost accounting.*

CCC Abbreviation of *Commodity Credit Corporation.*

CD Abbreviation of *certificate of deposit.*

CDC Abbreviation of *Commonwealth Development Corporation.*

Cecchini Report Formal name *The European Challenge, 1992*, a report published in 1998 about the expected outcomes from the 1992 programme for unifying the internal market of the European Community.

CEFTA Abbreviation of *Central Europe Free Trade Association.*

ceiling price The highest price allowed for a particular good or service. It can be imposed by authorities through market intervention or legal regulation.

census A national survey that provides information on population, economics and social matters. In the UK and USA a national census is taken every 10 years.

census of production A survey of the activities of production companies, recording such data as types of inputs, numbers of employees and types of products. The information allows economists to complete an *input-output* analysis of the economy.

Central African Customs and Economic Union (UDEAC) Union Douanière et Economique de l'Afrique Centrale, an organization established in 1966 to found a Central African common market with a common tariff. Its terms were revised in 1974.

Central American Common Market (CACM) A common market established in 1960 among Central American countries. It was revised beginning in 1973.

central bank A bank that carries out government economic policy, influences interest and exchange rates, monitors the activities of commercial and merchant banks, and usually issues currency. In this way it acts as the government's banker and is the lender of last resort to

C

the banking system. In the UK it is the Bank of England and in the USA the Federal Reserve Banks.

Central Europe Free Trade Association (CEFTA) An organization, similar to the European Free Trade Association (EFTA), formed by the Czech Republic, Hungary, Poland and Slovakia.

central government The highest level of government, superior to state governments (where they exist) and local government.

Central Government Borrowing Requirement (CGBR) The amount calculated by deducting private sector borrowing (by public companies and local authorities) from the *Public Sector Borrowing Requirement.*

centralization 1. In national terms, the concentration of economic planning centrally, as in a *centrally-planned economy.* 2. In a company, the retention of decision-making authority by the senior managers, who then delegate. Both forms are also termed central planning.

central planning An alternative term for *centralization.*

centrally-planned economy An economic system in which decision-making is made centrally by the state and the means of production (apart from labour) are collectively owned—hence the alternative name collectivism.

Central Statistical Office A UK government department that publishes various national economic statistics, including the *Balance of Payments Accounts* and the *National Income Accounts.*

CEO Abbreviation of chief executive officer (see *chief executive*).

certainty equivalent A statistical concept that is the certain outcome of a random event which gives the same satisfaction (utility) as the real distribution of expected outcomes, of importance in risk-taking decisions.

certificate A document that proves something, eg right of ownership or that certain actions have taken place.

certificate of deposit (CD) Essentially, a document (originally issued by merchant banks) declaring that a certain sum had been deposited with a bank. Sterling certificates of deposit refer to long-term fixed deposits of sums over £10,000 and therefore offer high interest rates.

certificate of origin An import-export document that declares the country of origin of goods. Customs authorities use such certificates to determine whether, for example, an import qualifies for a special tariff.

CES Abbreviation of *constant elasticity of substitution.*

CET Abbreviation of *common external tariff.*

ceteris paribus Latin for 'other things remaining equal'. It is used in economic analysis to study the effects of economic variants while assuming that all other factors remain the same.

CBBR Abbreviation of *Central Government Borrowing Requirement.*

CGT Abbreviation of *capital gains tax.*

Chamber of Commerce A UK voluntary organization that promotes and represents the interests of those involved in commerce in a particular geographical area. Chambers of commerce in other countries may be state-aided.

Chancellor of the Exchequer The chief finance minister of the UK government. He or she is a member of the cabinet in charge of the Treasury and presenter of the annual budget.

chartist A stock market or economic analyst who believes that trends (eg in price movements and so on) follow recognizable patterns and so predicts future trends with the aid of charts.

cheap money Also called easy money, money borrowed at a low rate of interest, usually consisting of funds made available by authorities wishing to encourage economic activity.

cheque The most familiar form of bill of exchange. A cheque is used to transfer funds from someone's account at a bank to somebody else. It is also a common way of withdrawing money from a current account.

Chicago school A school of economic thought associated with US economist Milton Friedman (1912-) and the Economics Department of Chicago University. Their key beliefs include nonintervention by government to try to control the economy, free markets (which best allocate resources), and the role of the money supply in determining inflation.

chief executive Also known as the chief executive officer (CEO), the person responsible for the day-to-day running of a company, usually the managing director.

C

Chinese wall   An artificial barrier erected in any business where confidentiality between departments is a legal requirement. For example, the Chinese wall has become necessary since the Big Bang changed the London Stock Exchange to a dual capacity system in 1986. The purpose of the wall is to prevent insider dealing.

circular flow of income   A simple model of how an economy works based on the movement of money and resources between producers and consumers. Producers pay money (wages and salaries) to workers who spend it on goods and services, thus returning it to the producers. Savings represent withdrawals from the income flow, whereas investments inject extra money into it. Similarly, on a national scale, taxes and imports are withdrawals and government spending and exports are injections.

City, The   The main financial district of London, situated in the City of London. It covers an area of roughly one square mile and for this reason is also sometimes known as the Square Mile.

City Code (on Takeovers and Mergers)   A voluntary system established in 1968 by a Takeover Panel and operated by the London Stock Exchange to regulate a code of conduct to be adopted in takeovers and mergers.

claimant count   The level of unemployment measured in terms of the number of people out of work and claiming unemployment benefit.

classical dichotomy   The anti-Keynesian postulate that, in any economy, the real variables depend on real factors and not monetary ones, and nominal variables depend on monetary factors and not real ones.

classical economics   The predominant school of economic thought that prevailed until about 1870, based mainly on the writings of economists such as Thomas Malthus (1766-1834), John Stuart Mill (1806-73), David Ricardo (1772-1823) and Adam Smith (1723-90). Unlike their predecessors, who thought that agriculture was key to the economy, they stressed the importance of manufacturing and labour, free competition and the minimum of government intervention.

classical unemployment   Unemployment that results when wages are too high for the level of productivity; not all the labour available can be employed at these wage rates. It can be reduced by lowering wages or increasing productivity

C

clearing bank A bank that is a member of a *clearing house* to facilitate the passing and clearing of cheques.

clearing house A financial institution that specializes in clearing debts between its members. (Clearing is the practice of organizing the payment of financial instruments). The best-known type is a banker's clearing house, which clears cheques between the major banks.

cliometrics The use of quantitative techniques, including *econometrics*, to interpret the economic past.

close company A company whose shares are held privately, by a few people (usually not more than five), and not traded on a stock exchange. The equivalent US term is closely-held company.

closed economy An economy that is self-sufficient in that it makes neither exports nor imports.

closed-end fund A fund with fixed capital, as opposed to an open-ended fund. Sums held by investment companies are closed-end funds (investment trusts).

closely-held company US term for a *close company*.

closing price The price of shares at the close of trading each day on a stock exchange.

club principle A way of apportioning common overhead costs to the individual members of a group who share goods or services.

CMEA Abbreviation of *Council for Mutual Economic Assistance.*

CNAR Abbreviation of *compound net annual rate.*

coalition A basically unstable alliance of people or companies with separate objectives who come together to adopt a common policy or strategy.

Coase theorem Economic efficiency is possible so long as all property rights are allocated and there is completely free trade in those rights (and there are no *transaction costs*). It was formulated by UK-born US economist Ronald Coase (1910-).

Cobb-Douglas function A *production function* relating aggregate output (of products) to the inputs (of capital and labour) used to produce it. It was corroborated in 1928 by US economists C. W. Cobb and P. H. Douglas.

C

cobweb model A simple cyclical demand model that reveals the fluctuating effect of time lags between producers' responses to a price change (such as the delay between sowing and harvest in farming).

coefficient of variation A statistical measure of variability relative to average size, equal for a range of values to the *standard deviation* divided by the *mean* value.

COGS Abbreviation of *cost of goods sold.*

coin A metal token that is *legal tender.* (The making of counterfeit money is called *coining*).

coincidence of wants The situation necessary for a barter transaction to take place—in the absence of money, each participant must want what the other has to trade.

collateral Also called security, anything (usually property) pledged against a loan, or the document that sets out the terms of such collateral.

collective bargaining The practice of workers in trade unions electing representatives to bargain on their behalf with management on such issues as wage levels and working conditions.

collective products Goods or more usually services that can be supplied (and charged) only to a group of people, because a single person's share cannot be varied independently. For instance a government-financed service such the army is a collective product charged to the whole (working) population through taxation.

collectivism An economic system in which all the factors of production are owned by the community and controlled largely by the state. An alternative term for *centrally-planned economy.*

collusion A usually tacit agreed course of action between independent companies to modify competition between them (eg by fixing prices). *See also cartel.*

Colombo Plan An agreement signed in Colombo, Sri Lanka, in 1950, and made permanent in 1980, by 24 Asian and Pacific Region countries for making available economic aid to developing countries in the area. Its full name is the Colombo Plan for Cooperative Economic and Social Development in Asia and the Pacific.

COMECON Abbreviation of *Council for Mutual Economic Assistance.*

commercial bank A bank that concentrates on cash deposit and transfer services to the general public. It may be a joint-stock bank or a private bank.

commercial paper A debt instrument that companies issue to raise capital.

commercial policy The use of tariffs, quotas, subsidies, export restraints and other barriers to trade by a government to control foreign trade.

COMEX Abbreviation of *Commodity Exchange of New York.*

commission Money paid to agents or other intermediaries for their services, usually as a percentage of the sum involved in the transaction.

commodity 1. Primary products and raw materials used in industrial processing and manufacture. 2. Raw materials and foods, especially goods such as cocoa, coffee, jute, potatoes, tea, and so on, that can be traded on a commodity market. 3. In economics, any tangible good that is traded.

commodity agreement An agreement between nations to stabilize or increase the price of a primary product (commodity) and thus reduce fluctuations in their balance of payments.

commodity broker A broker who deals in commodities, usually in a commodity market.

Commodity Credit Corporation (CCC) A US organization established in 1933 that gives farmers price support, providing loans to finance the marketing and export of farm produce (using the crops as security). It is owned and run by the government as part of the Department of Agriculture.

commodity exchange A commodity market on which actuals (commodities for immediate delivery) and futures (commodities for future delivery) are traded.

Commodity Exchange of New York (COMEX) A commodity market in metals established in 1870 which, together with the London Metal Exchange, has a leading role in the world. It deals mainly in futures contracts.

commodity market A market on which commodities are traded.

commodity price index A *leading indicator* of economic trends, a price

C

index of farm produce, mineral products and other commodities that are traded in bulk.

Common Agricultural Policy (CAP) An EU agreement on farming that aims to protect farmers of member countries, eg by subsidizing their produce and setting minimum prices.

common external tariff (CET) An import tariff charged by all members of a trading community (such as the EU) on goods being imported from non-member states.

common market Any market organization among countries that have a common external tariff (unlike a free-trade area). The EU is a modern example.

commons Air, public roads, sea fisheries and other resources that have no owner but are free to everyone. The dangers of exploitation of such resources has been termed 'the tragedy of the commons'.

common stock The US term for *ordinary shares.*

Commonwealth Development Corporation (CDC) UK public organization established in 1948 to help the economic development of overseas countries, particularly new members of the Commonwealth and particularly with agriculture.

communism A political and economic system in which all factors of production are owned and controlled by the state.

community charge A former UK local tax, commonly known as poll tax, which was levied on eligible adults between April 1990 and April 1993, when it was replaced by *council tax.*

community indifference curve In the theory of international trade, a graph that shows the quantities of various goods required to make each community member have the same utility level (as at some previous time). It thereby aims to reveal the community's 'tastes'.

company An enterprise that has been legally incorporated to produce certain goods or provide certain services, or to transact any other type of business. There are strict legal requirements of a company, as set out in the Companies Acts (*see company law*).

company director One of the principals of a company, in a public liability company (plc) appointed by its shareholders. Most companies have a group of directors (the board of directors) who act collectively as the senior management of the company, being responsible to the shareholders for its efficient running and future development. The duties and legal responsibilities of a director are defined in the Companies Acts. They include the compilation of an *annual report* and the recommendation of an annual dividend on shares.

company formation A series of stages involved in the setting-up of a new joint-stock company (formally termed incorporation), which include compiling a memorandum of association, drawing up articles of association, obtaining a certificate of incorporation, and issuing shares (to raise capital).

company law The legislation that applies to the creation and running of a joint-stock company. For example, the Companies Act 1985 is the chief legislation that applies to companies in the UK, defining a *limited company*, and *unlimited company* and a *public company*. The Companies Act 1989 was enacted to make UK company law conform to that of the European Union.

company limited by guarantee A company whose members are liable only up to the amount they guarantee to make available in the event of the company being wound up. The guarantors may or may not hold shares in addition. Charities and educational establishments are the most common organizations that form companies limited by guarantee.

company limited by shares The usual type of company, in which the members' liability is limited to their share holding. *See* *limited company*.

company registrar An officer of a company who maintains the register of shareholders and issues new share certificates.

company secretary A person who is responsible for ensuring that his or her company complies with company law. He or she is an officer of the company but need not be a director.

Company Security (Insider Dealing) Act 1985 UK law that made *insider dealing* illegal.

company taxation In the classical system, a company's profits are taxed before dividends are paid to shareholders (who then have to pay income tax on them). In the imputation system, a company's profits are regarded as shareholders' income and taxed, but no further tax is payable on dividends when they are paid to shareholders. In the UK

C

retained profits are taxed on the classical system (via **Corporation Tax**) and dividends are taxed on the imputation system (via **Advance Corporation Tax**).

comparability A desire for workers in one group or industry to earn wages that are comparable in level to those earned by similar workers in another group or industry. **Cost-push inflation** may result from wage increases gained in this way.

comparative advantage The economic state of being more efficient in one activity than in another, relative to a different country. For example, a country is able to produce cars twice as efficiently as another, but produces aircraft ten times more efficiently. In a free market, this country should export aircraft and import cars, and it is said that, in the production of aircraft, it has a comparative advantage over the other country.

comparative cost An expression of *comparative advantage* in terms of cost, being low for goods in countries that have a comparative advantage in producing them, and high in those with no such advantage.

comparative static equilibrium analysis Also called comparative statics, an economic or market analysis that looks at the differences between equilibrium positions and then tries to predict the new equilibrium assuming one of the variables alters.

compensated demand curve A redrawn market *demand curve* for a good that shows what would happen if consumers were to be compensated for price change effects.

compensating variation If a good becomes unavailable or its price increases, and in the absence of other price changes, the extra amount of money required to restore the original level of utility to a consumer. *See also equivalent variation.*

compensating wage differential Extra wages paid as compensation, for example to workers who have dangerous or dirty jobs or who have to work unsociable hours.

compensation In international trade, a single agreement under which an exporter agrees to supply goods and services in exchange for goods and services of an equivalent value supplied by the importer, which the exporter must then sell to finance his original sale. It is frequently used in *countertrading*.

compensation principle Also called the Hicks-Kaldor principle after UK economists John Hicks (1904-89) and Nicholas Kaldor (1908-86), the principle that if those who gain from a change in the economy could compensate those who lose from it, everyone would benefit—total economic welfare would increase.

competition The effort directed towards doing better than somebody else, especially among rival companies in the same market.

Competition Act 1980 UK legislation that empowered the Monopolies and Mergers Commission to investigate anti-competitive practices (such as refusal to supply goods or services to certain customers or purchase goods or services from certain suppliers).

competition laws The laws that control such anti-competitive actions as mergers, monopolies, restrictive trade agreements and takeovers. In the UK they include the *Competition Act 1980; Fair Trading Act 1973; Resale Prices Act 1964, 1976;* and *Restrictive Trade Practices Act 1956, 1968, 1976.*

competition policy Government policy that protects consumers' interests while encouraging the best use of economic resources. In the UK the *Office of Fair Trading* enforces any relevant legislation.

competitive advantage The collective factors that allow a company to do better than its rivals. These vary from well-established brands and cost-effective production methods to sole ownership of raw materials and other supplies.

competitive devaluation The use of currency devaluation to provide a cost advantage that improves a country's competitiveness—it can increase domestic prices (for extra revenue) or decrease export prices (for extra sales).

competitive market An open market in which goods and services are freely offered for sale by any number of sellers to anybody willing to buy, at prices agreed between them.

competitiveness Being able to compete with rival companies or nations and maintain market share. In markets for goods and services this usually depends on price and quality, although reputation (eg brand) may have a disproportionate effect.

C

competitive tendering The practice of asking rival companies to put in price bids for the supply of goods or services. In the public sector this may involving asking private companies to tender for the supply of goods or services that the public sector had hitherto supplied itself.

complementarity Describing *complementary goods*.

complementary goods Also termed complementary products, two goods that are related to each other in such a way that when demand for one increases, demand for the other rises at the same time. For example, cameras and photographic film are complementary goods, as are cars and petrol.

complementary products An alternative term for *complementary goods*.

complex monopoly A market in which two or more suppliers deliberately do not compete among themselves (offering buyers no choice based on price). *See cartel; collusion.*

compliance cost The cost to a company of complying with regulations, such as keeping records for Customs and Excise (for value added tax, VAT) or the Inland Revenue (for income tax etc.).

compound annual return (CAR) The total return on a sum invested or lent over a period of a year, including the return on interest previously accrued.

compound interest The rate of interest calculated by adding interest previously paid to the capital sum plus previous interest payment. After n years a sum S invested at x per cent compound interest is worth $S[100 + n)/100]^n$. *See also simple interest.*

compound net annual rate (CNAR) The return, after deduction of tax at the basic rate, of interest from a deposit or investment that includes the return on interest previously accrued.

computable general equilibrium model A economic model whose various equations can all be solved using a computer, and the effects of changes to any of them determined in terms of the economy as a whole. The more complex the model, the more powerful the computer has to be.

concealed unemployment Also called disguised unemployment, unemployment of those who are not earning and not seeking work. For example, during times of high unemployment, a housewife may wish to work but decides it is not worth trying to find a suitable job. This form

C

of unemployment is 'concealed' (or 'disguised') by the method of calculating unemployment figures in the UK. It can be said not to exist in the USA, where calculation methods enable the authorities to take such cases into account.

concentration Also termed market concentration, the extent to which a market is dominated by the major companies, either suppliers (seller concentration) or purchasers (buyer concentration).

concentration measure A measure of the distribution of companies in terms of their numbers in a market or an economy. The measure may be an absolute one, like the concentration ratio, or relative (*see **Lorenz curve***). Aggregate measures are concerned with the activities of only the larger companies.

concentration ratio A measure of the make-up of a market in terms of the sizes of companies (in terms of capital employed, number of staff or annual turnover). For example, the market may be dominated by a large number of small companies or a small number of large ones.

concerted practice A way of removing competition between rival companies which informally adopt similar policies regarding output and prices. *See also **cartel; collusion***.

concert party A group of people who come together secretly to act 'in concert', that is, to orchestrate a market in the group's favour. For example, two or more people may form a concert party to buy shares in a company in order to effect a takeover. Such action is illegal.

conditionality The way the International Monetary Fund allocates loans, making them conditional on the adoption of a particular policy by the borrowing nation.

condition of entry The ease or otherwise with which a new supplier can enter a market. There may be barriers to entry, which make this difficult, or free entry (where there is perfect competition).

Confederation of British Industry (CBI) An independent organization established in 1965 by combing the British Employers Confederation, the Federation of British Industry and the National Association of British Manufacturers. It represents industry in consultations with the government and promotes the activities of industry in the UK.

confirming house A type of export house that acts for foreign buyers, who use it like a UK office. The house places orders with UK exporters and thereby effectively becomes the buyer.

conglomerate A very large public company that is extremely diverse and probably international in its operations.

conglomerate merger A merger between companies whose business interests are not connected.

conjectural variation The achievement of equilibrium in an oligopoly by each supplier assuming that its rivals will to some extent follow any price or output change it makes.

conservative central banker A central banker who puts a higher value on the stability of prices in relation to economic activity than do the majority of people.

conservative social welfare function In estimating the effects of economic changes, putting greater emphasis on welfare reductions than on increases.

consistent preference If a person prefers X to Y and prefers Y to Z, for consistency he or she should prefer X to Z; this is a consistent preference. But preferences change either for the sake of variety or because of changes in taste. It is therefore safer to assume that peoples' preferences will not be consistent.

consol Abbreviation of Consolidated Stock or Consolidated Loan, a form of fixed-interest government security that has no redemption date.

consolidated accounts The combined financial statements of a group of subsidiary companies. Although each member of the group has its own profit and loss accounts, these must be consolidated to form accounts for the whole group, as required by the Companies Act. They are also called consolidated financial statements, group accounts or group financial statements.

consolidated fund An account at the Bank of England into which the UK government pays its income (from taxes and so on) and out of which it makes payments.

consortium A group of companies that come together to bid for a certain project. It is usually dissolved after that one project is completed. It is similar to a syndicate, but more short-term.

C

conspicuous consumption A consumer trend that involves the consumer buying goods (usually status symbols, such as sports cars, etc.), deriving satisfaction not from consumption of the goods themselves, but from being seen by other people to own them.

constant elasticity of substitution (CES) For a *production function*, the proportional changes in relative prices divided by the proportional changes is relative quantities is constant.

constant prices Prices that have been adjusted to take account of the current purchasing power of money; ie expressing prices in terms of a base year so that figures can be compared without being affected by inflation. *See also* **current prices**.

constant returns A situation in which the ratio of inputs to outputs of a production process is always the same—increasing one leads to a proportionate increase in the other.

constraint Something that prevents an organization from performing better. It may be a shortage of such things as labour, production capacity or raw materials, which must be remedied before performance levels can improve.

consultant An outside specialist (person or company) who is paid to give expert information or advice, generally about a commercial or technical matter.

consumables Also called consumable goods, materials that are used up in producing something, although not part of the prime cost (as are *direct materials*), such as abrasives, cleaning agents and lubricating oil.

consumer A person who buys goods for consumption.

consumer behaviour The way in which consumers choose to express their preferences in how they spend their money. There are many theories, but all seem to support the law of supply and demand (raise the price and demand falls).

consumer borrowing Also termed consumer debt, the amount consumers owe because they have used consumer credit.

consumer confidence A measure of how willing consumers are to spend their money. Worries about job security, for example, lower consumer confidence whereas optimistic views of future income raise it.

C

consumer credit 1. The credit made available to consumers by the sellers of goods and services. 2. Personal credit, such as a bank loan or incorporated into a hire-purchase agreement.

Consumer Credit Act 1974 Legislation in the UK that safeguards people who take out personal credit worth up to £15,000. It covers bank loans, credit cards, credit sale agreements, hire-purchase agreements and mortgages (bank overdrafts are excluded).

consumer durables Consumer goods of some technological sophistication that yield utility over a period of time, for example, clothing, cars, washing machines, and so on.

consumer equilibrium The point where a consumer's satisfaction (utility) from spending a fixed income is at a maximum. This occurs when the *marginal utilities* of the goods and services bought are proportional to their prices.

consumer expenditure Also called consumption expenditure, the money spent on private consumption (equal to about 60% of the UK gross domestic product). It can be apportioned among consumer durables, nondurables, housing and services.

consumer goods Goods that are consumed in use, either over a short period (eg foodstuffs) or over a longer period, such as motor vehicle tyres (or even the motor vehicles themselves).

consumerism A policy that bases business decisions on the best interest of the consumer (not the producer).

consumer nondurables Consumer goods that can be used only once and yield utility in the very short term, such as food and drink.

consumer preference The way a consumer decides how to spend his or her money. *See consumer behaviour.*

Consumer Price Index The US term for *Retail Price Index.*

consumer protection The laws and other measures designed to protect consumers, including advice to customers, supplying defective goods, consumers' health and safety, labelling of goods, weights and measures and the provision of consumer credit.

consumer rationality In demand theory, the assumption that consumers act rationally and can best judge their own interests, and therefore try to get the greatest satisfaction (utility) when they buy goods and services.

consumer sovereignty The idea that consumers ultimately determine what goods and services are produced (because it is they who buy them, although they can only chose from among those available).

consumer surplus A consumer's extra satisfaction (utility) from paying less for a good or service than he or she was willing to pay.

consumption The act of consuming, ie using goods or services that are thereby damaged or used up and cannot therefore be resold (at least, not at the purchase price).

consumption expenditure An alternative term for *consumer expenditure.*

consumption externality An external benefit or cost resulting from the activity of a consumer (such as the pleasure given by a display of flowers or the nuisance caused by a noisy motorcycle).

consumption function Broadly, the general relationship between consumption and the income that pays for it. For an individual, consumption rises as income rises, although not necessarily at the same rate (eg because of savings).

contango A stock exchange term for a delayed settlement of a deal (bargain) from one account to the next. A premium then becomes payable. The term is also used more frequently in futures trading to mean the opposite of *backwardation.*

contestability A measure of how easy it is for a company to enter or leave an industry. For instance there are no entry barriers to a perfectly contenstable industry.

contestable market A market for which there are no barriers to entry (such as sunk costs) or exit (such as unrealizable assets). A company already established in the market cannot charge above reasonable prices (it makes a normal profit) because of the ease with which a rival could enter the market.

contingent fee A fee that has to be paid only if an activity succeeds (such as a commission that is payable only if sales are made).

contingent liability A liability that may arise, depending on some contingency (which may be defined as something that will probably, but not certainly, happen at some time in the future).

C

contingent market A market in which contracts are completed only if certain things happen (eg a market in *options*).

contingent protection Import restrictions that are not invoked unless they are required (such as anti-dumping measures).

continuous compounding A method of calculating *compound interest* in which the compounding period is taken to be every instant of time. If interest is compounded at a rate of r per period, the effective interest rate is the same as interest compounded once per period at a rate of i, where $i = e^r - 1$ (and e is the base of natural logarithms).

continuous inventory Also called perpetual inventory, continuous audit or continuous stocktaking, a way of keeping a record of stock which is changed whenever an item is added to or removed from the stock. It is most commonly used in retailing, where stock turnover is fast.

contract A legally binding agreement between two parties, or the act of forming such an agreement. It may be verbal or, more usually, in writing.

contract curve An alternative term for *offer curve.*

contracted-out In general, describing an agreement to forego some activity (and possibly its benefits). For example, the term refers to a company that believes it can provide sufficient pension cover for its employees more economically using a private scheme than using the state pension system.

contract of employment A legally binding document that details the terms and conditions of somebody's job.

contribution Money earned or paid in addition to another sum, often used of extra profit that accrues once a product's breakeven point has been reached.

controlled economy An economy in which the government tries to control elements of economic activity by legislating for key areas rather than taking direct charge of the factors of production.

control total The total UK public expenditure, which is used by government departments in their yearly discussions about budgets.

convergence The aim, as detailed in the Maastricht Treaty, of bringing the currencies and economies of EU countries into line with each other, necessary before the universal introduction of a single currency and the European Monetary Union (EMU).

convergence criteria A set of conditions that European countries must satisfy if they were to adopt a single currency, as laid out in the Maastricht Treaty. In the event, the criteria were interpreted quite loosely and no applicant country was deemed not to have met them.

convertibility Describing the status of a currency that is freely convertible for another (without the need for official permission).

convertible currency A currency that is freely exchangeable for another currency, with no limit.

convertible loan stock Also known as convertible debentures, loan stock with the right of conversion into preference shares or ordinary shares at some time in the future. Government stock that can be converted into new stock (instead of repayment) is also known as convertible loan stock.

conveyance The transfer of ownership of land or other property.

cooperative An organization run by a group of people who each have a say in its management and a financial interest in its profitability. It may be a group of producers (such as farmers), consumers (in retail cooperatives) or the workers themselves (as in some Communist countries).

cooperative society A society of consumers and producers (or retailers) who share the profits of their cooperation.

coordination failure A situation in which two or more parties fail to benefit from activities that could happen but do not do so because the parties do not 'get their act together'. The classical example is a railway that is not built because of lack of freight to carry in a country that has rich mineral resources that are not extracted because there is no railway to carry them.

COP Abbreviation of *cost of production.*

core A densely populated central region of a country with good communications and infrastructure, as opposed to the sparsely populated periphery where such facilities are lacking.

corner a market To build a virtual monopoly in particular goods or services, so that the monopolist is able to dictate price.

C

corporate equity A company's net assets after paying off debentures, preference shareholders and other creditors. This is the amount available to ordinary shareholders if the company is wound up.

corporate governance The control of a joint-stock company, nominally in the hands of the shareholders but increasingly the role of professional managers (board of directors).

corporate income tax A tax paid by a company on its profits, as opposed to a tax on the owners' incomes. *See corporation tax.*

corporate planning An activity undertaken to plan the future aims of a company, covering such subject areas as new products, production targets and sales targets.

corporate sector The part of a company's economy consisting of trading companies which, together with the financial sector and personal sector, make up the private sector.

corporation A large company, usually with several subsidiary companies. In the USA, it is a company that has been incorporated under US law. The term there is therefore a virtual synonym for company; it is often abbreviated to corp.

corporation tax (CT) A tax levied on a UK company's profits. The rate depends on the amount of profit, starting at 10% for companies whose profits are less than £10,000, rising to 20% for companies with profits of between £10,000 and £300,000, rising to 30% for companies making more than £1.5 million. *See also advance corporation tax.*

corporatism A method of making decisions about the economy by discussions between centralized corporate organizations that represent employers and workers.

correlation of returns The degree to which the returns on an investment or project are favourable or unfavourable at the same time as the returns on a different one. The stronger the correlation, the less is the risk reduced by combining the two. Risk is reduced most if the two are independent or negatively correlated.

corset A restriction sometimes applied by the Bank of England on the amount of credit a bank can extend to its customers, usually in an attempt to control inflation. Its formal name is supplementary special deposits.

C

cost The amount of money that has to be expended to acquire something (goods or services), in most cases its price. A company's costs may be defined in a number of ways, such as acquisition cost, average cost, historical cost and replacement cost.

cost accountant An accountant who specializes in reckoning the cost of manufacturing a unit of product, taking into account such variables as cost of raw materials and labour, and thereby making a projection of probable cost at the planning stage of a project. This, in turn, can enable a manufacturer to tender a price to a prospective buyer. It is usually regarded as an area within management accounting. *See also management accountant.*

cost-based pricing The pricing of goods or services in terms of their production costs, as opposed to taking account of market conditions.

cost-benefit analysis An analysis of the total social costs and benefits of an economic project, generally in terms of money. The technique is used, for example, by public authorities to assess projects involving large-scale public investment such as a by-pass or motorway tunnel.

cost centre A specific operation within an organization that is charged separately for its own expenses (so that its costs can be accurately assessed).

cost curve A graph of cost (fixed, variable or both) versus output (quantity of goods produced). For short production runs, costs initially tend to fall with increasing output but after passing through a minimum the curve rises, showing that above a certain optimum output costs begin to rise.

cost-effective Describing something that gives value for money. As a relative term, it is used of an activity that has the greatest ratio of revenue (or benefit) to cost (among alternative activities).

cost function A relationship between cost and one or more variable quantities. A common example is $y = a + bx$, where y is total cost, a is total fixed cost, b is variable cost per unit and x is the number of units produced. Another equation could be constructed to relate the cost of repairs to a machine in terms of the number of hours it had been in use or the amount of product it had produced.

cost inflation The type of inflation that results when increases in prices or wages pass round the economy. Higher production costs lead to higher

C

prices, higher prices lead to demands for higher wages, and higher wages to some workers lead others to demand wage increases to preserve differentials.

cost minimization The practice of seeking the minimum cost at which a company is able to produce the output it requires.

cost of capital The average of the costs to a company of its various kinds of capital (bonds, debentures, loans, shares, retained profit, and so on).

cost of goods sold (COGS) The cost of items that are produced (or bought) and then sold (or resold). For a given accounting period, it is the value of stock at the beginning of the period plus the cost of goods produced (or bought) minus the value of stock at the end of the period.

cost of living In national terms, the amount of money each person has to spend in order to buy food and accommodation.

cost of living index Officially termed the Index of Retail Prices, an index related to the spending of an average family on the goods and services they need. Goods considered include a 'standard food basket', clothing, fuel, household goods and services, transport, drink and tobacco.

cost of production (COP) The cost of the materials and production process involved in producing a good, with an allowance for the cost of sales (but no profit).

cost-plus pricing A method of pricing in which the buyer pays the cost of an item plus a commission to the seller, as with a cost-plus contract. The term is also applied to a method of arriving at the selling price of goods or services by estimating the total cost to produce or provide them and then adding a percentage markup in order to make a profit.

cost price The price for a product that covers the costs of its production and distribution but with no profit for the producer.

cost-push inflation A type of inflation that results from price increases resulting from increased production costs.

cost schedule A table that lists total production costs for different levels of production. It can be used to draw *cost curves* and calculate *average costs* and *marginal costs*.

Council for Mutual Economic Assistance (CMEA *or* COMECOM) A group of Communist bloc countries that combined in 1949 with the aim of producing a self-sufficient economic bloc that could be coordinated from a central point (and to consolidate Soviet influence in the area). Its members were: Bulgaria, Cuba, Czechoslovakia, East Germany, Hungary, Mongolia, Poland, Romania, USSR and Vietnam. In 1991 is was superseded by the *Organization for Economic Cooperation and Development.*

Council of Economic Advisors A US agency within the Executive Office of the President that analyses the national economy and its various segments, advises the President on economic developments, appraises the economic programmes and policies of the federal government, recommends policies for economic growth and stability, and assists in the preparation of the annual Economic Report of the President to Congress.

council tax A UK local tax levied since April 1993 (when it replaced the *community charge*) on private properties based on their *rateable values. See also uniform business rate.*

counterparty credit risk In trading securities, the risk that the counterparty to a sale or purchase may fail to fulfil his or her obligations.

countertrading Barter; obtaining goods or services using means other than money.

countervailing credit Alternative term for *back-to-back credit.*

countervailing duty (CVD) An extra charge imposed on imported goods to offset subsidies received by the exporter.

countervailing power The marketing power that one economic group can use to protect itself by balancing the power of others. For example, large buyers and cooperatives can obtain discounts from suppliers and may even control prices.

coupon 1. A document attached to a bond, which must be detached and sent to the paying party in order for the bond holder to receive interest payments. Each payment is detailed on the coupon for each payment period. 2. An alternative term for interest that is payable on a fixed-interest security.

coupon interest rate The interest rate payable on a bond (related to its face value).

Cournot competition A type of competition in which each of the

C

competing companies assumes that the others will not change their outputs of products. The concept was first proposed by the French economist Augustin Cournot (1801-77).

Cournot duopoly A two-company example of *Cournot competition* in which each determines its output assuming that the other will not change its output.

covenant Broadly, any form of agreement; or more specifically, an agreement taken out between two parties, stating that one party agrees to pay the other a series of fixed sums over a certain period of time.

cover 1. Any form of security (ie collateral). 2. In financial futures, the buying of contracts to offset a short position. 3. The number of times a company could theoretically pay dividends to shareholders from its earnings. 4. To make enough money in selling products or services to pay for their production.

covered interest arbitrage A system in which money borrowed in one currency is converted into another and then invested, before selling it for a future delivery against the first currency.

covering A type of *hedging* to protect the value of currency received from international trade (by investing in the currency futures market).

CPS Abbreviation of *Current Population Survey.*

crawling peg exchange rate A form of fixed exchange rate in which the rate is allowed to fluctuate according to supply and demand, but within certain specified minimum and maximum limits. It is also known as a sliding peg rate.

creative accounting Also known informally as number fudging or window dressing, the creation of a favourable account sheet without resort to actual fraud.

creative destruction A decrease in the value of capital assets in one part of the economy as a result of technical advances in another part.

credibility How much people believe the policy statements of government and other authorities, especially those relating to inflation. It depends largely on past behaviour ('track record').

credit 1. A loan of money (made by a trader before requiring payment for goods or services). 2. A book-keeping balance that shows a profit (ie, on the right-hand side of the account). 3. A person's or company's financial standing. 4. To add a sum to an account.

credit account Also called a charge account, an account offered by some retail stores and chains which allows a customer to purchase goods on the spot (usually by means of a plastic card) and to pay for them at the end of the accounting period or in instalments.

credit control 1. method employed by a company to ensure that its debts are paid within a reasonable time. 2. As part of monetary policy, the government regulation of borrowing (eg by specifying minimum deposits and payback periods for hire purchase agreements).

credit creation An alternative term for *bank-deposit creation.*

credit cycle The idea that fluctuations in credit cause trade cycles. The ease of obtaining credit from banks and other lenders creates an economic boom, but defaults in repayment then cause a slump. When lending restarts the cycle continues.

credit freeze An action by banks (under the government's direction) to restrict the extension of credit to customers. It is also called a credit squeeze.

credit guarantee Insurance against default provided for a lender by a credit guarantee organization. The *Export Credits Guarantee Department* is a UK government-run scheme of this sort.

creditor A person or company that lends or is owed money. In company accounting, creditors who are due to be paid within a year are classified as current creditors; creditors who are not due to be paid until after a year are classified as long-term liabilities.

creditor nation A nation that has a surplus on its balance of payments (it has positive net foreign assets).

credit rating A rating assigned to a person or company that assesses creditworthiness.

credit-rating agency An organization that collects and sells data about a person's or company's creditworthiness.

credit rationing The imposition of a limit on overall lending by a bank or other lender (as an alternative to raising interest rates, which could increase the number of bad debts).

C

credit risk When a loan is made, the risk that the borrower will be unable (or unwilling) to repay the principal and any interest owing.

credit sale A purchase that is paid for at a future date, usually in instalments (ie using instalment credit). Unlike **hire purchase**, it confers ownership as soon as the contract is signed.

credit squeeze An alternative term for *credit freeze*.

credit transfer A method of paying money into another person's bank account.

credit union In the UK, a non-profit making mutual organization that offers facilities for savings, makes small loans, and may provide basic personal insurance within a local area. In the USA and some European countries, it is a member-owned, democratically governed, non-profit making cooperative that provides financial services to members and whose earnings are returned to the members.

creeping inflation A type of inflation in which prices rise moderately but continuously over a long time, regarded as not a bad thing by some economists.

cross-elasticity of demand The percentage change in the demand for one good divided by the percentage change in the demand for a different good. It may be positive (an increase in demand for good X results in a similar increase in demand for good Y) or negative (the result is a decrease in the demand for Y).

cross-section analysis The analysis of various companies' financial statements for a single accounting period (as opposed to time-series analysis, in which a single company's statements are analysed over several time periods).

cross-section data Information about a number of factors—people, companies or even nations—that relates to the same period of time, as opposed to time-series data which comprises information about a single factor in successive periods of time.

cross-subsidization The financing of a loss-making activity using profits obtained elsewhere. It may be employed by a company to allow price cutting (to undercut a rival), new-product development or diversification into new markets. In a social context, loss-making services (such as a country bus route) can be financed by a cross-subsidy from other income (such as from urban bus routes).

C

crowding out An effect in which increased government spending reduces the level of spending in the private sector. For instance government borrowing can adversely affect interest rates, discouraging private investors.

CT Abbreviation of *Corporation Tax.*

CTT Abbreviation of *capital transfer tax.*

cum coupon Describing a security that is passed from one holder to another with *coupon* (enabling the holder to claim interest payments) attached. *See also ex coupon.*

cum dividend Describing shares that are sold with the right of the new holder to claim the next dividend payment. It is sometimes abbreviated to cum div. *See also ex dividend.*

cumulative preference share A kind of *preference share* whose holder can claim any dividends not paid in earlier years, as long as the company has funds to pay them. Even then, eventual payment is guaranteed before payment to holders of ordinary shares.

cum new Describing shares that are sold with the right to claim participation in any outstanding scrip or rights issue. *See also ex new.*

currency 1. Coins and banknotes that are used as *legal tender.* 2. An alternative term for cash. 3. In banking, the general term for foreign currency.

currency appreciation Under a floating exchange rate system, a rise in the value of one currency in terms of other currencies (making exports dearer and imports cheaper, thus tending to reduce any balance of payments surplus). A large upward change is termed revaluation.

currency depreciation Under a floating exchange rate system, a fall in the value of one currency in terms of other currencies (making imports dearer and exports cheaper, thus tending to reduce any balance of payments deficit). A large downward change is termed devaluation.

currency risk Also called exchange rate risk, the potential loss that could be incurred from a movement in exchange rates. Foreign investment, foreign lending and foreign trade can all incur such risk, which can be minimized in the short term by investing in the currency futures market.

C

current account 1. An account at a bank or building society for the day-to-day deposits and withdrawals of cash. It is a type of sight deposit. 2. For a particular period of time, an outline of a country's trade with other countries, both in visibles (goods) and invisibles (services).

current account deficit In a nation's balance of payments, a current account that has expenditure in excess of receipts.

current accounts In company accounting, an account detailing interdepartmental or intercompany balances, or an account detailing transactions of a partner in a partnership which do not relate to his or her capital.

current account surplus In a nation's balance of payments, a current account that has receipts in excess of expenditure.

current asset Money owed to a person or company that should be received within a year of the date of the balance sheet (as opposed to a long-term asset).

current cost accounting (CCA) Also known as inflation accounting, a method of accounting that takes changes in pricing due to inflation into account, adjusting the values of assets, costs, and so on.

current expenditure Expenditure on assets for resale, such as raw materials, rather than fixed assets. It is also known as above-the-line expenditure.

current liability Money owed by a person or company that should be paid within a year of the date of the balance sheet (as opposed to a long-term liability).

Current Population Survey (CPS) A US Census Bureau survey that compiles economic data about US households.

current prices Prices that have not been adjusted to take account of the current purchasing power of money (eg prices that were current at the time that economic data was collected). *See also constant prices.*

Customs and Excise The UK government department charged with levying indirect taxes, including customs duty on imports, excise duty on certain home-produced goods (such as petrol) and value-added tax (VAT). It formal name is Board of Customs and Excise.

customs barrier A high level of customs duty that makes trade difficult. It is also known as a tariff barrier.

customs drawback When imported goods are re-exported, or used to manufacture goods that are then exported, a rebate of the customs duty originally paid.

customs duty A duty levied on imports by the Customs and Excise, either as a protectionist measure or simply to raise revenue for the government.

customs union A group of nations between which there is free trade and which employ a *common external tariff* in their trade with non-union nations (unlike a free-trade area where there is a variable external tariff).

cut-throat competition Intense competition that threatens the survival of one or all of the competing parties.

CVD Abbreviation of *countervailing duty.*

cyclical adjustment The adjustment of varying economic data to values that would pertain if total activity remained at its normal level or followed its normal trend.

cyclical fluctuation Short-term variations in an economic variable, generally about a steady trend (*see secular trend*).

cyclically adjusted budget deficit The government's *budget deficit* recalculated to show what it would be at normal levels of activity (*see cyclical adjustment*).

cyclically adjusted public sector borrowing requirement The government's *public sector borrowing requirement* recalculated to show what it would be at normal levels of activity (*see cyclical adjustment*).

cyclical unemployment Unemployment that results from movements in the trade cycle (eg during a recession).

C

D

data mining Looking for correlations in economic data (often using computers) with a view to forming general theories. It is frowned on by many statisticians because any correlation might be coincidental, although there are standard tests of significance that can be applied.

dated security A security, such as a bill of exchange or a bond, that has a stated date for repayment (redemption date) of its nominal value. It may be described as short-dated or long-dated.

dawn raid The buying of a significant number of a target company's shares at the start of a day's trading, or before the market becomes aware of what is happening, often at a price higher than normal. The purpose of a dawn raid is to give the buyer a strategic stake in the target company, from which he or she may launch a takeover bid.

DCE Abbreviation of *domestic credit expansion.*

DCF Abbreviation of *discounted cashflow.*

DCR Abbreviation of *domestic content requirements.*

DE Abbreviation of *Department of Employment.*

deadweight burden of taxes The difference between the revenue raised by taxation and the harm it does (eg fewer goods are sold if the indirect tax on them is raised).

deadweight debt A debt that is not covered by or incurred in exchange for real assets. For example, part of the National Debt taken on to pay for war is a deadweight debt.

deadweight loss When a product's output is kept less than optimum under perfect competition (eg when a monopolist restricts output to keep up prices), the reduction in consumers' and producers' surpluses is termed the deadweight loss.

dealer 1. Anybody who is engaged in trading (usually on their own account) on a financial market. 2. An overseas agent who acts as an intermediary between an overseas exporter and a home importer.

dear money Describing money that is difficult to find for borrowing or investment and even then at only very high interest rates.

death duty Also called estate duty, a former tax levied in the UK until 1975 on the estate of someone who has died. It was superseded by capital transfer tax, which was itself replaced in 1986 by *inheritance tax*.

death rate The average number of deaths per year per 1,000 population.

debenture A long-term loan to a company made at a fixed rate of interest and usually with a specified maturity date, generally between 10 and 40 years. Fixed debentures are secured against a specified company asset, floating debentures against its assets generally. Debenture holders are numbered with the company's creditors, and in the event of liquidation have preferential claims on the company. Debentures may be treated as tradable securities.

debit A sum owed by or a charge made on a person or organization, ie a *debt* as it is described in accounting. In double-entry book-keeping, for example, a debit appears on the left-hand side of an account, where it represents an increase in assets or expenditure (corresponding to a decrease in liabilities, owners' equities or revenues).

debt A sum of money, or value of goods or services, owed by one person, group, company or nation to another. Debts arise because the seller allows the purchaser *credit*. Assignable debts may be transferred in whole from one person to another. In commerce, especially in the USA, the term is also used to describe the whole of a company's long-term borrowings.

debt burden *See burden of debt.*

debt-collection agency A firm that charges a commission for collecting its client's outstanding debts. *See also factoring.*

debt crisis The situation that arises when a major debtor cannot or will not service a debt (ie make interest payments) or settle a debt (ie pay it in full). Mere fear on the part of the lender that this might happen contributes to the debt crisis.

debt deflation A reduction in spending that results from too much debt on the part of individuals or companies (who prefer to reduce the debt than to spend or borrow further).

debt financing A method a company uses to raise funds, by issuing bonds, mortgages or notes.

D

debt for equity The substitution of an equity stake for a debt that is proving difficult to recover, despite the good prospects of the borrower.

debt management The management of a debt (corporate or national) to minimize the cost and to make sure that money is available for repayments and interest.

debt neutrality The concept that borrowing money to finance spending has the same effects as does financing it in another way.

debtor A person, company or nation that owes money, goods or services to another.

debtors A company's balance-sheet assets that consist of debts due to it (short-term or long-term).

debt service ratio In international finance, a nation's annual repayments on its foreign debt divided by the value of its exports (in hard currency).

debt servicing The payment of interest on a debt.

decentralization The distribution of the constituent parts of a company or government to a variety of geographical locations. The advantages include the availability of cheaper labour (that is likely to be offset initially by the cost of relocating key personnel), increased efficiency and, in the case of government, the provision of incentives to industry to consider non-metropolitan locations.

decreasing-balance depreciation Also called declining-balance depreciation or reducing-balance depreciation, a way of determining depreciation charges by reducing the book value of a fixed asset at the beginning of a specified accounting period by a constant percentage (derived by taking into account the acquisition cost, depreciable life and scrap value of the asset).

decreasing returns A situation in which the figure given by outputs divided by inputs decreases as inputs increase.

deep discounted stock Also called zero coupon stock, loan stock issued at a greater discount than other stock of the issuer, providing lower (or zero) interest.

default A failure to comply with the terms set out in a contract. Legal proceedings may follow if the matter cannot be settled amicably.

defence spending Government expenditure on armaments and the military (as opposed to civil spending).

deferred rebate A rebate (or discount) to a buyer that is retained by the seller for a specified time in order to build up customer loyalty.

deferred share A share with special dividend rights, often allocated all company profits remaining after a given percentage has been paid on other kinds of shares. Such shares are usually issued to the founders of a company.

deficiency payment A farming subsidy paid by the government when selling prices for produce fall below pre-set government targets.

deficit An excess of expenditure over income, or liabilities over assets; it is therefore a loss.

deficit financing The financing of an excess of expenditure over income (a budget deficit) by borrowing. *See **public sector borrowing requirement**.*

deflation A persistent decrease in prices, generally caused by a fall in the level of economic activity within a country; the opposite of inflation. It should not be confused with *disinflation*.

deflationary gap The difference between the actual level of investment and the level necessary to restore full employment.

deindustrialization An ongoing decrease in the contribution to national income by the industrial sector. Often a fall in the numbers of people employed in industry accompanies it, as often does a rise in the contribution made by the services sector.

delivered pricing The practice of calculating the price of goods for sale that includes the cost of delivery.

delivery note A document that advises a recipient of the intended delivery of goods or that accompanies goods on delivery.

Delors Report A report published in 1989 that proposed the adoption of a single currency and a common monetary policy by the European Community (now the EU). It was prepared by a committee under the chairmanship of President of the Community Jacques Delors and had the full title *Report on Economic and Monetary Union for the European Community*.

delta A stock exchange classification of shares that are traded on the *Alternative Investment Market.* They are generally relatively inactive and stable shares in small companies.

demand 1. A desire for possession of a particular good or service at a specified price expressed by those able and willing to purchase it. 2. A request, such as a request for payment of a debt.

demand curve A relationship between demand and price, in the form of a graph that plots the likely demand for a product at various prices.

demand-determined output The situation that arises when output is determined only by demand, as occurs during a depression.

demand for money Also termed liquidity preference, the amount of money people want to retain. It is generally determined by the amount of transactions people wish to make (*transactions motive*), the way they think interest rates will move (*speculative motive*) and how uncertain they feel about the future (*precautionary motive*).

demand function A mathematical expression that links the demand for a good or service with changes in an independent variable such advertising expenditure, credit availability, buyer's income, price of the product, prices of other goods, and so on. It is also called the Marshallian demand function after the UK economist Alfred Marshall (1842-1924).

demand inflation A general rise in prices (inflation) that results from excess demand (at a time when there are insufficient resources to meet it).

demand management Controlling the level of an economy's aggregate demand by means of fiscal and monetary policies. It attempts to remove or moderate economic fluctuations such as the business cycle, targeting the balance of payments, inflation or unemployment.

demand-pull inflation Overall price rises resulting from excess demand in an economy (ie there are not enough goods and services to meet the demand for them).

demand schedule A table of price variations of a product and the quantities demanded at each price.

demarcation A dividing line that separates the activities of one group of workers in a company (such as maintenance engineers) from another group (such as maintenance electricians).

demerger The splitting of a company into two or more independent parts, either by floating them separately on the stock exchange or by selling them off.

demographic transition The way a country's population alters with increasing economic development, gradually changing from high birth rates and high death rates, though a period of rapid population growth as death rates fall, to a levelling off of population with low birth rates and low death rates.

demographic unemployment Unemployment that results from a fairly rapid increase in the number of workers available, often because of migration.

demography The study of human populations and how they change in nature and number over time.

denationalization The privatization of a previously nationalized industry by floating the company concerned on the stock exchange and selling shares to members of the public or to institutions. In the UK, denationalized industries include British Telecom, British Gas and British Airways.

Department of Employment (DE) A UK government department that puts the government's employment laws and policies into practice. It also runs local employments offices (Job Centres) and organizes industrial training schemes.

Department of Social Security (DSS) A UK government department that puts the government's social security policies into practice. It collects National Insurance contributions and pays out various state benefits and pensions.

Department of the Environment (DOE) A UK government department that regulates local authorities and monitors the environment, especially with regard to pollution.

Department of Trade and Industry (DTI) A UK government department that advises and controls business, finance and overseas trade, according to the government's policies.

depauperization The relief of poverty (generally through economic growth).

dependency culture A situation in which the provision of benefits to those in need increases their likelihood of needing (or at least accepting) them.

dependency ratio In an economy, the number of people of non-working age (either because they are too young or too old) divided by the number of working age, usually expressed as a percentage.

depletable resources Resources that can be used only once, such as fossil fuels and other minerals, unlike renewable resources such as wind or tidal energy.

depletion theory The branch of economics that studies the rates at which natural resources are used up.

deposit An initial payment made on an item to reserve it, or an initial payment for something bought on credit or by hire purchase. The term is also used for goods or money placed with a bank or other financial institution.

deposit account A bank account that pays interest, although usually notice has to be given before funds may be withdrawn (it is a type of time deposit).

Depository Institutions Deregulation and Monetary Controls Act (DIDMCA) US legislation that removed the limit on interest rates for passbook savings accounts (which thereafter followed market trends).

depreciation A positive decline in the real value of a tangible asset because of consumption, wear or obsolescence. The concept of depreciation is widely used for the purpose of writing off the cost of an asset against profit over an extended period (its depreciable life), irrespective of the real value of the asset. See *accelerated depreciation; decreasing-balance depreciation.*

depressed area A part of a country that has lower-than-average levels of income and higher levels of unemployment than elsewhere.

depression A major and persistent downswing of a trade cycle, characterized by high unemployment and the underutilization of other factors of production. A less severe downswing is known as a slump or recession.

deregulation The removal of controls and the abandonment of state supervision of private enterprise. One of the most notable recent deregulations was that of the London Stock Exchange.

derivative A transferrable, often high-risk, security, such as a future or an option.

derived demand A demand for a product that depends on the simultaneous demand for another related one. For example, a demand for tyres depends in turn on a demand for motor vehicles.

devaluation A reduction in the relative value of currency. The devaluation may be relative to an absolute value (eg the gold standard) or, more usually, to other relative values (eg other currencies).

developed country A country with an advanced economy, with a large service sector and a large industrial sector (although there is a move to increasing services at the cost of industry). Average per capita income is also high.

developing country A country that is beginning to industrialize, but which is still too poor to do without foreign aid. Developing countries are characterized by improving standards of health, wealth (standard of living), education, capital investment and productivity, and by a broadening of the economic base.

development area An economically depressed area suitable for reindustrialization. Development areas are designated by the state and incentives are provided to help to attract new businesses to the area, to encourage the relocation of existing businesses, and to enhance the prospects for employment.

development economics The branch of economics that studies how developing countries attain sustained economic growth through increasing their productive capacity (agricultural and industrial) and improvements in infrastructure.

DIDMCA Abbreviation of *Depository Institutions Deregulation and Monetary Controls Act.*

diffusion of innovations The spreading around an economy and among nations of new ideas and objects, usually by copying or adaptation.

diminishing marginal product An alternative term for *diminishing returns.*

diminishing marginal utility The observation that as a consumer uses more of a product, his or her satisfaction (utility) with it gradually decreases.

diminishing returns A concept that suggests that as additional units of one factor of production are added, the relative increase in output will eventually begin to decline. For example, a factory can increase its output by employing more labour, but unless other factors of production (eg machinery) are also increased each additional employee will be working with a smaller proportion of the other, fixed, resources available.

direct cost Also called variable cost, the cost of materials, items or activities (including labour) that are directly involved in the production of goods, and without which those goods could not be produced in the short term. The prime cost is the total of direct expenses, direct labour and direct materials.

direct investment 1. Company money spent on physical assets, such as plant and machinery. 2. Investment in a company's overseas operations by buying an existing foreign operation or creating a new one.

directive European Union (EU) legislation that states what has to be done within a given timescale, without defining how it is to be done.

direct labour Members of a company's workforce who are directly involved in the production of goods or services. For example, a welder is a member of the direct labour force whereas an estimator is not.

direct materials Materials that directly become part of a company's product or cost unit.

director One of the principals of a company, in a public liability company (plc) appointed by its shareholders. Most companies have a group of directors (the board of directors) who act collectively as the senior management of the company, being responsible to the shareholders for its efficient running and future development. The duties and legal responsibilities of a director are defined in the Companies Acts.

direct taxation A system of taxation whereby companies and individuals pay tax on income directly to the authorities (Inland Revenue in the UK, Internal Revenue Service in the USA) or through an employer, as opposed to indirect taxation, in which tax is added to the prices of goods and services.

D

dirigisme The willingness of a government to intervene in the country's economy; the opposite of laissez-faire.

dirty float A partly-managed floating exchange rate in which the central bank continues to intervene in the market for its own currency.

discomfort index A measure of a country's economic difficulties given by the sum of the annual rates of inflation and unemployment. It was devised by the US economist Arthur Okun (1928-80).

discount To make a reduction in the face value of an article (or the list price), generally in order to make the purchase more attractive to a customer or perhaps for paying by cash. Bulk discounts and trade discounts are also sometimes available. Discounts are shown as expenses in a company's profit and loss account. The term has several other meanings.

discounted cashflow (DCF) A method of assessing a company's investments according to when they are due to yield their expected returns, in order to indicate cashflows and the present worth of the future sum. In this way it is possible to determine preferences for one of a number of alternative investments.

discount factor Also called present-value factor, a factor that, when applied to a predicted annual cashflow, converts it to a present value. It is equal to $1/(1 + r)^t$, where r is the **hurdle rate** and t is the duration of the project concerned.

discount house An organization whose main activity historically is discounting bills of exchange. Today discount houses deal mainly in Treasury bills and other short-term government debt instruments that are issued at a discount but redeemed at their face values.

discounting The act of making a *discount* or applying *discount factors*. More specifically, it is the practice of selling a debt at a discount to an institution (*see discount house*).

discounting the future The practice of assigning a lower value to future receipts than to the same sum received now. The various possible (unrelated) reasons include: the recipient might by then be no longer alive to receive it; the recipient may by then be more wealthy so that the sum involved is much less significant (has a much lower marginal utility); or the debtor may not pay up.

discount market That part of a money market that involves the buying and selling of short-term debt between the commercial banks, the discount houses and the central bank.

discount rate An interest rate applied to future earnings to convert them to present values. It is the cost of capital rate of interest or hurdle rate used with a discount factor in calculating a discounted cash flow.

discount window A method by which a bank gets short-term funds from a central bank, either by securing a loan or by issuing Treasury bills.

discretionary competition policy A way of judging whether economic changes are, overall, good or bad by looking at the implications of individual mergers, takeovers, restrictive trade practices, and so on.

discretionary policy A policy that is left to the policy-makers to decide, as opposed to an inflexible *rules-based policy* (which may be inappropriate for something as complex as the workings of the economy).

discretionary spending Expenditure that a government organization can make but is not legally obliged to do so (as opposed to *mandatory spending*).

discriminating duty Also called discriminatory tariff, an import duty or tariff set at a different level from other similar ones to discourage or favour a certain commodity or a certain exporting country.

discriminating monopoly A monopoly in which the monopolist sells its goods or services at two or more different prices or to two or more different sectors. For example, an electricity supply company may sell electricity at a cheaper rate to industrial users than to domestic users, in an attempt to dissuade the larger industrial users from changing to cheaper forms of power.

discrimination The differential treatment of imports depending on where they come from. *See customs union; discriminating duty.*

discriminatory tariff An alternative term for *discriminating duty.*

diseconomies of scale An increase in the average cost of a product that may occur in the long run as the scale of production increases beyond a certain level. There could be various causes: transport costs (to and from the manufacturing plant); congestion within the plant; problems with administration and management of a large-scale operation;

D

problems with recruitment and labour relations; problems with the disposal of waste.

disembodied technical progress　An increase in output (productivity) without adding to input or investing in new equipment resulting from better technical knowledge of the existing equipment. *See also embodied technical progress*.

disequilibrium　A situation in which a plan or project cannot be implemented either because equilibrium has not been attained or it has been lost. It generally leads to a process of change (*see dynamic analysis*).

disguised unemployment　An alternative term for *concealed unemployment*.

dishoarding　A reduction in previously-hoarded stocks of goods (or money).

disincentive　Anything that lessens the incentive to save or work, such as high marginal tax rates. In extreme cases it may make it pay not to work (people receiving unemployment benefit may be better off than if they accepted low-paid work).

disinflation　The curbing of inflation by the adoption of mild economic measures such as the restriction of expenditure. Other measures include increasing interest rates and the deliberate creation of a budget surplus. Disinflation is a mild form of deflation, which by contrast indicates an uncontrollable fall in prices.

disintermediation　The withdrawal of a financial intermediary from a negotiation. The term may also be applied to the flow of funds from lenders to borrowers 'off the balance sheet' without the intervention of an intermediary (such as a mortgage broker).

disinvestment　The withdrawal or sale of an investment. Governments and companies sometimes decide to disinvest from nations whose economic or political complexion offends them.

disposable income　That part of a person's income that he or she may dispose of in any way, ie, what is left after taxes have been paid.

dissaving　A preference for spending rather than saving.

distorted price　A price for a good or service that is not indicative of the actual cost of making it available. For example the seller may be a monopolist who controls the market.

distribution 1. The transport, allocation and placement of raw materials or goods to and from a factory to warehouses and shops. 2. Payments made by a company from its profits (ie dividends). 3. The apportioning of a scrip issue or rights issue of shares.

distribution channel The route followed by a product from its producer to its ultimate purchaser.

distribution cost The expense incurred by a company in advertising, selling and delivering goods, including the costs of packaging, insurance, and postage or transport. It is also known as distribution expense or distribution overhead.

distributive efficiency The efficiency of a market in getting its products from the suppliers to the consumers. This requires minimization of distribution costs (transport, storage and handling) and selling costs (advertising, packaging and other costs of sale).

disutility The lack of satisfaction a consumer feels in consuming a product or in performing work (generally assumed to decrease with the former and to increase with the latter).

divergence indicator For members of the *Exchange Rate Mechanism*, a measure of how far their exchange rate differs from their central parities with the European currency unit (Ecu).

diversification The extension of the range of goods and services offered into new areas, either material or geographical. By extension the term may also be applied to attempts by local authorities or central government to attract a variety of industries to an area heavily dependent upon a single industry, particularly one in decline.

divestment The sale or liquidation of parts of a company, generally in an attempt to improve efficiency by cutting loss-making business and/or concentrating on one product or industry. Divestment is therefore the opposite process to merger.

dividend A share in the profits of a limited company, generally paid annually. Dividends are usually expressed as a percentage of the nominal value of a single ordinary share. Thus a payment of 10p on each £1 share (or 10c on each $1 share) would be termed a dividend of 10%. They may also be expressed in terms of the dividend yield, which is the dividend expressed as a percentage of the share value. Dividends are determined by the directors of a company and are announced at the

D

end of the annual general meeting (AGM).

dividend control A government restriction that limits or prevents the payment of or an increase in company dividends.

dividend cover The degree to which a dividend payment on ordinary shares is covered by profits earned. Thus a company that declares after-tax profits of $10m and makes a total dividend payment of $2m on ordinary shares is said to be 'covered five times'. An uncovered dividend, on the other hand, is a payment made at least partly from reserves rather than current profits.

dividend policy A company policy, agreed by the board of directors, regarding the allocation of profits between shareholders (in the form of dividends) and reserves.

dividend warrant An order to a company's bankers to pay a specified dividend or interest to a shareholder or other investor.

dividend yield A yield calculated in relation to the current market price of the investment; the dividend divided by the share price.

division of labour The splitting of a job or other task into small repeating parts that can each be done by one person.

divorce of ownership from control An acknowledgement of the fact that, in many companies, actual control lies with the senior management (board of directors) and not with the shareholders (the owners).

dollar standard A system in which countries peg their exchange rates to the US dollar (and hold most of their currency reserves in dollars).

domestic content requirements (DCR) A condition imposed by some countries that imported goods should contain a certain amount of components made within that country using domestic labour and materials.

domestic credit expansion (DCE) A measurement of the growth of a nation's money supply which allows for changes in the balance of payments by deducting net foreign currency reserves from the figure for the money supply itself. It is thus a measure of domestic liquidity.

domestic distortion A factor that causes a nation's internal economy to differ from the usual state in which any change that increases

D

somebody's welfare lowers somebody else's (the so-called **Pareto optimality**). Discriminatory taxation and a monopoly situation are examples of such distortions.

domestic economy The internal economy of a nation.

domestic market The market for goods and services that exists within a country, as opposed to the international market that is reached by exports.

domestic product The value of the total production from enterprises that operate within a country, no matter who owns them. Compare with **national product**.

domestic rates A method of local taxation, in operation until 1990, that levied a tax on property according to its **rateable value**. It was replaced by the **community charge** (poll tax), itself later superseded by **council tax**.

dominant firm A company that supplies a major proportion (more than a quarter) of a particular good or service, which may give it an advantage in negotiating price from the producer. See also **monopoly**.

dominant strategy A strategy that is the best to follow (or is as good as any alternative) no matter what others do—an option that is seldom available except in **game theory**.

dominated strategy A strategy that it is wrong to follow, no matter what others do. See **dominant strategy**.

double counting The danger of trying to find an economy's total output by summing each company's gross sales without subtracted what they purchase from other companies.

double-entry bookkeeping A method of recording financial transactions under two parallel headings, debits and credits, so that all accounts must balance (thus preserving the equality of the accounting equation).

double-figure inflation Inflation that has reached a rate of more than 10 per cent.

double taxation A situation in which something is taxed more than once. For example, the income of a non-resident may be taxed in his or her home country as well as in the country of residence. **Double-taxation agreements** aim to avoid this happening.

double-taxation agreement An agreement between two countries that the income of non-residents should not be taxed both in their home country and in their country of residence.

Dow Jones Index Formal name the Dow Jones Industrial Average, often called simply the Dow Jones, a security price index used on the New York Stock Exchange and issued by the US firm of Dow Jones & Co. (publishers of the Wall Street Journal). It is based on the average closing prices of a selection of 30 quoted companies.

down payment Another term for a *deposit* against the purchase of goods or services.

downside risk The amount a person stands to lose when taking a risk.

downsizing 1. To reduce the size of a company's workforce (ie making employees redundant), usually to make financial savings. 2. To move applications from (large) mainframe computers to (small) personal computers (PCs).

downward-sloping demand curve A *demand curve* that shows that demand decreases as price rises. This is the usual situation, as opposed to an *upward-sloping demand curve* (demand increases as price falls).

drawing rights A method by means of which members of the International Monetary Fund (IMF) that have balance of payments difficulties get financial help. Each member has a quota, up to 25% of which can be drawn on demand. *See also* **Special Drawing Rights**.

DSS Abbreviation of *Department of Social Security.*

DTI Abbreviation of *Department of Trade and Industry.*

dual economy An economy that contains both labour-intensive low-technology sectors such as traditional agriculture and, independent of them, capital-intensive high-technology sectors, a situation that sometimes occurs in a less developed country.

duality A recognition that a problem (such as one in economics) expressed using one set of variables can also be expressed using a totally different set. For example, finding the maximum utility for certain incomes and prices can alternatively be considered as finding the minimum cost of achieving a certain level of utility; the results are the same.

dumping The sale of surplus goods overseas at extremely low prices (often less than cost price). It may be done to get rid of excess production, to earn foreign exchange or to harm foreign industry. It is frowned upon and countries may take retaliatory action (such as the imposition of antidumping duty)

duopoly A market in which there are only two competing companies. Because competition between duopolists is particularly fierce and destructive, there tends to be some form of implicit or even explicit agreement to share the market (eg on a regional basis).

duopsony A market in which there are only two purchasers of a type of goods or services, but a number of competing suppliers.

durable goods Goods that are not consumed by their use but which endure for a reasonable period of time. Some manufacturers of durables incorporate a form of obsolescence to ensure a continuity of demand.

Dutch disease Named after the effects on the economy of the Netherlands after the discovery of natural gas, the way in which a rise in one export increases a nation's exchange rate, thus hampering the sales of other exports (and increasing the competition between home-produced goods and cheaper imports).

duty Broadly, any tax levied by a public authority, particularly that imposed on imports, exports and manufactured goods. *See also excise duty*.

dynamic analysis A type of economic analysis that studies the way that an economy changes between one equilibrium state and another.

dynamic equilibrium An equilibrium whose contributing variables change over time (as opposed to *static equilibrium*).

dynamics An analysis of the behaviour of variable elements.

D

E

earmarking A direct relationship between a certain tax and certain government spending. It would exist in the UK, for example, if the money collected from issuing Road Fund Licences were spent on the roads (which it is not).

earned income Income received in exchange for labour, rather than derived from investments (for UK tax purposes, the definition does, however, include some pension payments and state benefits).

earnings drift The tendency for salaries and wages to rise faster than basic rates per unit of labour, perhaps because of bonuses, overtime and other special arrangements between employers and employees.

earnings per share (EPS) A method of expressing the income of a company, arrived at by dividing the net annual income attributable to the shareholders by the number of shares. Earnings per share can then be used to calculate the price/earnings ratio of the company.

earnings yield A hypothetical figure that provides a reliable measurement of the worth of an investment. It is reached by relating a company's divisible net earnings to the market price of the investment (earnings per share divided by market price, expressed as a percentage). Sometimes, with reference to fixed-interest securities, the term is used interchangeably with flat yield.

easy fiscal policy A policy of increasing government expenditure while at the same time cutting taxes, ignoring the resulting budget deficit and rise in government debt, sometimes pursued during times of depression.

easy monetary policy A policy of giving economic activity a stimulus through low interest rates and wide availability of credit, sometimes pursued during times of depression.

EBRD Abbreviation of *European Bank for Reconstruction and Development.*

EC Abbreviation of *European Community.*

ECGD Abbreviation of *Export Credits Guarantee Department.*

e-commerce Commerce carried out electronically, particularly over the Internet.

E

econometrics A branch of statistics that uses mathematical models to test economic hypotheses, describe economic relationships, and forecast economic trends. Econometrics is employed to produce correlated quantitative data rather than to prove economic causation.

economic aid The giving of financial (and sometimes physical) help to developing countries. It may include money and technical and managerial skills.

economically active population A country's labour force, that part of the population employed in the production of goods and services.

Economic and Monetary Union (EMU) A plan to bring together the currencies and monetary policies of the EU member states, as laid down by the Maastricht Treaty. There would thus be a single currency (the *euro*) and a single central bank . The plan was implemented in January 1999, but not all member states (including the UK) initially took part. By January 2002, all but a few of the member states (including Denmark, Norway, Sweden and the UK) had adopted the euro as their currency.

Economic and Social Research Council (ESRC) Formerly the Social Science Research Council, a UK quango that finances postgraduate training and research in economics and social sciences.

Economic Community of West African States (ECOWAS) An organization of 16 West African nations based in Abuja, Nigeria. By the 1975 Treaty of Lagos (revised 1993) they formed a customs union, and at Freetown, Sierra Leone in 1981 they agreed to remove trade restrictions between member states.

economic development The per capita increase in national income over time. Broadly, the rate of economic development is a way of expressing the growth of an economy and can be used to determine the relative growths of a number of competing or allied economies. It is often used as a simple guide to the health of an economy.

economic doctrines The various schools of thought about economics that have arisen over the years, such as classical, Keynesian, monetarist, neoclasical, and so on.

economic efficiency A measure of how well economic resources are allocated to minimize cost and maximize output.

E

economic growth An alternative term for *economic development.*

economic history The study of economics from a historical perspective.

economic imperialism The economic domination of developing countries (mostly ex-colonies) by advanced countries or multinational companies.

economic indicator One of several measurable variables used to study change in an economy. In addition to these variables, economists study such factors as production indices, unemployment trends, the amount of overtime worked and levels of taxation.

economic man A hypothetical person, often nominated in economic models, who behaves in a totally rational way—and, therefore, also in a completely self-interested way.

economic model A way of dealing with economic variables to examine their relationships, predict the effects of changes to them and work out their probable implications to the economy as a whole.

economic policy The measures taken by a government to attain its economic targets by manipulating the economy.

economic refugee A person who leaves his or her country for economic (rather than political) reasons. The term embraces both tax exiles and those who leave a country in which employments prospects are bleak.

economic rent A payment for the use of a resource which is not the reason for its availability. For example, a landowner may receive an economic rent for an area of unimproved land, or for a highly-paid solicitor whose only other possible occupation would be a low-paid clerk. The economic rent is the difference between the two rates of pay.

economics The study of a society's commercial activities in terms of the production, distribution and consumption of goods and services, and how resources should be allocated.

economic sanction An alternative term for an embargo on trade with another country, almost always for political reasons.

economic statistics Numerical information about levels of income and production, exports and imports, inflation, unemployment and so on as collected and published by the government and other organizations.

economic theory The production of reliable economic models based on

E

human behaviour and measurable economic variables to produce hypotheses that can be tested.

economic union An agreement between two or more countries to do away with trade barriers with each other and to apply common tariffs on imports from non-union members.

economies of scale A reduction in the average cost of production with an increase in amount of production, generally made possible by the large size of a company or industry. Internal economies of scale are defined as those enjoyed by a large single company or operation and are, broadly, made possible by the distribution of indirect costs and improvements in technology, which increase the optimum level of output. External economies of scale are those associated with an industry or location. For example, a concentration of ship-building companies on a river leads to the creation of a large pool of skilled labour which can be drawn on if one company wishes to expand.

economies of scope A reduction in the average cost of production with an enlargement of the range of a company's related activities, which can result in cost savings through shared equipment and labour.

economism The theory that economics is the chief aspect of society to the exclusion of all others (unless they are restated in economic terms).

economize To reduce costs of production. It can be achieved in several ways: to get higher output from the same input, to get the same output from less input, or to get the same output using a cheaper input.

economy 1. The financial and productive apparatus of a nation, or a nation defined in terms of its economic activities. 2. (The exercise of) frugality or cost-reduction.

ECOWAS Abbreviation of *Economic Community of West African States.*

ECSC Abbreviation of *European Coal and Steel Community.*

Ecu See *European currency unit.*

EEA Abbreviation of *European Economic Area.*

EEC Abbreviation of *European Economic Community.*

EEOC Abbreviation of *Equal Employment Opportunity Commission.*

effective demand A desire for goods or services (demand) that is backed by the ability to pay.

E

effective exchange rate A weighted average of a country's exchange rate and that of its significant trading partners.

effective interest rate *See interest yield.*

effective protection The actual protection gained by a home producer when there is a tariff on competing imported products or no tariff (or a lower tariff) on material imported to make the product.

effective yield The yield calculated as a percentage of the price of an investment.

efficiency In general, a measure of the use of resources. High efficiency is achieved by getting the most output from the least input. In a manufacturing company, for example, efficiency can be measured in terms of the standard hours allowed for a certain amount of production and the actual hours taken to achieve it (known as the efficiency ratio).

efficiency audit A check on how efficiently a company is running, either by comparing its performance with what is theoretically possible or by comparing it with that of other similar companies.

efficiency-equity trade-off The dilemma between making decisions on the basis of efficiency only or on the basis of fairness (equity). For instance, it would be economically efficient to tax children's clothing, but unfair on the lower-paid with big families who spend a proportionately larger part of their incomes on it.

efficiency-wage hypothesis The theory that employers may benefit from paying workers more than is justified by their marginal productivity. Better-paid workers—those with higher living standards—are generally better motivated, more productive and more conscientious and loyal.

efficiency markets hypothesis The theory that an efficient (financial) market is one in which all information relevant to price is reflected in the price, and any new information is quickly incorporated ('news soon gets around').

efficient resource allocation The recognition that if a person, company or country allocates resources efficiently it cannot reallocate them to increase the worth of one objective without causing a decrease in another.

EFTA Abbreviation of *European Free Trade Association.*

E

EIB Abbreviation of *European Investment Bank.*

eighty/twenty rule A rule of thumb that states that 80% of benefits (or disbenefits) come from 20% of items or objects. It is also known as the Pareto analysis after the Italian economist and engineer Vilfredo Pareto (1848-1923).

elastic Describing something that responds to change (*see* the following entries).

elasticity 1. The proportional change in a variable divided by the proportional change in another; it is therefore a pure ratio. For example, the proportional change in the amount of a good sold divided by the proportional change in its price is termed *price elasticity.* 2. The ability of a bank to meet demands for currency and credit when needed and to reduce their availability when this is needed (eg when there is overexpansion).

elasticity of demand A measure of how responsive demand for a product is to a change in some independent variable (such as income or price).

elasticity of expectations The proportional change in the expected value of an economic variable divided by a proportional change in its current value, which can have significant effects on the stability of a market.

elasticity of substitution A measure of the change in use of a commodity (by substituting one commodity for another) related to a change in its price.

elasticity of supply A measure of how responsive the supply of a product is to a change in some independent variable (such as price).

elasticity of technical substitution The rate at which one input can be changed to another (eg capital to labour) without affecting output.

eligible bill In the UK, a bank bill that is issued by a bank entitled to discount acceptances at the Bank of England (an eligible bank); it may be rediscounted at the Bank of England. In the USA, another term for *eligible paper.*

eligible liabilities The liabilities for which a bank has to hold a specific percentage of reserves.

eligible paper In the USA, a banker's acceptance that may be rediscounted at the Federal Reserve Bank.

E

e-mail A service provided by a number of organizations (notably Prestel in the UK and the Internet worldwide) that allows two computer users linked by modem and telephone lines to deposit messages on each other's machines.

embargo A prohibition on the export or import of specified goods to or from a particular country or bloc, generally for political reasons.

embodied technical progress Advances in technical knowledge that can be used only by installing new equipment (in which the technical advances become embodied). *See also* **disembodied technical progress**.

emerging market A security market in a newly industrialized country (such as those in Eastern Europe and eastern Asia).

Emerging Markets Traders Association (EMTA) An organization established in New York in the late 1980s for overseeing trade in bank loans to emerging nations. Brady bonds and eurobonds were included in its remit in 1990.

EMI Abbreviation of *European Monetary Institute*.

emolument A salary and other benefits, particularly those paid the holder of high office.

empirical testing The testing of a theory or hypothesis against empirical (actual) data.

employee A person working for somebody else to provide (in economics terms) labour in return for salary or wages, as opposed to somebody who works for himself or herself (ie is self-employed).

employee stock ownership plan (ESOP) A US scheme that lets employees buy shares (stock) in their own company.

employee share-ownership schemes Any scheme that enables employees buy shares (stock) in their own company, such as the US *employee stock ownership plan*.

employer A person or company that employs a workforce in exchange for wages and salaries.

employers' association An organization that represents the interests of employers, usually in a particular industry or sector of the economy. It negotiates with trade unions and makes representations to government.

E

employment   1. The act of employing somebody. 2. The provision of work. 3. The state of having a job.

Employment Acts   UK legislation, passed in 1980, 1982, 1988, 1989 and 1990, that deal with conditions of employment, trade unions and, latterly, the employment of women and young people.

EMS   Abbreviation of *European Monetary System.*

EMTA   Abbreviation of *Emerging Markets Traders Association.*

EMU   Abbreviation of *Economic and Monetary Union.*

endogenous   Describing something that results from the workings of a system (as opposed to exogenous, which derives from outside the system).

endogenous growth   The growth in an economy that in the long term arises out of the workings of the system.

endogenous money   The part of the money supply that arises from the activity of banks within the economic system, as opposed to money supplied from outside (eg by government).

endogenous preference   A consumer's preference that does not derive from his or her innate nature but depends on experience—it has resulted from the effect of outside factors.

endogenous variable   An economic variable that is quantified by other variables within the system—it has an effect on and is affected by the relationship embodied in the relevant economic model.

energy tax   A tax on energy consumption, advocated by some economists as a disincentive to consume (irreplaceable) fossil fuels.

Engel curve   A graph that shows the relationship between the level of income and the spending on (consumption of) a particular good at a particular price. It graphically illustrates *Engel's law*.

Engel's law   As a consumer's income increases, he or she tends to spend an increasing fraction of the additional money on luxuries and a smaller fraction on staple goods. It was formulated in 1857 by the German statistician Ernst Engel (1821-96).

enterprise   Any undertaking, but particularly a bold or remarkable one; or the quality of boldness and imagination in an undertaking.

E

Enterprise Allowance Scheme A UK scheme that pays a weekly allowance to an unemployed person who wants to set up a business.

enterprise culture A social attitude that favours enterprise, being willing to try new ways of conducting business, to take risks and to make (and retain) profits.

Enterprise Investment Scheme A UK scheme dating from 1994 (when it superseded the Business Expansion Scheme) that allows tax relief on money invested in certain small businesses (that are not quoted on the Stock Exchange).

enterprise zone A geographical area in which economic activity is promoted by the government. Small businesses are encouraged, and the relocation of companies and industries to enterprise zones is helped by the provision of various incentives.

entitlement program A programme of US schemes for mandatory (ie non-discretionary) payments of benefits such as Medicare and social security.

entitlement A mandatory benefit, ie one to which the beneficiary has a legal right.

entrepôt A location where imported goods are re-exported without any further processing.

entrepôt trade A trade based on the re-export of imported goods. The exporter may be entitled to a refund of any customs duty paid (drawback), unless the goods are exported directly from a bonded warehouse.

entrepreneur A person who controls a commercial enterprise—the risk-taker or profit-maker—the person who assembles the factors of production and supervises their combination. The term also has the connotation of somebody who has an idea and then finds the money to back it.

entry and exit The appearance of companies in an industry and the disappearance of other companies, as new companies are established and other ones diversify, go into liquidation, or merely cease to trade.

envelope curve A graph that shows the maximum outputs that can be attained from a combination of two or more independent inputs.

E

environmental accounting Also known as green reporting, a method of including in a company's accounts attempts to detail the costs and benefits of the company's activities as they affect the environment.

environmental audit Also known as a green audit, an audit that reveals the impact of a company's activities on the environment.

environmental economics The part of economics that studies the effects of the consumption (and abuse) of natural resources.

environmental impact assessment A European Union requirement for member governments to make an assessment of how any proposed project is likely to affect the environment (such as destroying habitats or causing pollution).

Environment Protection Agency (EPA) A US federal organization that conducts research into pollution and the environment.

EPA Abbreviation of *Environment Protection Agency.*

EPS Abbreviation of *earnings per share.*

Equal Employment Opportunity Commission (EEOC) A US federal organization, established by the Civil Rights Act 1964, that deals with all aspects of discrimination in employment.

equal pay The contention, set out in the UK in the Equal Pay Act 1970, that people doing the same job should be paid the same irrespective of age, sex or race.

equalization grant A UK government grant to smaller local authorities that have an inadequate base from which to raise sufficient money through local taxation.

equalizing wage differential Extra money paid to a worker in an undesirable job, because it is dangerous, dirty, involves unsocial hours, and so on.

equation of international demand The ratio at which the products of one country exchange with those of another is in equilibrium when the amount an importer will import (at this ratio) equals the amount an exporter will export.

equilibrium The theoretical situation in a market where supply and demand are equal.

equilibrium level of national income 1. The national income level at which the total of government spending, exports and investments equals the total of imports, savings and taxes. 2. The national income level at which aggregate demand and aggregate supply are equal. 3. The national income level at which the economy's plans for buying and selling are in synchrony.

equilibrium price The market price for a good or service at which the demand exactly equals the supply.

equilibrium quantity The quantity of a good or service demanded (and supplied) in an equilibrium market where the price is such that demand equals supply.

equity In general terms, the concept of fairness, of central importance to a branch of law distinct from common law, and as such having a significant effect on all kinds of contracts, dealings and trusts. The term also has various specific meanings. 1. The ordinary share capital (risk capital) of a company. 2. A company's net assets. 3. The residual value of common stock over the debit balance of a margin account. 4. The difference between the market value of a property and the outstanding mortgage on it. In the last definition, if the amount still owing is greater than the present market value of the property, the mortgagor (borrower) has negative equity in the property.

equity-efficiency trade-off The difficulty of maximizing average consumption in an economy and at the same time equalizing that consumption throughout the population.

equity withdrawal The practice of obtaining or increasing a mortgage and using the money for purposes other than buying or improving the mortgaged property. It is virtually equivalent to borrowing money with the property as security.

equivalent variation If a good's price falls or a new good becomes available, and in the absence of other price changes, the extra amount of money required to restore the original level of utility to a consumer. *See also **compensating variation**.*

ERM Abbreviation of *Exchange Rate Mechanism.*

escalator The UK government policy of raising excise duty of petrol and tobacco by more than the annual rate of inflation.

escalation clause Also called an escalator clause, a condition in a long-term contract that sets out the agreement concerning rising costs (of, eg, raw materials or labour) during the term of the contract.

E

escape clause A clause in a contract that allows one or other party to withdraw from the contract should certain events take place. For example, in a lease, it is possible to have a clause that allows the lessee to withdraw should the lessor increase the rent.

ESOP Abbreviation of *employee stock ownership plan.*

ESRC Abbreviation of *Economic and Social Research Council.*

Estimates The UK government's proposals for spending in the coming financial year as set out in the budget (and requiring parliamentary approval).

ethical Describing an action that conforms to the moral constraints of an industry or society. *See also* next entry.

ethical investing Investment made in a company that is not active in anything that the investor thinks is antisocial or unethical in its dealings. Thus some investors would not put money into companies that deal in or manufacture animal furs, armaments, tobacco products, and so on.

Euratom Abbreviation of *European Atomic Energy Community.*

euro The standard currency unit of the European Monetary Union, introduced at the beginning of 2002 (but not adopted then by Denmark, Norway. Sweden and the UK).

eurobond A medium- or long-term bearer bond denominated in a eurocurrency. Eurobonds are issued by governments or multinational companies. The eurobond market developed in the 1960s and is independent of the stock market.

eurocurrency Currency of any nation held offshore in a European country. The eurocurrency markets deal in very large-scale loans and deposits rather than the purchase or sale of foreign exchange. *See also euro; Euromarket.*

Euroland A theoretical political association comprising European Union countries that adopted the euro in 2002.

Euromarket 1. A market in which eurocurrency is traded. 2. A market for currencies from countries other than the one in which the market is located. 3. Any market in *Euroland.*

E

European Atomic Energy Community (Euratom) An organization of

European Union member states that was set up to develop the Community's peaceful exploitation of nuclear energy in commerce and industry.

European Bank for Reconstruction and Development (EBRD) A financial institution, established in London in 1990, which encourages open-market practices and private enterprise in Central and Eastern Europe.

European Central Bank (ECB) The European Union's central bank, proposed in 1995 and intended to be established in 1988 and functional by 1998, as formulated by the Maastricht Treaty. Its main task is to deal with the single European currency (euro) and lay down monetary policy throughout the EU.

European Coal and Steel Community (ECSC) An organization founded in 1952 by France, Italy, West Germany and the Benelux countries (Belgium, the Netherlands and Luxembourg) to establish a common market for coal and steel and to abolish quotas and tariffs among members. It merged with the European Economic Community in 1958.

European Commission A major institution of the European Union, established in 1967, responsible for implementing the Treaty of Rome. It introduces EU legislation and reconciles disagreements between members.

European Community (EC) Short form of the European Economic Community (EEC), now called the *European Union (EU)*.

European Council The European Union's executive organization, comprising the foreign ministers and other ministers of the member states and chaired by the President of the European Commission.

European currency snake An agreement reached in 1972 among the members of the European Community to so manage exchange rates that they moved in relation to each other (with fluctuations limited to within $\pm 2\frac{1}{4}\%$). It was superseded in 1979 by the *European Monetary System*.

European Currency Unit (ECU) Unit of account dating in use by the European Economic Union (EEC) from 1979 and now by the European Union (EU). The value of the ECU is calculated by taking a weighted average of the current value of EU member-states' own currencies. It exists on paper, but is used to settle intra-Union debts and in the

E

calculation of Union budgets. Because it is an inherently stable currency, the ECU is increasingly favoured in the international money markets as a medium for international trade. *See also euro.*

European Development Fund A fund, set up in 1975 by the *Lomé Convention*, to provide aid to the Lomé signatories.

European Economic Area (EEA) A European free trade area, established in 1994 by agreement between the European Union (EU) and the European Free Trade Association (EFTA). Its members consist of the countries of the European Union plus Iceland, Liechtenstein and Norway.

European Economic Community (EEC) An association of some twelve European nations, established in 1957 by the Treaty of Rome, that were joined by a customs union and committed to the promotion of free trade within the boundaries of the community, now renamed the *European Union (EU)*. The founding members were Belgium, France, Germany, Italy, Luxembourg and the Netherlands. Later members include Austria, Denmark, Finland, Greece, Ireland, Portugal, Spain, Sweden and the UK . It was often abbreviated to European Community (EC) and was originally known as the Common Market.

European Exchange Rate Mechanism (ERM) *See Exchange Rate Mechanism.*

European Free Trade Association (EFTA) A trade association, established in 1960 between several west European countries, some of whom left when they joined the European Union.

European Investment Bank (EIB) A bank established in 1958 with headquarters in Brussels, administered by the Finance Ministers of its member countries. Its main business is making loans, financed chiefly by public bond issues.

European Monetary Institute (EMI) An institute created in 1991 under the Maastricht Treaty to manage the currency reserves of the European Union's central banks, with a view towards a single monetary policy and the use of the European currency unit (ECU).

European Monetary System (EMS) A system established in 1979 for stabilizing exchange rates between European Union member states. It was seen as a step towards a European Central Bank and a single currency as part of European Monetary Union.

E

European Monetary Union (EMU) One of the aims of the Maastricht Treaty that would result in all European Union member states having a common currency.

European Regional Development Fund An fund founded in 1975 by the European Community to provide financial aid to counter imbalances within and among member states.

European Single Market The aim to totally integrate the economies of European Union member states, to have been achieved by 2002 under the terms of the Single European Act 1986.

European Union An association of European nations formerly known as the European Economic Community (EEC) or European Community (EC), and before that the Common Market. It is intended that in the long run all the factors of production may be moved within the community at will, and remaining customs barriers are expected to be removed in the near future. The EU operates a protectionist policy by maintaining common tariffs on imports, and generates a substantial part of its income from import duties and value-added tax. In finance, its committed aims include a European Monetary System (EMS), and all that it entails.

evolutionary theory of the firm The idea that the survival of a company takes place by a gradual process of evolution, based on the correct choice of actions in the prevailing economic situation, in turn determined by the skill of the policy-makers—or perhaps mere serendipity.

ex ante Latin for 'from before' or 'before the event': what is expected to be the position after some future event. *See also* ***ex post***.

excess capacity A capacity to produce goods or services over and above the current rate. Excess capacity is more strictly used to denote the increase in production necessary to bring the average production cost to a minimum. *See also* ***spare capacity***.

excess demand A demand for goods or services that exceeds the quantity supplied (at the existing price). It generally leads to price rises.

excess profit An alternative term for *above normal profit*.

excess profits tax A tax paid on a company's profit over and above a level that is thought to be normal. These profits are caused by

E

economic conditions that favour the company but act against the interests of the majority.

excess supply A situation in which the amount of goods or services supplied is greater than the demand (at the existing price). It generally leads to price cuts.

exchange Broadly, any transaction between one entity and another (formally, a reciprocal transfer).

exchange control The control of foreign exchange dealings by the government, either by restrictions on trade or by direct intervention in the market. Exchange controls help a government to exert some influence over the international value of its own currency. They were abolished in the UK in 1979.

exchange economy An economy in which people use barter or money to obtain what they cannot produce for themselves.

Exchange Equalization Account Also called Foreign Exchange Equalization Account, the UK government's account at the Bank of England in which it deposits the nation's gold and foreign exchange reserves. It may be used by the Treasury, under the Bank's management, for intervention in the foreign exchange market to stabilize the foreign exchange rate.

exchange exposure The extent of the risk that results from quoting assets or liabilities in a foreign currency, because variations in the exchange rate can affect the values.

exchange rate The price at which one currency may be exchanged for another. Such transactions may be carried out on either the spot or forward markets, and are usually conducted either to permit investment abroad or to pay for imports. There is, in addition, considerable speculation on the exchange rates.

exchange rate band The limits between which an exchange rate may vary. For example, the Exchange Rate Mechanism at one time required most members of the European Monetary System to hold their exchange rates within $\pm 2\frac{1}{4}\%$ of an agreed rate.

Exchange Rate Mechanism (ERM) An European Union regulation that restricts variations in the exchange rates of its member states to within closely defined limits. It is a vital feature of the European Monetary

E

System. Britain and Italy left the ERM in 1992.

exchange rate regime The system that establishes the exchange rates between different currencies. Such regimes vary from freely-floating rates to fixed ones tied to the gold standard, with crawling peg systems in between (*see crawling peg exchange rate*).

exchange rate risk An alternative term for *currency risk.*

Exchequer In its widest meaning, the central depository of UK government funds. As the department charged with the supervision of the nation's economic affairs, the Treasury is responsible for ensuring that all monies due to the government are paid to the Exchequer, and all spending approved by Parliament is paid for out of Exchequer funds.

excise duty A duty levied on home-produced goods, either to control consumption and thus influence spending, or to raise revenue. Goods that currently attract excise duty in the UK include alcohol, petrol and tobacco. In the USA, a similar levy is known as excise tax.

exclusive dealing An arrangement between a producer and a distributor or seller that one will deal only with the other, such as a manufacturer who sells through only one retailer or a retailer who stocks only one manufacturer's brand.

ex coupon Describing stock that does not give the purchaser the right to the next interest payment due to be paid on it.

ex dividend Often shortened to ex div, describing stock that does not give the purchaser the right to the next dividend payment, or to any dividend payment due within a specified period, generally the next calendar month. However, he or she does have the right to receive subsequent dividends.

exercise price Also known as striking price, the price at which an option for purchase or sale of a security is exercised.

Eximbank Short form of *Export-Import Bank of the United States.*

exit To leave a market by selling all relevant stocks and shares, or to cease production.

exit price The price attained below which a company will cease production of a particular good or service (because it is not worth its while).

E

ex new Describing shares that are sold without the right to claim participation in any outstanding scrip or rights issue. *See also* **cum new.**

exogenous expectation An expectation that is not accounted for but assumed to be the result of some (unnamed) factor outside the system.

exogenous money The part of the money supply that enters the economic system from outside (ie from the government), as opposed to money created by the banking system (endogenous money).

exogenous variable An economic variable that is unaffected by other variables within the system.

expectations Prospects; that which is expected. Expectations of future business activity are one of the most important influences on investment and thus have a significant effect on the level of unemployment.

expectations-augmented Phillips curve A version of the *Phillips curve* (which relates wage rises to demand pressure) that takes into account expected price rises due to inflation.

expected utility The anticipated average satisfaction (utility) from future consumption or the possession of assets of uncertain benefit flow.

expected value The anticipated average value of an economic variable.

expenditure The money spent on attaining (or trying to attain) some objective; outgoings.

expenditure changing The adoption of an economic policy that is designed to change total spending, generally by means of a new fiscal or monetary policy.

expenditure method A way of working out domestic product at market prices by totalling the spending by various economic sectors, such as the government, consumers and investors. *See also* **income method; output method.**

expenditure switching The adoption of an economic policy that is designed to divert existing spending from one place to another, such as from imports to home-produced goods (by the imposition of tariffs).

expenditure tax A tax on spending, ie an indirect tax that is included in the price of a good or service and therefore paid by the buyer (consumer).

E

explicit cost The cost to a company of using an input (capital or labour) that it purchases from outside, ie that it does not own.

exploitation 1. Taking an unfair advantage of a person (such as an immigrant worker) or group of people (such as those in an less developed country exploited by a multinational company). 2. Making the best use of a resource, such as minerals or fish stocks.

exportables The kinds of goods or services that can be exported (whether or not they actually are).

export concentration The limiting of exports to a small range of goods or services or to a small range of importers, each of which making the exports vulnerable to sudden changes in demand or buyer policy.

export control Government restrictions on goods leaving the country (exports).

export credit Financial facilities or delayed payment terms made available to foreign buyers.

export credit agency An organization that provides credit to exporters or provides guarantees to exporters who grant credit to their customers.

Export Credits Guarantee Department (ECGD) UK government department, part of the Department of Trade and Industry (DTI), established in 1991 and partly privatized that makes available export credit insurance and guarantees to repay banks that give credit (over two years or more) to exporters.

export duty A tax levied on exports. Export duties tend to discourage exports and adversely affect the balance of payment, and for these reasons they are seldom used.

Export Import Bank of the United States (Eximbank) A bank established by the US government in 1934 to provide loans to foreign importers of US goods and services. It also refinances and guarantees export credit provided by US banks.

export incentives Government incentives designed to encourage exports. They include direct-tax incentives, subsidies, favourable terms for insurance and the provision of cheap credit.

export-led growth A kind of economic expansion that is stimulated mainly by exports (which become the *leading indicator*). This type of growth is less likely to create balance-of-payments difficulties than is growth led by domestic spending.

E

export multiplier The overall increase in a nation's national income divided by the increase in export income (ie the demand for its exports) that produced it.

export promotion Actions by government that encourage the sale of exports, such as help for overseas for exporters and domestic *export incentives*.

export restraint agreement An arrangement between two countries, one an exporter and the other an importer, to limit the trade in certain products in order to protect the importer's domestic producers.

exports Goods or services that are sold outside their country of origin (visible exports) or to non-residents (invisible exports).

export subsidy A subsidy paid to domestic companies by a government so that they can lower the prices of their exports. It may take the form of money (contrary to international agreements), low-interest credit or tax concessions.

ex post Abbreviation of *ex post facto*, Latin for 'after the event'. It describes the position that arises after a certain event has taken place. *See also ex ante.*

exposure to risk A lending organization's risk—how much it would lose—if certain borrowers were to default on repayments.

external balance A situation in which a nation spends the same amount abroad as other countries spend with it. As a result, it has a *balance of payments equilibrium. See also internal balance; internal-external balance model.*

external diseconomy An increase in cost resulting from an economic activity that does not accrue to the company carrying it out but is spread over the community as a whole. Examples include traffic congestion and pollution.

external economy A decrease in cost resulting from an economic activity that does not benefit the company carrying it out but benefits the community as a whole. Examples include public parks and restored historic sights.

external growth A type of growth that originates outside a company, as through an acquisition or merger (as opposed to internal expansion through organic growth).

E

externality An increase or decrease in cost resulting from an economic activity that does not accrue to the company carrying it out. *See external diseconomy; external economy.*

external labour market The policy of recruiting employees on the open market, outside the company concerned (as opposed to using the *internal labour market*).

extrapolative expectations The expectations that result from assuming that, in the short term at least, everything will continue more or less as it is at present.

E

F

face value Also called nominal value, the price or value written on something, such as the par value of stocks or shares or the denomination of a banknote.

facility A general term for any kind of loan, usually from a bank.

factor A person or company that undertakes *factoring*.

factor cost The value of goods and services at the prices paid to producers (equal to market price less indirect taxes plus any government subsidies).

factor endowment The stock of *factors of production* that a country has to produce goods and services, important in determining its exports and imports (international trade).

factor income The income that comes from selling products of the *factors of production*, including wages (from labour), rent (from land and property), and dividends and interest (from investments).

factoring A method of managing the trade debts of another organization. Commonly, a company sells due debts to a factor at a discount. The factor then makes a profit by recovering the debts at a price nearer the face value. Factoring relives companies of the burden of administering debts and gives them access to cash before payment is made.

factor input The *factors of production* that come together to produce a product (output) in the form of goods or services.

factor-intensity The concentration of the various *factors of production* used to produce a product (output) in the form of goods or services.

factor market The 'market' in which *factors of production* are traded, their prices reflecting the current supply and demand. It is not a physical market (eg *see labour market*).

factors of production A collective term for those things necessary for production to take place. They are usually divided into the following categories: capital, labour and land, to which may be added organizational ability (ie, management).

F

factor payment A payment made for one of the *factors of production* to its owner for its use to produce a product (output) in the form of goods or services.

factor price equalization A tendency for a reduction in the international variations of relative prices of factors that results from international trade, a tendency that trade barriers and international transport costs tend to oppose.

factor price The cost of the services of one of the *factors of production*, such as interest for capital, rent for land and wages for labour.

factor productivity The value of a factory's, company's or industry's output expressed per unit of factor input. The factor most commonly analysed in this way is labour.

fair trade A less emotive term for *protectionism*, as a counter to 'unfair' competition.

Fair Trading Act 1973 UK legislation that established the *Office of Fair Trading* , which provides government ministers with advice about mergers, monopolies and restrictive practices in trade and industry.

fallacy of composition The mistake of thinking that what is true for one person or group is also true for the whole community.

family expenditure survey A yearly government survey of the spending patterns of UK households. It is used for, among other things, selecting the 'basket' of goods and services on which to base the *Retail Price Index.*

FAO Abbreviation of *Food and Agriculture Organization.*

farm subsidy A government payment to farmers, which may be compensation for not growing beyond the quota of a particular crop or a price support payment (to prevent having to sell at unprofitable prices).

FCO Abbreviation of *Federal Cartel Office.*

FDI Abbreviation of *foreign direct investment.*

FDIC Abbreviation of *Federal Deposit Insurance Corporation.*

feasible set In an economic model, the allocations of resources that meet all the constraints.

F

FED or Fed Abbreviation of *Federal Reserve System.*

Federal Cartel Office (FCO) The US organization that implements *antitrust laws* by monitoring all company mergers.

Federal Deposit Insurance Corporation (FDIC) A US regulatory organization that authorizes banks and insures depositors against their failure.

federal fiscal system A fiscal system, such as taxation and authority spending in the USA, that operates at both state and federal level. Each may subsidize the other if necessary.

federal funds Deposits held by US federal reserve banks that bear no interest.

Federal Open Market Committee (FOMC) A committee that determines the monetary policy of the US Federal Reserve System, particularly with regard to its open market operations.

federal reserve bank Any of the USA's central banks, each of which is controlled by a state government.

Federal Reserve Board The board that controls the growth of US bank reserves and the money supply.

Federal Reserve System (FED or Fed) The US central bank system, under which 12 regional federal reserve banks are governed by the Federal Reserve Board in Washington, appointed by the President. Like the Bank of England in the UK, it sets banking policy and controls the money supply.

Federal Trade Commission (FTC) A US organization that encourages competitive business and shapes competition policy, opposing price discrimination and other constraints on trade.

fiat money Any paper money that a government decrees is *legal tender.*

fiduciary issue Money issued by the Bank of England backed by securities, mainly in the form of the government's debt to the Bank. It is termed fiduciary because of the public's trust that the government will repay the debts backing the issue.

FIFO Abbreviation of *first-in, first-out.*

F

final good An alternative term for final product.

final income The income a person or household is left with after payment of taxes, but including any benefits received.

final product Also termed final good, a product that is made for consumption rather than as an intermediate for the production of other products.

Finance Act Annual UK legislation that enforces the measures set out in the government's budget.

finance company Generally an alternative term for *finance house*, although it may be applied to other businesses in the financial sector.

finance house A company that provides funding (credit), eg for hire-purchase agreements. The finance house pays a trader in full, and charges interest to the purchaser of goods provided by the trader.

financial accounting The branch of accounting that deals with the recording and classifying of a company's transactions, providing a true and fair view on the company's (annual) balance sheet.

financial asset Any asset that is cash or will yield or can be converted to cash, such as bills, bonds, options, shares and swaps.

financial capital A company's capital that takes the form of holdings of cash and trade credit given to customers.

financial derivative A security with a value based on an underlying asset, such as a commodity or currency. They include futures, options, swaps and other derivatives that may be traded on a suitable market.

financial future A contract for the delivery of a financial instrument (ie a currency) on a future date. Financial futures are used to hedge against the rise and fall of interest and exchange rates.

financial institution A bank, building society, finance house or other institution that collects, invests and lends funds.

financial instrument *See financial security.*

financial intermediary A bank, building society, finance house or other business that collects funds (from depositors or members) to use for making loans (to borrowers). Any person or organization that sells insurance (but is not an employee of an insurance company) is also regarded in the UK as a financial intermediary.

F

financial market Any market in which people trade *financial assets*, such as a foreign exchange market, futures market, money market or stock exchange.

financial ratio Also called accounting ratio, a ratio—calculated from figures in a company's accounts—that is used to assess its performance or financial viability by market analysts and potential investors. There are many such ratios, such as earnings per share, fixed asset turnover, gross margin, interest cover, liquidity ratio, net profit percentage, proprietorship ratio, rate of collection of debtors, rate of payment of creditors, rate of return of gross assets, rate of return on shareholders' equity, rate of stock turnover, total asset turnover and working capital ratio.

financial sector The sector of the economy that deals mainly in long- or short-term borrowing and lending. It consists of *financial institutions* and their intermediaries.

financial security Any financial instrument that is used to borrow money and thus raise capital. They include bills, bonds, debentures, stocks and shares issued by companies, financial institutions and the government.

Financial Services Act 1986 (FSA) UK legislation, in force since April 1988, introduced to prevent abuse of the deregulated stock exchange system, principally by placing all people and institutions involved in financial services under the authority of a self-regulating organization (SRO).

Financial Services and Markets Act 2000 (FSMA) UK legislation enacted to expand the regime of financial regulation introduced by the Financial Services Act 1986 to all financial services.

Financial Services Authority (FSA) A UK regulatory organization, established in 1997, that regulates the financial services industry and monitors financial services sold to the general public.

Financial Times Actuaries All-Share Index An index of 800 financial and industrial shares and fixed-interest stocks traded on the London Stock Exchange (representing 98% of total market value), published daily since April 1962.

Financial Times Industrial Ordinary Share Index (FT 30) Also known as the Financial Times 30 Index, an index of changes in prices of 30 major industrial and commercial ordinary shares on the London Stock

F

Exchange, updated hourly during the working day. The index value of 100 was set on the base date of 1 July 1935.

Financial Times-Stock Exchange 100 Share Index (FT-SE 100 or Footsie) An index of shares of the 100 largest UK companies, a weighted average of which is updated every minute during the working day. The index value of 1000 was set on the base date of 3 January 1984.

financial year A period of twelve months, beginning at any time in the calendar year, used for company accounting purposes. Or, for purposes of corporation tax, it is the period of twelve months beginning on 1 April to which the tax applies. *See also fiscal year.*

fine tuning An attempt to make short-term fine adjustments to control fluctuations in the level of economic activity using fiscal and monetary measures. Lags in the production of data and the notorious difficulty of long-term forecasting make this an extremely difficult exercise.

firm 1. Strictly, under UK law a firm is a partnership of professionally qualified people, such as accountants, civil engineers, lawyers or surveyors. In this case, the firms are legally distinct from companies and do not, for instance, issue shares. Also the liability of individual partners is not (and legally cannot be) limited. 2. In economics, a firm is the basic decision-making and producing unit. This includes any company or business, including partnerships and sole traders. *See theory of the firm.*

firm objectives The aims of a company ('the firm') in producing goods and services and their effects on *market conduct*. These may alternatively emphasize growth, profits or sales revenue.

firm-specific human capital Specialized work experience or skills that only one type of employer values, perhaps because the employer has a monopoly or a unique production process.

first-degree price discrimination A type of price discrimination in which the price is fixed at the maximum consumers are willing to pay. *See also second-degree price discrimination; third-degree price discrimination.*

first-in, first-out (FIFO) An accountancy principle whereby stock-in-trade is assumed to be issued to customers in the order that it is received. Thus, stock currently held may be valued at current prices.

F

first-mover advantage The idea that companies (or countries) that establish a new product or industry gain a competitive advantage that others find difficult or impossible to overcome.

fiscal drag An effect during times of inflation in which pay increases push employees into higher tax brackets (giving the government a higher proportion of incomes).

fiscal federalism The practice in a country with both central and regional government of sharing the revenue from taxes and the costs of public works between them. Usually central government receives the money from taxes and makes grants to local government.

fiscal neutrality The idea that the economy should be distorted as little as possible by the running of the tax system (eg value-added tax should be levied at the same rate over all items—a neutral policy—or consumers will concentrate spending on low-tax items).

fiscal policy Also termed budgetary policy, the attempts to manage economic activity by controlling government spending and taxation. The policy is tightened by raising taxes or cutting public spending; it is loosened by lowering taxes or increasing government expenditure. The actual choices are reflected in the shaping of the budget (the government's fiscal stance).

fiscal stance *See fiscal policy.*

fiscal year A period of twelve months for the purposes of tax calculation. In the UK the fiscal year runs from 6 April to the following 5 April. In the USA, the term can be synonymous with *financial year.*

Fisher effect The effect that inflation has on the interest rate of a bond or loan. The nominal rate is the real interest rate plus the rate of inflation. It was named after the US economist Irving Fisher (1867-1947).

Fisher equation An expression, also called the quantity of money equation, that links money and prices: the stock of money multiplied by its velocity of circulation equals the output of goods and services multiplied by the price level. It was named after the US economist Irving Fisher (1867-1947).

fixed asset Also known as a capital asset, an asset that is used in furtherance of a company's business, such as machinery or property.

F

fixed charge 1. Part of the charge, usually made for a service, that is unchanged no matter how much a service is used. Examples of utilities that levy fixed charges are electricity, gas and some telephone companies. 2. Also called a specific charge, a charge that gives a creditor the right to have an asset sold and the receipts put towards repayment of a debt that is outstanding. A legal mortgage is an example of such a fixed charge.

fixed cost Also called a fixed expense, a cost that does not vary with short-term changes in the level of output or sales (such as heating costs, business rates, and certain other overheads).

fixed exchange rate An exchange rate that a government attempts to control and fix in the short term by instructing the central bank to buy or sell foreign exchange reserves, or by introducing tariffs.

fixed factor input In a production process, a *factor input* (such as plant and equipment) that cannot be varied in the short-term.

fixed factor An alternative term for *fixed factor input.*

fixed-interest security A security for which the income is fixed and does not vary. Such securities include bonds, debentures and gilt-edged securities.

fixed investment An investment in plant, equipment or any other durable capital goods, which cannot be written off for several years.

fixed target In macroeconomics, a specific target value of an economic quantity such as balance of payments equilibrium, full employment, economic growth and stability of prices.

fixprice An economic model that has fixed prices in the short term while other quantities vary faster than prices. See also *flexprice.*

flag carrier A company that is thought to add to a country's prestige (eg a national airline) and for this reason should receive government support if necessary.

flag of convenience A flag flown by a merchant vessel registered in a country whose manning, taxation and safety requirements are less stringent than elsewhere, to the advantage of the shipowner.

flat yield Also known as running yield, the interest rate expressed as a percentage of the price paid for a fixed-interest security.

flexible manufacturing system (FMS) A production method that uses

F

automation and computers to produce small batches and which can be rapidly adapted to produce other similar things.

flexible price A price that can vary, up or down, to clear a market. Most primary products—agricultural produce, fuels and minerals—have flexible prices whereas those of industrial products are generally much less flexible.

flexible wage A wage that can vary, up or down, to maintain equilibrium in the labour market. Downward flexibility—involving wage cuts—is very seldom achieved.

flexprice An economic model that has quantities fixed in the short term while prices vary faster than prices. *See also fixprice.*

flight capital Capital that is hurredly removed from one country that seems to be politically (or economically) unstable, and taken to a more stable environment.

flight from money During times of high inflation, the tendency not to use domestic currency (but instead to use exchange or barter).

floating capital Capital invested in wages paid, work in progress and anything other than fixed assets.

floating charge A charge over a company's assets that comes into effect only if a specified event occurs (such as liquidation of the company).

floating currency A currency whose value varies up and down according to its supply and demand.

floating debenture A *debenture* (loan to a company) with a charge on the company's assets as security.

floating debt A short-term debt, generally applied to government borrowing.

floating exchange rate Also known as a free exchange rate, an exchange rate that is not in any way manipulated by a central bank, but which moves according to supply and demand.

floating interest rate An interest rate for a loan that rises and falls in response to an appropriate index.

floating pound The pound sterling left to the laws of supply (with no central bank or governmental intervention) and demand to find its own level on foreign money exchanges.

F

floor price The lowest price to which a commodity is allowed to fall before some sort of intervention (such as severely restricting the supply or buying up stocks at that price).

flotation The process of selling shares in a company to raise capital and be listed on a stock exchange.

Flow of Funds Accounts A US national statistical system developed by the Federal Reserve Board and published regularly since 1947. It is constructed to show the financial activities of the US economy in a manner that enables them to be related to the non-financial activities of economic functions that turn out income, savings, foods and services.

flow An economic process that varies over time, such as expenditure and income (as opposed to *stock*, such as debt or the labour force, which are measured at one particular time).

fluctuation A movement of prices up or down on a market. Downward fluctuation is also known as slippage.

FMA Abbreviation of *flexible manufacturing system.*

FMS Abbreviation of *flexible manufacturing system.*

FOMC Abbreviation of *Federal Open Market Committee.*

Food and Agriculture Organization (FAO) A United Nations international organization, founded in 1945 with headquarters in Rome, that aims to improve the productivity of agriculture throughout the world. It provides training, makes technical assistance available and carries out research into various aspects of farming, fishing and forestry. It is also concerned with standards of human nutrition, especially in less developed countries.

food subsidy A subsidy on the price of food, which can thereby be available at less than its true cost to the producer or seller.

Footsie Popular name for the *Financial Times-Stock Exchange 100 Share Index.*

forced savings Savings that do not involve a conscious decision to save but which nevertheless accumulate. Examples include government taxes that contribute to retirement pensions.

forecasting Estimating future economic or financial events, such as costs (outgoings), revenues (income), or both.

F

foreclosure If a property has been mortgage, ie, it stands as security against a loan, the lender may take possession and ownership of the property of the borrower fails to pay off the loan. Such an act of possession is known as foreclosure (and in the UK requires a foreclosure order issued by the court).

foreign aid Economic assistance, most often in the form of loans or investments, given to developing and Third World countries. In times of emergency, it may also take the form of humanitarian aid.

foreign currency From a UK point of view, any money of a non-UK country.

foreign currency-denominated borrowing The borrowing of money in a currency that is different from that of the borrower. It is an anti-inflationary device for government borrowing, and may be cheaper when domestic interest rates are very high.

foreign direct investment (FDI) The investment in assets overseas or in the overseas operations of a company.

foreign exchange (F/X) The currency (or credit instruments) of a foreign country, and the buying and selling of such currencies.

foreign exchange controls The restrictions placed by a central bank on the amount of foreign currency available. It restricts imports and helps to reduce a balance of payments deficit.

Foreign Exchange Equalization Account *See Equalization Account.*

foreign exchange market (FOREX) A market where foreign currencies are traded by foreign exchange brokers (intermediaries) and foreign exchange dealers (bank employees). Options and futures on forward exchange rates are also traded.

foreign exchange reserves Also termed international reserves, gold or foreign currency held by a government or central bank, to be used for intervention in the *foreign exchange market* (usually because of balance of trade problems).

foreign investment The acquisition of another country's assets through any form of investment. It serves to stimulate economic growth in the investing nation and helps to maintain a favourable balance of payments.

F

foreign sector The part of an economy that deals with trade and other transactions with countries overseas. It includes exports, imports and the transfer of capital by bankers and investors, and is a major factor in determining the balance of payments.

foreign trade multiplier The increase in domestic product divided by the value of extra exports that produced it. The extra income to the overseas importing country may allow it to purchase even more from the exporting country, while at the same time the home demand for imports will increase (because of the extra spending power).

FOREX Abbreviation of *foreign exchange market.*

forfaiting A specialist banking service by which the bank buys foreign debts at a discount without recourse, thus removing the risk to the seller of non-payment.

forty-five degree line On a graph of income against expenditure, a line that joins points at which the two are equal. There is a similar forty-five degree line on graphs of other pairs of economic variables.

forward contract A contract to purchase goods or foreign currency at a price agreed today (spot price) for delivery at a specified future date.

forward exchange market A market in which people make contracts to purchase and supply foreign currency at a fixed price at some fixed date in the future (a *forward contract*).

forward integration The taking on by a company of activities at a subsequent stage of production or distribution (which could be carried out by another company). For example, an oil production company undertakes forward integration when it invests in refineries, tankers and petrol stations.

forward market A market in (contracts or options for) currencies or goods that are to be delivered at some future date.

forward price A price quoted for goods not immediately available or not yet manufactured. The forward price is usually lower than the eventual retail price because it takes into account only the estimated costs of manufacture at some future date. More specifically, it is the price quoted on a futures deal.

fractional banking A practice in which a government requires its banks to keep a fixed fraction between deposits (cash reserves) and liabilities.

F

franc fort French for *strong franc*, a policy of pinning down inflation by tying the exchange rate of the domestic currency to that of a foreign county with a history of low inflation. It was introduced in the late 1980s and early 1990s by Belgium and France, which tied their currencies to the German deutschmark.

franchise A licence bought by a retailer of goods or supplier of services (the franchisee) that entitles him or her to sell the products of a particular manufacturer (the franchisor) under a particular trading name. This system enables the manufacturer to have direct control over who sells the goods, and often gives the seller exclusive rights to sell those products in his or her area.

franked investment income A company's investment income that has already been taxed at source.

fraud The illegal practice of obtaining money from people under false pretences. For example, fraud is committed if facts pertaining to a contract are purposefully misrepresented. Fraudulently diverting one's company's or employer's money for one's own use is embezzlement.

free entry Also called freedom of entry, a situation in which there is nothing to obstruct new entrants to a market (*see* **barrier to entry**).

free exit Also called freedom of exit, a situation in which there is nothing to prevent a business from leaving a market (*see* **barrier to exit**).

free good A plentiful good, such as air or water, that is regarded as being freely available and incapable of limiting an economic activity.

free market A market that operates essentially by the laws of supply and demand. Or, on the stock market, a situation in which a particular security is freely available and in reasonably large quantities.

free-market economy Also called a private-enterprise economy, an economy in which resources are allocated purely on the basis of supply and demand in a free market.

freeport A type of *free trade zone* that encompasses the area around a port.

free rider A consumer who is unwilling to pay for something that (he hopes) somebody else will pay for, usually involving **public goods**.

free trade A concept of international trading where there are no tariff barriers between countries.

F

free trade agreement (FTA) An agreement between nations to abolish all tariffs between the two countries.

free trade area (FTA) A region in which the countries concerned have signed a *free trade agreement*.

free-trade zone An area, defined by customs, in which goods or services may be employed or produced without attracting duties, tariffs or taxes. For example, a company that makes goods for export out of imported materials benefits from not having money tied up in duties.

freedom of entry An alternative term for *free entry*.

freedom of exit An alternative term for *free exit*.

frictional unemployment Unemployment that results from the movement of people between jobs. Thus although there may be enough jobs to go round, some people may experience periods of unemployment between the finish date of one job and the start date of the next.

friendly society An organization (first coming to existence in the UK in the 17th century, to help to provide working people with some form of security) that provides mutual benefits to its members, such as life assurance and pensions, in return for yearly subscriptions.

fringe benefit An item that is given to an employee as part of his or her payment but apart from wages or salary (such as a company car, health insurance, or goods at a discount). Fringe benefits are usually taxable.

fringes Colloquial US abbreviation of *fringe benefits*.

front door A popular term for the Bank of England's practice of lending money to discount houses in order to inject cash into the money market.

front-end charge A charge such as administrative costs or commission included with the first repayment of a loan or the first payment of an insurance premium, with the result that the first payment is larger than the remainder.

frozen assets Assets that may not be converted into ready money without incurring a loss of some kind, or which may not be converted because someone has claim on them or there is an order that they may not be transferred. The latter is also called a frozen fund. *See also* **liquid assets**.

FSA Abbreviation of *Financial Services Authority*.

F

FSMA Abbreviation of *Financial Services and Markets Act 2000.*

FTA Abbreviation of *free-trade agreement* and *free-trade area.*

FTC Abbreviation of *Federal Trade Commission.*

full costing A costing method in which all of a company's costs (direct and overhead) are charged to a product or service.

full-cost pricing A way of fixing a product's selling price to make sure that it covers all the costs incurred in producing and supplying it (alternatively known as total absorption costing).

full employment A major aim of macroeconomics, a situation in which all available labour is utilized, thus allowing an economy to maximize its production (and gross national product). It is generally taken to exclude *frictional unemployment.* Most economists agree that true full employment is unattainable.

full employment budget The government's budget as it would appear if there were full employment (and taxation remained the same).

full employment national income The gross domestic product as it would be if there were full employment (and taxation remained the same).

full-line forcing The action of a supplier who insists that a retailer must stock the full range of that supplier's products (and cannot choose just one or a few).

functional income distribution The distribution of national income classified in terms of capital (dividends, interest and profits), labour (wages and salaries), or some other *factor input. See also personal income distribution.*

fundamental disequilibrium Under a fixed exchange rate system, a situation in which a country has a long-standing balance of payments deficit or surplus (generally necessitating devaluation or revaluation).

funded debt Generally, any short-term debt that has been converted into a long-term debt.

funding 1. The substitution long-term debt for short-term liabilities. 2. Government borrowing from the non-bank private sector.

funding operation The conversion of a floating debt (short-term, fixed interest rate) into a funded debt (long-term, fixed interest rate).

F

future good A good that is contracted to be delivered at a future date. See *futures*.

futures Contracts that are made for the delivery of eg currencies or commodities on a future date at a pre-agreed price. Futures markets provide an opportunity for speculation, in that contracts may be bought and sold (with no intention on the part of the traders to take delivery of the goods) before the delivery date arrives, and their prices may rise and fall during that time.

futures market A market that deals in *futures* and options on bonds, commodities, foreign currencies are shares.

F/X Abbreviation of *foreign exchange.*

F

G

GAB Abbreviation of *General Agreement to Borrow.*

gains from trade The extra benefits (consumption and production) that international trade provides to a nation—benefits that are not available to an autarky.

galloping inflation An alternative term for *hyperinflation.*

game theory The application of stylized logic to deduce the consequences of various possible strategies and actions in making economic and industrial policy decisions, just like competing players in a game. And as in a game, each 'player' does not know what the others are going to do. *See*, for example, *prisoner's dilemma; zero-sum game.*

gamma A stock exchange designation for a share that is traded infrequently and then in only small quantities.

GAO Abbreviation of *General Accounting Office.*

GATS Abbreviation of *General Agreement on Trade in Services.*

GATT Abbreviation of *General Agreement on Tariffs and Trade.*

GDP Abbreviation of *gross domestic product.*

GDP deflator The price index equal to the ratio of GDP at current prices to an index of GDP at base-year prices. It provides a way of finding out whether there has been a real rise or fall in gross domestic product (GDP) in a given year.

gearing The proportion of long-term debt to equity finance on the balance sheet of a company. More specifically, it is the ratio of borrowed capital to total capital employed, expressed as a percentage (the gearing ratio). It is sometimes known by the equivalent US term leverage.

GEMU Abbreviation of *German Economic Monetary Union.*

General Accounting Office (GAO) A US organization that ensures that funds approved by Congress are spent in the way that was intended.

General Agreement on Tariffs and Trade (GATT) An international organization, established in 1947 with headquarters in Geneva,

Switzerland, and now with more than 100 member countries, whose object is to negotiate on matters of trade policy, notably the reduction of tariffs and other barriers to free trade.

General Agreement on Trade in Services (GATS) An international agreement on trade and services. It was formulated as part of the *Uruguay Round* negotiations in 1994 under the *General Agreement on Tariffs and Trade.*

General Arrangements to Borrow (GAB) An agreement established in 1962 under which the International Monetary Fund may call upon the major industrialized nations to borrow money if required.

general equilibrium The economic situation in a group of unrelated markets where none of them has any excess demand or supply (ie each component market is in equilibrium).

general equilibrium analysis The study of how a change in economic variables in one sector of the economy impacts on other sectors (and the consequent feedback that affects the original sector). *See also partial equilibrium analysis.*

General Household Survey A UK survey of a sample of households that provides data about household spending and the labour force.

general human capital The qualifications and skills, such as literacy, that can be used in a wide range of jobs (as opposed to specialized skills that apply to only one or two occupations).

generalized system of preferences A scheme introduced in 1971 for the reduction or removal of tariffs on the import of specified goods from certain developing countries.

general partnership A partnership in which each partner shares equally in the running of the firm.

geometric mean A type of average determined for a group of n positive numbers by taking the nth root of their product.

German Economic Monetary Union (GEMU) Following the reunification of the former East and West Germany in 1990, the process of bringing together their monetary and economic policies.

Giffen good A good that violates the general law of demand. When the price of a Giffen good (such as a cosmetic product) increases, the demand for it increases—instead of falling off, as would normally be

G

expected. It was named after the UK economist Robert Giffen (1837-1910).

gilt-edged security　A security that carries little or no risk, in particular government-issued stocks, which are known as gilts for short. In the USA, the term gilt-edged refers to bonds issued by companies with a good reputation for dividend payment and with a good profit record.

gilt repos　Introduced by the Bank of England on 1996, a market in (agreed sales and repurchases of) gilt-edged securities.

gilts　Shortened term for *gilt-edged securities.*

gilt strip　A type of gilt-edged stock issued from late 1997 by the Bank of England. It is issued at a discount to compensate for the fact that no interest is paid (until maturity).

Glass-Steagal Act 1933　A US Act of Congress that separated the activities of commercial and investment bankers (so that banks could not lend to companies in which they had also invested).

globalization　The increasing internationalization of all markets, industries and commerce.

glut　An overabundance in the supply of a good or service which, unless it can be stored cheaply, will make its price fall significantly.

GM　Abbreviation of *gross margin.*

GNMA　Abbreviation of *Government National Mortgage Association.*

GNP　Abbreviation of *gross national product.*

GNP deflator　A price index that aims to remove the effect of price changes and produce only real changes in gross national product (GNP), which is concerned with output not monetary values.

gold　A precious metal, widely and historically used as a primary medium of exchange independent of the value of national currencies. *See bullion; gold standard.*

gold and dollar reserves　The stock of gold and US national currency held by the US government or central banks.

gold and foreign exchange reserves　The same as *gold and dollar reserves,* but with national currencies other than the US dollar included in the stock.

G

golden handcuffs A contractual arrangement between a company and its employee whereby the employee has a strong financial incentive (other than the loss of normal salary) to remain with the company, such as a low-interest mortgage or share options that expire if the employee resigns.

golden handshake A gratuitous payment made by a company to an employee who is leaving, or has recently left. Such payments may be made out of goodwill, or to maintain good relations with an ex-employee, or to induce an employee to resign where there are no grounds, or dubious grounds, for statutory dismissal or redundancy.

golden hello A payment other than normal salary paid to en employee on joining a company in order to induce him or her to do so.

golden parachute A term in a contract of employment whereby the employer is bound to pay the employee a substantial sum of money in the event of dismissal or redundancy.

golden rule A 'law' which states that an economy can maximize the long-term value of its per capita consumption if its balanced growth rate equals the marginal product of capital (profit and interest).

gold-exchange standard A type of *gold standard* in which hard currencies (such as US dollars) are used as well as gold.

gold parity For a nation on the *gold standard*, the official par value of its currency in terms of gold.

gold reserves Funds held by a nation in the form of gold. They fluctuate with the balance of payments and are used for international transactions.

gold standard A monetary system used internationally in which gold is used to finance trade and balance of payment deficits. In a country on the gold standard, the central bank (or government) makes its currency freely convertible into gold.

Goodhart's law When a commercial bank's lending is regulated by central bank controls, the commercial bank finds other ways of lending that are not regulated.

goods Physical items manufactured, sold or exchanged, from raw materials to finished products (as opposed to services, for which no physical items are transferred).

G

goodwill The value of a business over and above the book value of its identifiable or physical assets. Or it is the amount paid on acquisition of a business over and above its current market valuation (including any stock). It can refer, for example, to the literal good will of the established customers of a retail business (shop or restaurant) whose benevolent habit (or custom) of using it can be quantified.

Gosplan The former Soviet Union's central planning agency, which drew up the successive five-year plans.

government broker A firm formerly nominated by the Bank of England for dealing with new issues of gilt-edged securities, now replaced by a number of market-makers in gilts.

government debt Also called national debt, any money owed by central government to domestic and overseas lenders.

government expenditure Also called public expenditure, any spending by central government, such as on real goods and services (eg armaments and police force) and transfer payments (eg interest payments, pensions and various benefits).

Government National Mortgage Association (GNMA or Ginnie Mae) A US government-owned corporation that guarantees payment on mortgage-backed pass-through securities.

government production The part of a country's income that comes from factors and services owned by central or local government. It includes rents, and revenue from state-owned utilities and services.

government securities Treasury bills, gilt-edged securities and any other government fixed-interest paper. They are sold as a means of borrowing, often to offset a budget deficit.

government spending on real goods and services *See government expenditure.*

government transfer payments *See government expenditure.*

gradualist monetarism The policy of slowing down the growth rate of the money supply until it gets close to the growth rate of the economy in order to stabilize inflation.

Gramm-Rudman Act 1985 US legislation, sponsored by Gramm, Rudman and Hollings and introduced in stages, aimed at amending the

G

Constitution to make it unconstitutional to run a deficit budget.

grant in aid A US federal grant made to poorer state or local governments for the maintenance of essential public services.

gravity model The theory that contact between different places (such as a consumer and a shop or a pair of trading nations) is inversely proportional to the distance between them. It is so called because the law of gravity follows a similar inverse-square law.

Green Book The informal name for the *Unlisted Securities Market*, published by the London Stock Exchange, setting out requirements for entry into the *Unlisted Securities Market* and associated regulations.

green currency The currency of an EU country (based on the European Currency Unit, ECU) that uses an artificial rate of exchange to protect farm prices from fluctuations in the real rates of exchange.

greenfield development Also called green grass development, a project for the construction of a new factory or processing plant where none existed before (by contrast with the extension or replacement of an existing facility).

green issues Economic issues that arise because of environmental considerations, such as climate change, deforestation, erosion, habitat loss and pollution.

green pound A notional unit of currency used in the administration of the Common Agricultural Policy of the European Union to determine the relative prices (and hence subsidies) of farm produce from the different member countries.

green revolution The large recent improvement in farming methods and productivity in less developed countries. It is due mainly to better varieties of crops and farm animals and the increasing use of pesticides and fertilizers.

Gresham's law An overvalued money of equal legal tender power tends to displace an undervalued money; that bad money (mutilated or debased money) drives good money out of circulation; or that cheaper money supplants dearer money. The principle was named after Sir Thomas Gresham (1519-79), Master of the English Mint under Queen Elizabeth I who, while not the first to recognize it, clearly enunciated it and gave it official standing.

G

grey market Any semi-legal market, usually for goods that are in short supply; it is one that keeps within the letter if not the spirit of the law. The term is most usually applied to the market dealing in any stock or share whose issue has been announced but which has not yet taken place. Traders therefore gamble on the eventual selling price of the issue when it comes onto the market. *See also* **black market.**

gross Describing an amount that has not had any (justifiable) deductions made from it. After such deductions it is described as *net.*

gross domestic capital formation The level of total investment in a country, including that by companies owned by non-residents but excluding investment overseas by domestic companies.

gross domestic fixed capital formation The part of investment in a country that consists of durable goods (fixed capital) rather than work in progress or stocks (circulating capital).

gross domestic product (GDP) A measure of the value of goods and services produced within a country, normally in one year. GDP does not take into account the value of goods and services generated overseas. It is sometimes also known as gross value added. *See also* **gross national product (GNP).**

gross domestic product at factor cost The gross domestic product (GDP) at market prices, ie the GDP adjusted to take account of subsidies (which are added) and indirect taxes (which are subtracted).

gross fixed investment The total amount spent on fixed investment, without any reduction to take into account depreciation of capital stock (unlike net fixed investment, which does allow for capital consumption).

grossing up A calculation of a gross amount from the net amount by adding back the amount deducted.

gross interest The interest on a deposit or investment before deduction of income tax.

gross investment The spend on investment in capital goods including depreciation (ie including the cost of replacing obsolescent and worn out equipment).

gross margin (GM) Also called gross profit or gross profit margin, the price at which goods are sold minus what they cost, usually expressed as a percentage of the selling price. More formally it is the difference

G

between a company's sales revenue and the cost of the goods sold, ignoring costs of administration, distribution or finance.

gross national product (GNP) A measure of the value of all goods and services produced by a country, including those produced overseas, usually in one year. *See also gross domestic product (GDP)*.

gross national product at factor cost The gross national product (GNP) at market prices, ie the GNP adjusted to take account of subsidies (which are added) and indirect taxes (which are subtracted).

gross profit Alternative term for *gross margin*.

gross trading profit Alternative term for *gross margin*.

Group of Five (G-5) Five leading industrial nations (France, Germany, Japan, the UK and the USA), which meet from time to time to discuss common economic problems.

Group of Seven (G-7) Seven leading non-communist nations consisting of the *Group of Five* countries with the addition of Canada and Italy.

Group of Ten (G-10) Also known colloquially as the Paris Club, the ten countries Belgium, Canada, France, Germany, Italy, Japan, the Netherlands, Sweden, the UK and the USA. These countries signed an agreement in 1962 to increase the funds available to the International Monetary Fund and to aid those member countries with balance of payments difficulties.

growth 1. The process of increase in an activity, entity or quantity. 2. The speed of increase in an activity, entity or quantity.

growth rate 1. The proportional (eg pecentage) rate of increase of an economic variable in a given period of time, usually a year. 2. The change in the financial status of a company over a period of time, usually expressed as a percentage of profits or revenue. 3. Of a country's population, the difference between the birth rate and the death rate.

growth recession A situation in a country's economy in which the gross national product and unemployment are both slowly increasing.

guarantee A promise to pay the debt of somebody else in the event that the debtor defaults. Guarantee is also the name given to a document stating that goods or services are of good (merchandizable) quality.

G

H

Hang Seng Index An index of share prices quoted since 1964 on the Hong Kong Stock Exchange.

hard arbitrage The borrowing of a (considerable) sum of money from a bank and re-lending it profitably on a secondary market, a device disliked by central banks.

hard budget constraint A spending limit imposed on a company or public organization whose breach would have disastrous results (to the company or organization and its employees).

hard currency A currency, widely used in international trade, from a country with a stable and prosperous economy. It is thus in high demand and preferred to less stable or legally restricted currencies.

hard landing A recession that results from trying to check inflation by applying severe measures to reduce excess demand but thereby undermining business confidence. *See also* ***soft landing.***

hard loan A loan lacking any concessions; it uses market interest rates, a risk premium (depending on the borrower's creditworthiness), a specified maturity date, a repayment schedule and a specified currency.

harmonization The aim of bringing common principles and standards to financial reporting worldwide, and particularly within the European Union.

harmonized system A method used in international trade for classifying goods, each being given an HS number.

Harmonized Index of Consumer Prices (HICP) The European Union's standardized measure of inflation, established in 1997, which compares changes in the cost of living among member states.

Harrod-Domar economic growth model A theoretical economic model which specifies that national income should grow at a rate that satisfies the equilibrium national income condition (that, over a given period, savings equal investment). It was devised in 1939 by the UK economist Roy Harrod (1900-78) and, independently, E.D. Domar.

Harrod-neutral technical progress A type of technical advancement that increases labour's efficiency, thus saving labour. The idea was put forward by the UK economist Roy Harrod (1900-78). *See also* **Hicks-neutral technical progress.**

Heckscher-Ohlin model A theoretical economic model to describe international trade. It predicts that a country exports goods that use its most plentiful factor (such as labour) and imports goods that use its least plentiful factor (such as capital), which tends to equalize the relative prices of the factors in different countries. It was named after the two Swedish economists who devised it. *See also* **comparative advantage.**

hedging A method of protecting against price fluctuations, commonly on the commodities futures market. The term is also used to describe the practice of protecting against fluctuations in exchange rates (by buying forward) to minimize risks and possible losses.

Herfindahl index A measure of a market's seller *concentration ratio* that takes into account the total number of companies and their share of total market output (their size distribution).

Herstatt risk The risk of making a loss on a currency transaction when one side of the deal has been completed but completion of the other side is delayed. It is named after a German bank which made such a loss in 1974.

heteroscedacity The property of having different variances (as when the variations of data are not consistent with their being random samples from the same population).

Hicksian demand function If the level of consumer satisfaction (utility) remains constant, a relationship between a consumer's demand for a commodity and its price. If the price rises, the consumer is assumed to be compensated so that he or she feels the same satisfaction as before the price rise. It is named after the UK economist John Hicks (1904-89) who first described it in 1934.

Hicks-neutral technical progress A type of technical advancement in which, for all factors, the average and marginal products change in the same proportion. The idea was put forward by the UK economist John Hicks (1904-89). *See also* **Harrod-neutral technical progress.**

HICP Abbreviation of *Harmonized Index of Consumer Prices.*

H

hidden price reduction An increase in the real value of a good or service occasioned by a increase in its quality or quantity rather than by a fall in its price (such as an increase in the weight of detergent in a packet sold at the same price as previously).

hidden price increase A decline in the real value of a good or service occasioned by a decrease in its quality or quantity rather than by a rise in its price (such as an decrease in the weight of detergent in a packet sold at the same price as previously).

hidden reserve Also called secret reserve, a reserve that is not declared on a company's balance sheet.

hidden tax A tax included in the price of goods or services so that it is not obvious to the purchaser. It includes most forms of indirect taxation, such as excise duty on alcohol, petrol and tobacco.

hidden unemployment An alternative term for *concealed unemployment*.

high-powered money Money in a form that a commercial bank can use for its *reserve assets* which, if added to those assets, could lead to *bank-deposit creation*.

high-tech Describing any business that makes extensive use of modern technology, especially electronic systems and particularly computers.

hire purchase (HP) A form of credit, normally extended on consumer goods, in which the customer takes and uses the goods and pays for them in instalments (with interest) over an agreed period of time. The seller can in theory repossess the goods at any time if the hirer defaults on payment (unlike with a *credit sale*). The finance for such business usually comes from a *finance house*.

Hire Purchase Act 1965 A UK Act of Parliament that formerly defined regulations that apply to hire purchase agreements. It was superseded by the *Consumer Credit Act 1974*.

hiring Paying a sum of money (usually expressed as so much per hour, day, week, etc.) for services or the use of goods (eg equipment or transport). The employment of casual labour is also sometimes termed hiring.

historical cost The cost of an asset at the time it was acquired, rather than the current cost of its replacement. It is also called acquisition cost or original cost; some US accountants prefer the term sunk cost.

hit-and-run entry Action of a company that enters a market expecting to make a quick profit and then possibly retire from that market. For this to work, their must be few or no barriers to entry and exit.

hoarding A deliberate holding of money or products that does not yield interest or profit.

holding company A company that exists to hold shares in other companies, which are (depending on the level of shareholding) its subsidiaries. An immediate holding company is one that holds a controlling interest in another company but, in turn, the immediate holding company itself may be owned by a holding company. It is also known as a parent.

homogeneous products Identical goods or services from rival suppliers available in the same market. They are perfect substitutes for each other and all of the suppliers have to charge the same price.

homoscedasticity The property of having the same variance (as when the variations of data are consistent with their being random samples from the same population).

honararium Money paid to a professional such as an accountant or a solicitor when he or she does not request a fee.

horizontal diversification Diversification into industries or businesses at the same stage of production as the diversifying company. For example, a suit manufacturer might diversify into leisurewear, or a yacht builder into the construction of motor boats. *See also* ***vertical diversification.***

horizontal equity The idea that people with similar incomes should receive the same treatment (eg with regards to taxation).

horizontal integration An amalgamation of companies in the same stage of production, and which are therefore likely to possess similar skills and benefit from economies of scale.

horizontal merger A merger between two companies that are at the same stage in the production process. *See also* ***vertical merger.***

hostile takeover bid An attempt to purchase control of a company that is unwelcome to some of the target company's shareholders and directors.

hot money An informal term for money obtained illegally (eg, by fraud or theft). In business, however, the term is more often used for money that is moved rapidly and at short notice from one country to another to take advantage of changes in short-term interest rates or to avoid imminent devaluation of a currency.

Hotelling's law A principle which states that it is logical for all producers of goods and services to make their products as alike as possible (with the consequence of reducing variety for the consumer). It was postulated in 1929 by US economist Harold Hotelling (1895-1973).

household In economics terms, a group of people who share the same accommodation and also share decision-making about economic matters (even if only one of them is a wage-earner).

household production The output of a cottage industry—production of goods and services within a household. It is significant economically only in less developed countries.

HP Abbreviation of *hire purchase.*

human capital The value of a company's employees.

human-resource planning Also termed manpower planning, the identification of future requirements for human resources (labour) and other aspects of personnel management (such as recruitment and training).

hundred-per-cent gold backing The situation of a bank that holds a stock of gold of equal value to the currency it issues, regarded as unnecessary as having gold as the currency itself.

hurdle rate In capital budgeting, the rate of interest that a proposal must exceed before it is given consideration; ie, the required rate of return. It is usually related to the cost of capital, taking into account any risk factors.

hyperinflation Inflation (a general increase in price levels) that is running extremely high, also known as galloping inflation.

hypothecation A firm of shippers may borrow money from a bank using as security the cargo it is currently shipping. In this case, the bank takes out a lien on the cargo and this is conveyed in a letter of hypothecation. In the USA, hypothecation is the act of putting up securities as collateral on a margin account.

hypothesis testing The use of statistical methods to test the validity of a hypothesis (such as estimating the probability that a particular deduction results from a sampling error). It aims to avoid accepting 'facts' when there is good reason to doubt their validity, and to avoid not accepting 'facts' when there no good reasons to doubt them.

I

IADB Abbreviation of *Inter-American Development Bank.*

IBEX Abbreviation of *International Bank for Economic Cooperation.*

IBRD Abbreviation of *International Bank for Reconstruction and Development.*

ICC Abbreviation of *Interstate Commerce Commission.*

IDA Abbreviation of *International Development Association.*

idle money An alternative term for *inactive money.*

IEA Abbreviation of *International Energy Agency.*

IFC Abbreviation of *International Finance Corporation.*

IHT Abbreviation of *inheritance tax.*

illegal activity Any economic activity (such as drug smuggling) that is omitted from the national income accounts because it is illegal.

illiquidity A situation in which an asset is not easily converted into cash, or in which a person is not able to raise cash quickly and/or easily.

ILO Abbreviation of *International Labour Organization.*

IMF Abbreviation of *International Monetary Fund.*

immersizing growth A growth of production that actually reduces welfare, as could happen if a country's major export provided most of the world market. Further production would cause oversupply and a worsening of the country's terms of trade, so that export revenue could actually fall.

immobile factor An economic factor that is not easy to move (between industry sectors, geographical regions or even countries) when the opportunity to do so is available. Labour is the factor most often affected, although it may also apply to capital.

impact effect The initial short-term effect of an alteration in an economic variable (before secondary effects have time to take place). For example, a sudden increase in demand can drive up prices for a while before producers can react to meet the extra demand.

imperfect competition A system of competition in which the goods are not homogeneous, ie they are not perfect substitutes for each other. This dissimilarity gives the producer a small amount of control over price. It is also known as monopolistic competition.

imperfect market Any market that does not enjoy free competition, good communications, regular demand and uniform goods.

implicit contract A mutual agreement, eg about trading terms, made where a formal written contract is not practicable (perhaps because of uncertainty about future production or prices). The two parties trust each other to behave in a reasonably way if circumstances change.

implicit cost Also called imputed cost, a cost that is assumed to arise from using an asset owned by the user. Although it does not actually exist, it is included in accounting records in order to be able to compare overall costs with another operation that does incur such a cost.

importables Goods or services that could be imported (whether or not they actually are).

import ban Also called an embargo, a ban on specified imports, often for political rather than economic reasons.

import controls Quotas (specifying quantities of goods) or tariffs (taxes) designed to limit the amount of imports, usually to protect the home market.

import deposit A deposit consisting of a percentage of the value of its imports that an importer is required to make (with an institution such as the central bank, as nominated by the government). It is a type of *import restriction.*

import duty A government tax levied on imports.

imported inflation A type of inflation that results from rises in the prices of a country's imports, perhaps because of a lowering of the exchange rate or an increase in foreign prices. Such price rises can have a knock-on effect by raising production costs and hence the prices of domestic products.

import licence A government document that authorizes the importation of (specified) goods.

import penetration A measure of the home market share taken by importers.

import propensity The part of the national income that is spent on imports.

import quota The amount of a particular good that a government allows to be imported (from a particular source).

import restrictions Government controls on the amount of goods that can be imported, usually because there is an adverse trade balance.

imports Good and services purchased by a country's residents but produced overseas. Goods physically entering the country are termed visible imports; incoming services are termed invisible imports.

import schedule A graph that shows national income plotted against the proportion of it spent on imports.

import substitution A method of reducing the imports of a less developed country by replacing them with home-produced goods, thus also reducing the expenditure of foreign currency and stimulating industrialization. It is usually achieved using import quotas and tariffs.

import surcharge A temporary tax that is levied on imports (in addition to any tariff), generally to reduce a balance of payments deficit.

imputed cost An alternative term for *implicit cost*.

imputed income The income that the owner of an asset is assumed to have from using the asset when it could have earned rent (such as the rent that an owner-occupier could have received for his or her house).

inactive money Also called idle money, money that is not invested in a financial asset or on deposit—it is not in circulation.

incentive A positive motive (sometimes artificially generated) for performing some task.

incentive bonus Extra money offered or paid to an employee to encourage harder work (and therefore greater productivity). It is also called a productivity bonus.

incentive compatibility A group situation in which each person has his or her own incentive to behave in such a way as to benefit the group as a whole.

incentive pay scheme A method of paying wages or salaries in such a way as to give each employee an incentive to work harder or more productively. Bonuses and profit-sharing are two ways of achieving this.

incidence of taxation The location of the real burden of a tax. For example, the burden of a direct tax (such as income tax) is located with the person who pays it, whereas an indirect tax (such as value-added tax) can be passed on to somebody else.

income Money, goods or services received from an activity. Income may be a return on one of the factors of production—a salary, rent, interest or profit—or it may be a transfer payment made for other reasons, such as a pension or unemployment benefit. The definition also includes non-monetary income, such as the benefit a company or individual derives from the possession of assets. For a company it is therefore the amount by which revenue and gains exceed expenses and liabilities (debts).

income-consumption curve A graph that plots the relationship between income and the amount of product demanded (consumed).

income distribution The way that total national income is apportioned between the various factor inputs (functional income distribution) or between the suppliers of factor inputs and consumers or others (personal distribution of income).

income effect The change in the real income of a consumer that results from a change in the prices of products. The effect is usually positive, ie a fall in price leads to an increase in demand.

income elasticity of demand With prices held constant, the proportional increase in the amount demanded divided by the proportional rise in income. For example, for a good with a high positive income elasticity of demand, such as a luxury, a higher proportion of income is spent on it as income increases, whereas for a good with a low income elasticity of demand, such as a staple good, a less higher proportion of income is spent on it as income increases. The income elasticity of demand is negative for an *inferior good*.

income from employment The income from wages and salaries earned by working for somebody else, such as another person, company or government organization.

income from self-employment The income from working for oneself (an unincorporated business), eg as a partner or sole trader.

income method The totalling of the factor incomes of the members of an economy to establishing the domestic product, usually employing the information from tax returns. See also *expenditure method*.

income redistribution Any way of changing the pattern of personal income distribution within an economy to get a more equitable distribution of wealth and thus generally for social motives. Methods include welfare payments to the low-paid, specified minimum wages and a progressive taxation system (in which high-income earners pay proportionately more tax).

income tax A direct annual tax levied on *income* such as on fees, salaries and wages. In accounting terms it is regarded as an expense or, if not yet paid, a liability.

income velocity of circulation The total national income divided by the total stock of money in an economy. *See velocity of circulation.*

inconvertible Describing money that cannot be exchanged for gold of equal value. UK currency has been inconvertible since the country left the gold standard in 1931.

increasing returns A situation in which productivity rises disproportionately with an increase in output.

incumbent firm A company that is already established in a market, and so is normally in a stronger position that a new entrant (because of reputation, customer loyalty, sunk costs and so on).

indexation A form of index-linking that ties, say, income to the retail price index and therefore prevents a fall in real wages during a period of inflation. Annuities, pensions or taxes may also be index-linked. The term also describes an adjustment (the indexation allowance) to the value of an asset to take into account a change in the retail price index. This prevents the owner of the asset from having to pay capital gains tax on a gain that was due entirely to inflation.

index number A weighted average that permits the comparison of prices or production over a number of years. The components elected for comparison are weighted according to their importance and then averaged. Figures are compared to those for a base year, selected for its typicality and usually given the index number 100 or 1000.

Index of Industrial Production An index of the physical production volume from an economy's productive sectors. It excludes public and private services, and is based on construction, mining, manufacturing and public utilities.

Index of Retail Prices The formal name of an indicator popularly known as the *cost of living index.*

indicative planning A method of using input-output analysis and similar techniques to set long-term targets and ways of achieving them with the overall aim of controlling the economy. This combination of decentralization and central planning has been successful in France and Japan, but not in the UK.

indicator A measurable variable used to suggest overall change among a group of linked variables too complex to yield to simple analysis. Thus a variety of economic indicators—such as price, income, imports, exports, money supply and so on—are studied in an attempt to estimate the state of a national economy.

indifference curve For two products that provide the same satisfaction (utility), a graph that shows the various combinations of the two. Sets of such curves are called indifference maps.

indifference map *See indifference curve.*

indirect investment An investment in bonds, debentures, stocks, shares or any other financial security.

indirect labour Workers who are not directly involved in a production process (such as cleaners, maintenance staff and supervisors). In other words, all labour that is not *direct labour.*

indirect materials Materials that are not included in a final product but which are necessary for its production (such as cleansers and lubricants).

indirect production The production of goods for sale by employing labour and machinery and using a system of divided labour in order to make a profit (as opposed to direct production, in which everyone merely makes the things that he or she requires and none is sold).

indirect taxation A system of taxation in which tax paid to one person or organization (often a retailer) is then paid to the Inland Revenue or Treasury. Excise duty and value-added tax are forms of indirect taxation.

indirect utility function A function that relates consumer satisfaction (utility) to prices and incomes (as opposed to a direct utility function which relates utility to consumption and work done).

indivisibility The inability of a machine or production process to produce fewer than a certain large number of units (without working inefficiently at less than optimum capacity).

induced consumption The part of a change in expenditure on total consumption that results from a change in national or disposable income (the other part is *autonomous consumption*, which does not change with income).

induced investment The part of a change in real investment that results from a change in national income (ie in output). The other part is *autonomous investment*, due to long-term factors such as technical improvements.

industrial classification The classifying of similar economic activities into markets or industries. The UK's Standard Industrial Classification (SIC), latest revision 1980, has ten Divisions (categories) which are subdivided into Classes, Groups and Activities, making 334 in all.

industrial country A country whose gross domestic product (and exports) include a large proportion of industrial production, such as the members of the *Organization for Economic Cooperation and Development* and most of the members of the *Council for Mutual Economic Assistance*.

industrial democracy The concept that every company employee— workforce as well as management—should have a say in the way it is run. *See also social charter.*

industrial economics The branch of economics that deals with how production activities are organized in terms of both companies and markets.

industrial espionage An attempt by one company or group to gain access to confidential information about another, generally to acquire commercial advantage and improve efficiency by imitation.

industrialization The process of developing the manufacturing side of an economy, generally by moving capital and labour from agriculture into industry.

industrial policy An economic policy that promotes industry—its development, efficiency, expansion, competitiveness, modernity, training, and so on.

industrial sector Also called the secondary sector, the part of an economy that is concerned with the production of goods (both intermediate and final), as opposed to the primary sector (raw material extraction and agriculture) and tertiary sector (services).

industry An agglomeration of companies involved in the production of goods. The term is usually applied as a generic for a group of companies manufacturing very similar products, eg 'the car industry'.

industry demand for labour The demand for labour in an industry as determined by the rate of wages or, at fixed wages, by the rate of output.

inelastic Describing an economic variable that is relatively unaltered by a change in another related variable.

inelastic demand A situation in which a price increase (for goods or services) does not produce a proportionate decrease in demand. It usually occurs with necessities or goods with a very strong brand image.

inelastic supply A situation in which a price increase (for goods or services) does not produce a proportionate increase in supply.

inequality of incomes The income differences between individual earners or households, or between different groups, regions or nations. Inequality among individuals in a particular society can often be correlated to the possession (or lack of) job skills and training, while inequality among households may depend on the number of wage-earners.

infant industry A newly-established national industry in the early stages of growth.

inferior good Also called inferior product, a good for which the demand falls (at any given price) as income rises; ie the income elasticity of demand is negative (eg the demand for small cars by large families).

inflation A persistent general increase in the level of prices. Strictly defined, it includes neither one-off increases in price (occasioned by, for example, a sudden scarcity of one product) nor any other increases caused by real factors. Its causes include an excess of demand over supply and increases in the money supply, perhaps brought about by increased government expenditure, which causes a decline in the real value of money.

inflation accounting An alternative term for *current cost accounting*.

inflation-adjusted Describing wages that have been modified to maintain real income by increasing pay in line with inflation. The term may also be applied to the economist's technique of discounting price changes to obtain a truer picture of quantitative changes in output.

inflationary gap At full employment, the amount by which aggregate demand (total spending) exceeds the output level. Prices rise because of increase in demand, but all resources are fully accounted for (and so output cannot increase). This leads to *demand inflation*.

inflationary spiral An increase in the rate of inflation that is self-sustaining because of simultaneous rising input costs and the resultant price increases. It is also termed price-wage spiral because rising prices lead to demands for higher wages—again increasing input costs.

inflation target Within a government's monetary policy (or the policy exercise by the central bank), a given level of inflation that is accepted as part of that policy.

information agreement An agreement by which companies provide information to each other, generally through a central agency such as a trade association. The information can include conditions of sale, discounts, selling prices, and so on.

information technology (IT) An area of microelectronics that combines computing and telecommunications technology to organize, store, retrieve and transfer information.

infrastructure The public utilities of a nation. Also known as social overhead capital, the infrastructure includes roads, railways, airports, communications systems (eg telephones), housing, water and sewerage systems, and other public amenities.

inheritance tax (IHT) A tax paid on inheritances by heirs, often calculated in relation to the closeness of the relationship between the heir and the deceased person. In the UK, capital gains tax now covers income from inheritances.

initial conditions The starting position that is assumed to apply to any economic system, used to calculate its later positions.

injection Spending on domestic goods and services other than consumer spending, ie that comes from outside the household sector (eg from exports, government spending and investment).

Inland Revenue A UK government department whose major responsibility is the collection of various taxes, such as income tax, capital gains tax and corporation tax. Its full name is the Board of the Inland Revenue.

innocent entry barrier A barrier to entry that is not deliberately meant to be restrictive, such as those caused by natural, technical or social conditions (eg expensive production techniques or market or production experience).

innovation An original idea that has been developed into a saleable product (product innovation) or usable production technique (process innovation).

input-output analysis The measurement and study of how goods and services flow between the various sectors of an economy, both as inputs and as outputs. The method was developed from 1941 by the Russian-born US economist Wassily Leontief (1906-).

input The services of factors of production (eg capital and labour) or supplies (eg fuel, intermediate products and raw materials) that have to be used in a production process.

input price The price that has to be paid for the services of factors of production (eg capital and labour) or for supplies (eg fuel, intermediate products and raw materials).

inside money Money that counts as an asset to the company or individual who holds it but is a liability for somebody else, as opposed to outside money for which there is no such liability.

insider dealing Also called insider trading, illegal profitable transactions made on the basis of privileged information available as a result of working inside an organization. Most insider dealing concerns trading in stocks and shares whose value is likely to be affected by the release of news that only a few people are aware of.

insiders and outsiders People who have a job (insiders) and those who do not (outsiders). It can be argued that workers and their trade unions keenly look after the jobs of the insiders but do less to create job opportunities for outsiders, thus maintaining unemployment.

insolvency A state in which total liabilities (excluding equity capital) exceed total assets; it is therefore the inability to pay debts when called to do so. If insolvency is chronic, bankruptcy or liquidation generally follow.

Insolvency Act 1986 A UK Act of Parliament that details how an insolvent company can be dealt with. Among the choices are winding up (if there is no way of saving the company) using an administrator or receiver; appointing an administrator the reorganize the company (to the best interests of creditors and shareholders); or recapitalization through a voluntary agreement between the company and its creditors.

instalment Part payment of a debt, such as one undertaken as part of a *credit sale* or *hire purchase* agreement. Instalment payments fall due at fixed and specified intervals and when totalled equal the original debt, usually with the addition of interest.

instalment credit *See credit sale.*

instalment plan The US term for *hire purchase.*

institutional economics A theory of economics that criticizes the reliance on mathematical models which ignores the (non-economic) role of institutions such as the legal, political and social structure of an economy.

institutional investor A corporate rather than individual investor; a company that invests funds on behalf of clients, generally intending to reap profits only in the long term. Institutional investors include banks, insurance companies, pension funds and unit trusts. In the UK, institutional investors hold from 50% to 70% of all negotiable securities.

insurance A contract under which the insurer agrees to provide compensation to the insured in the event of a specific occurrence, eg loss of or damage to property. In return, the insured pays the insurer a premium, usually at fixed intervals. The premium varies according to the insurer's estimate of the probability that the event insured against will actually take place.

intangible asset A non-monetary asset that is neither physical nor current. The many examples include brand names, copyright, franchises, goodwill, leases, licences, mailing lists, patents and trademarks. It is sometimes known as an invisible asset.

intangibles For any investment project, those benefits (and costs) that cannot be assessed accurately, or at least not in terms of money. Examples include the improvement or spoiling of views as a result of major earthworks such as those accompanying road building.

integration An amalgamation of two or more companies to improve efficiency. Also, an industry is said to be integrated if profits from different partaking companies are compatible.

intellectual property An expression of the theory that ideas as well as tangible inventions are unique to one person or a group and should be patentable. Currently intellectual property has no clear legal standing in many countries, other than in copyright.

Inter-American Development Bank (IADB) A bank founded in 1959, with headquarters in Washington, DC, that provides financial aid for economic development in 28 Caribbean and Latin American countries. Canada, Israel, Japan, the USA and 18 European countries are also members.

interest A charge made by a lender to a borrower in exchange for the service of lending funds. It is usually expressed as a percentage of the sum borrowed for a specific period (normally a year), termed the interest rate, but it may be paid in kind. Interest is also payment made by a bank or building society to customers who deposit money with them. *See* **compound interest; simple interest.**

interest cover The ratio of earnings to the fixed-interest payments necessary to service loan capital. It is an indication of how vulnerable a company is to fluctuations in profit or interest rates.

interest-elasticity of the demand for money A measurement of how changes in interest rates affect the demand for money.

interest equalization tax A US tax on overseas borrowings in the USA, levied to reduce the amount of capital leaving the country.

interest rate The interest charged to a borrower or paid to an investor, usually expressed as a percentage per annum (*see* **interest**).

interest rate futures Financial futures purchased as a hedge against an adverse change in interest rates. If interest changes on the hedger's financial instruments produce a loss, the futures contract offsets it.

interest-rate swap An exchange of two interest-rate payments in a transaction, in which a borrower of lower creditworthiness benefits from the higher interest rate available to a borrower of higher creditworthiness (who makes a profit on the deal).

interest yield On a fixed-interest security, the rate of interest expressed as a percentage of the price paid. It is also termed the effective interest rate or running yield.

interfirm conduct The ways in which companies react with each other in a market, ranging from total interdependence to total independence. *See also* **collusion**.

interim dividend Any dividend other than the final dividend declared by a company at the conclusion of each trading year. Interim dividends may be made as a reward for a particularly good economic performance or simply as an effective advance on the final dividend, which will be correspondingly reduced in value. Many UK companies quoted on the stock market make interim dividend payments per annum; it is unusual for a firm to exceed this frequency of interim payments.

interim report A short statement published at the end of the first half of a public company's financial year, detailing results for the previous six months and declaring any *interim dividend*.

inter-industry trade A type of trade between countries in which the exports of one country are different from the imports of another and are usually products of different industries, dependent mostly on their abilities to produce goods at a competitive cost. *See also* **intra-industry trade**.

interlocking directorates The situation in which somebody is a director of two or more different companies.

intermediate product Also called an intermediate good, a product that is an input for the production of a *final product*.

intermediate technology The use of non-traditional techniques, based on modern science, to produce goods by employing labour-intensive methods. It is advocated for less developed countries that have plenty of available labour but lack the skills or capital to establish modern large-scale manufacturing.

intermediation The activities of banks, building societies and other financial institutions in making funds deposited with them available to creditworthy borrowers.

internal balance A situation in which an economy's level of activity maintains a stable rate of inflation, such as when there is full employment and prices remain constant. It is an objective of macroeconomics. *See also* **external balance;** *internal-external balance model.*

internal economies of scale A fall in a company's average production costs with increasing output, generally through better utilization or enlargement of plant.

internal-external balance model An economic model that seeks to combine *internal balance* (full employment and stable prices) with *external balance* (balance of payments equilibrium).

internal financing The cash generated within a company's own accounts (such as retained profits) or from its own resources (such as assets or working capital).

internal growth An alternative term for *organic growth.*

internalization The cost saving resulting from a company's desire to control its overseas operations, rather than use another company for that purpose.

internalizing externalities Ways of getting external costs (or benefits) taken into account by the people producing them when they are making decisions.

internal labour market The policy of recruiting among existing junior employees for more senior positions (as opposed to using the *external labour market*).

Internal Market The integrated market, originally planned for 1992, that was to assure the free movement of funds, goods and labour throughout the countries of the European Union.

internal rate of return (IRR) The discount rate at which, applied to the expected pattern of cash expenditure and income of a capital project, would give a net present value of zero. It may be compared with the return on alternative investments, or on some target rate of return.

Internal Revenue Service (IRS) The US equivalent of the UK's *Inland Revenue.*

International Agreement for Guidelines on Officially Supported Export Credit Commonly known as Consensus, an agreement between members of the Organization for Economic Cooperation and Development on how much they will subsidize the interest rate on loans to purchaser's of their own country's exports.

International Bank for Economic Cooperation (IBEX) A financial organization established in 1949 that acts as the central bank for the Communist-based Council of Mutual Economic Assistance (CMEA), later (1991) superseded by the Organization for Economic Cooperation (OEC).

International Bank for Reconstruction and Development (IBRD) Part of the World Bank, established in 1945 with headquarters in Washington, DC, to help economic reconstruction in countries after World War II. It makes loans to developing nations or guarantees loans from other sources. The bank's capital comes from the member nations of the International Monetary Fund .

international commodity agreement An agreement aimed at helping developing countries by stablizing foreign exchange earnings and the incomes of their producers, which is in turn achieved by trying to stabilize the prices of commodities that are traded internationally (by setting an 'official' price). The primary commodities concerned include cocoa, coffee, olive oil, rubber, sugar and wheat. The first agreement (for coffee) was made in 1962.

international competitiveness A measure of how well a county competes in international trade against other countries.

international debt The money that borrowing countries owe to the rest of the world. *See* **debt servicing.**

International Development Association (IDA) An organization founded in 1960 as part of and financed by the International Bank for Reconstruction and Development (World Bank) to give advice and aid in the form of long-term low-interest (or no-interest) loans to the poor less developed countries.

International Energy Agency (IEA) An organization founded in 1974 by the Organization for Economic Cooperation and Development (OECD) to try to stabilize the trade in oil and reduce members' dependence on supplies of oil.

International Finance Corporation (IFC) An organization established in 1956 by the International Bank for Reconstruction and Development

(World Bank) to raise capital to instigate growth in a developing country's private sector.

International Labour Organization (ILO) A United Nations organization (originally established in 1919 under the Versailles Treaty) that aims to improve working conditions, living standards and social justice throughout the world.

international liquidity Also called international money, those money assets (such as gold, reserve currency or special drawing rights) that can be used to finance international trade or a balance of payment deficit.

International Monetary Fund (IMF) An international organization, established in 1944 after the Bretton Woods conference, to organize and administer the international monetary system. It was designed to help countries in financial difficulties, especially with their balance of payments. It makes loans and provides financial advisers.

international monetary system The markets in foreign exchange that determine exchange rates and provide finance for the movements of capital between countries and for international trade.

international reserves An alternative term for *foreign exchange reserves*.

international trade The exchange of goods and services between countries—exports and imports.

International Trade Commission (ITC) A US government organization established in 1974 (when it superseded the United States International Trade Organization) whose main function is investigating claims that a particular import is damaging a home industry.

Internet A message-forwarding system that interlinks computers worldwide. Its applications grow daily, and include e-mail, banking, shopping and entertainment, as well as other types of information access and transmission. It is funded largely by the sites that receive or relay messages (not the senders), although access may not be free. Any statement about the number of users is out of date immediately, because of the rate of current growth, but at the beginning of the year 2002 there were an estimated 50 million users.

Interstate Commerce Commission (ICC) A US organization that controls traffic across state boundaries (by pipeline, railway, road or waterway).

I

intertemporal budget constraint The constraint that the spending of an individual, company or government must be limited to the funds it has available over a lengthy time period.

intertemporal substitution The exchange of present consumption/ production for similar consumption/production in the future (and vice versa).

intervention The action of a central bank in the foreign currency markets when it buys or sells currency in an attempt to control its exchange rate.

intervention mechanism A type of *intervention* employed by the European Monetary System to stabilize exchange-rate relationships as agreed between members. It provides short-term (75-day) finance to the central bank of a country whose exchange rate is under pressure, or grants short-term monetary support or medium-term financial assistance.

intra-industry specialization The type of specialization in which different companies specialize in (different) specific products in the same industry, thereby lowering costs (through economies of scale) and pleasing consumers (by providing variety).

intra-industry trade A type of trade between countries in which the exports of one country are in the same category as the imports from another and are usually products of the same industry, usually because of economies of scale (small quantities of high-cost goods are exported, large quantities of low-cost goods are imported). *See also* **inter-industry trade.**

intra-marginal intervention The intervention by the central bank or other authority in foreign exchange markets before the exchange rate reaches its permissible limit (effectively narrowing the band in which the exchange rate is allowed to fluctuate).

inventory A list of the stock of raw materials, goods in production (work in progress) or finished goods owned and stored by a company, giving details of their cost, value and price. In the USA, the term inventory is synonymous with **stock.**

inventory investment An investment in inventory—raw materials, work in progress and stock of finished goods. As production proceeds, investment in the early stages becomes an investment in the later ones.

It may be deliberate (eg to meet an anticipated seasonal increase in demand) or unintentional (because of an unanticipated fall in demand). *See also **just in time***.

inverse elasticity rule The principle that, when prices are rising, it is best from the producer's point of view to make the highest increases on products that have the most inelastic demand—people will continue to buy them even at the higher price. Price-sensitive products should be given the lowest proportional increase.

investment 1. The purchase of something that is expected to increase in value, generally with a view to selling it for a profit at a later date. Although the 'something' could be goods or property (real assets), the term most commonly applies to financial instruments such as bonds, commodities, futures, options, shares, stocks, unit trusts and warrants. Interest-bearing accounts in banks and building societies, savings banks, annuities, endowments, pension plans and life assurance policies are also types of investments. There is no formal distinction between investment and savings, although the latter is generally taken to mean 'putting by' regular small sums (*see **savings***). 2. To an economist, investment covers spending that results in economic growth (such as money spent on the purchase of machinery or the building of plant that will produce goods and services for sale). In this sense, it extends to funds applied to the improvement of the infrastructure, and the term may also be applied to expenditure on human resources.

investment appraisal The assessment of the anticipated costs and income from a capital investment (over its whole life). It may be carried out in terms of cashflows or profits, from a short- or long-term perspective.

investment centre The area of a company that is responsible for costs, revenues and any related investment. It may be as small as a section or as large as a subsidiary company.

investment incentive An inducement to the private sector to make capital investments, offered by local or national government. It may consist of a government grant or exemption from or a reduction in tax, or accelerated depreciation on capital assets. *See also **enterprise zone***.

investment income A company's income from outside investments (as opposed to revenue from normal business activities).

investment schedule A graph that shows he relationship between investment and national income. The total investment is the sum of autonomous investment (independent of the level of national income), replacement investment (needed to maintain the existing capital stock) and induced investment (in response to increased demand).

Investment Services Directive (ISD) A directive of the European Union, issued in 1966, that deals with cross-border transactions by investment banks and dealers in securities.

investment trust An investment scheme, similar to a *unit trust*, in which a small investor is able to invest in a range of securities through the agency of the scheme's managers.

invisible asset *See intangible asset.*

invisible balance A country's balance of trade in *invisibles* (services).

invisible earnings Income earned from payment for services rather than goods, on a national scale. Invisible earnings include profits from tourism, shipping, and the provision of insurance, banking and other financial services. They are also called invisibles.

invisible export The sale of a service, such as banking, shipping or insurance, to an overseas buyer. Revenue from tourism (eg from foreign tourists in the UK) is also regarded as an invisible export.

invisible hand The way in which the prices on a market adjust themselves without anybody being consciously involved. The term was first used by the Scottish economist Adam Smith (1723-90).

invisible import The purchase of a service from an overseas supplier.

invisible trade The trade in services rather than in tangible goods.

invisibles A collective term for invisible exports and imports.

invoice A document that summarizes a business transaction and often doubles as a request for payment. A formal invoice lists and describes the goods (or services) ordered and details their price, and usually records the dates and times of dispatch and delivery.

involuntary unemployment A type of employment in which the unemployed worker is willing to work at current wage rates but there are not enough job opportunities. *See also* **Keynesian unemployment.**

inward investment An alternative term for *foreign investment.*

irredeemable security Also called undated security, a consol, debenture, preference share or other financial security that has no redemption date. The original sum borrowed does not have to be repaid but a fixed rate of interest is payable for ever.

IRR Abbreviation of *internal rate of return.*

IRS Abbreviation of *Internal Revenue Service.*

IS curve In macroeconomic models, the investment-saving curve which is a plot of the equilibrium positions at which the combination of national income (gross domestic product) and interest rate makes savings and investment the same.

ISD Abbreviation of *Investment Services Directive.*

IS-LM model In theoretical macroeconomics, a plot of national income (gross domestic product) versus interest rate. Where the *IS curve* (on which savings equal investment) and LM curve (on which the supply of money equals the demand to hold it) cross, the market for goods and the market for money balances are both in equilibrium.

isocost curve A graph that shows the combinations of *factor inputs* (such as capital and labour) that can be purchased for the same amount of money.

isoquant curve A graph that shows the combinations of *factor inputs* (such as capital and labour) that produce the same output.

issue The quantity of a particular new stock or share and the method by which it is offered to the public. In an issue by tender, stocks and shares are issued by the process of inviting tenders above a certain stated minimum price and then selling to the highest bidder.

issued share capital The amount of a company's authorized share capital that has actually been taken up (ie sold to investors).

IT Abbreviation of *information technology.*

ITC Abbreviation of *International Trade Commission.*

I

J

J-curve A graph that illustrates the delay between devaluation (or depreciation) of a country's currency and a change in the balance of trade. At first the prices of exports fall and those of imports rise, worsening the trade balance, but after a while the opposite happens—exports rise and imports fall

JIT *See just in time.*

job acceptance schedule The combination of aspects of a job that somebody seeking work will accept—usually a mixture of location, prospects, wages and working conditions. The mixture often varies, depending on whether the job-seeker is or is not currently employed.

jobber Also known as a stockjobber, a member of the London Stock Exchange who deals in securities with stockbrokers and other jobbers, but not directly with the public. Formerly, the activities of jobbers and stockbrokers were kept separate on the London exchange. Now jobbers have been replaced by *market-makers*. In the USA, a jobber is any middleman between a wholesaler and a retailer, or a person on a stock exchange who deals in securities that are worthless (eg junk bonds). The US synonym for a jobber in the UK sense is *dealer*.

joint and several The concept by which joint debtors (eg, two or more partners in a partnership) are responsible for the debt, both jointly and as individuals. Joint and several liability gives the lender the recourse to each of the partners in the debt in the event of default.

joint costs Expenses that are shared between two or more products, sometimes difficult or impossible to allocate precisely between them and so work out their independent costs.

joint demand A demand for two or more goods or services that are used together (such as cars and tyres). As a result, a change in the demand for one causes a change in the demand for the other.

joint product One of two or more products of similar value that are produced simultaneously by the same process.

joint production costs The costs of two or more products that are produced together by a single process and cannot be identified separately until a stage in production called the separation or split-off point. The costs are allocated to the individual products in accordance with their respective sales values at the separation point.

joint-profit maximization A situation in which rival companies, rather than compete, coordinate their policies on prices and output so as to maximize their profits. *See also cartel; collusion.*

joint-stock company An alternative name for a *limited company.*

joint supply A situation in which two or more goods are produced together using the same supply. A change in the production of one good results in a change in the production of another (but only if their proportions can be varied).

joint venture A situation in which one (reporting) entity has a long-term contractual interest in another which is controlled jointly by the reporting entity and some other venture. The reporting entity details in its accounts its share of assets, cash flows and liabilities of the joint venture.

Juglar cycle A *business cycle* about 9 or 10 years long identified in 1862 by the French economist Clément Juglar (1819-1905).

junior debt A debt that ranks after another (is subordinated), termed the senior debt, when it comes to payment in the event of default.

junk bond Also sometimes called a high-yield bond, a bond issued by a company with a low credit rating.

just in case The maintaining of buffer stocks for a production and distribution processes, just in case supplies become hard to get or there is a sudden increase in demand. Because of the amount of capital this ties up, it is not favoured as much as *just in time.*

just in time (JIT) A method of minimizing the costs of holding stocks (of raw materials, work in progress and finished goods). It requires careful planning and scheduling, and reliable sources of supply. *See also just in case.*

J

K

Kennedy Round A large-scale renegotiation of international tariff agreements, within the limits of the General Agreement on Tariffs and Trade (GATT), initiated by US President Kennedy in 1963.

Keynesian Describing a school of economic thought, named after UK economist John Maynard Keynes (1883-1946), who was greatly influential in the 1930s. Keynesians believe that the best way to bring about economic change is by government intervention in the form of market controls and public investment.

Keynesian unemployment A type of employment in which unemployed workers are willing to work at current wage rates but there are not enough job opportunities and simultaneously companies cannot sell as much product as they want—there is an excess in the supply of both labour and goods (and a lack of demand for both). The idea was introduced by UK economist John Maynard Keynes (1883-1946).

Keynes Plan A set of proposals by the UK economist John Maynard Keynes (1883-1946) presented at the Bretton Woods Conference in 1944 by the UK Treasury. It proposed the establishment of an international clearing union (a combination of commercial bank and clearing house) and an international monetary unit (the *bancor*). The plan was rejected in favour of the US proposal to set up the International Monetary Fund.

Know-How Fund Established after the collapse of central planning in the former Soviet Union and Eastern Europe, a UK government organization that provides technical help for the transition into market economies.

Kondratieff cycle A very long *business cycle* of about 50-60 years between boom to recession. It was based on an analysis of many years' economic statistics by the Russian economist Nicolay Kondratieff.

L

Labor-Management Relations Act 1947 *See Taft-Hartley Act.*

labour The people used in the production of goods or services; the workforce, one of the main factors of production. In economics it is taken to include employed workers, self-employed people and the unemployed. It is one of the chief *factors of production.*

labour economics The part of economics that deals with the demand for and supply of labour, including such things as hours of work, training, redundancy, wages and working conditions.

labour force Also called working population, the number of people in a country who are available for work, including the employed, self-employed and unemployed.

Labour Force Survey (LFS) A regular survey that analyses the labour market, particularly with a view to accurately counting the number of unemployed (not merely those claiming unemployment benefit).

labour hoarding The keeping on of more employees than a company actually needs for its level of output. It saves redundancy payments and ensures that labour is immediately available to meet a sudden increase in demand.

labour-intensive Describing an industry or process in which labour is the most important and costly factor of production, such as one in which the major cost is the payment of salaries, incentives and bonuses. Service industries or those operating job production or batch production tend to be labour intensive.

labour-intensive firm A company that uses a large input of labour and proportionately small amounts of capital to produce goods or services. A group of such companies defines a labour-intensive industry.

labour intensity The relative amount of labour in the input to a production process. *See labour-intensive.*

labour market The supply and demand for labour, which is the main determiner of wages and salaries.

labour theory of value A classical economic theory that the value of goods or services is determined by the amount of labour required to produce them, an oversimplification that ignores all other *factor inputs.*

labour turnover The rate at which employees leave a company or other organization, equal to the ratio of the number of people who leave in a year to the average number of employees (usually expressed as a percentage).

Laffer curve A diagram that illustrates a nonlinear relationship between tax rates and tax revenues for an economy, as popularized by US economist Arthur Laffer.

LAFTA Abbreviation of *Latin American Free Trade Association.*

lagging indicator A measurable variable (such as unemployment) that does not change until a while after the indicated item (such as a downturn in the economic activity). *See also* **leading indicator.**

LAIA Abbreviation of *Latin American Integration Association.*

laissez-faire An economic and market policy that favours a free market system over any form of government control or intervention.

land In economics, any natural resource as a factor of production (including the oceans).

landlord The owner of buildings or land, who can charge rent for their use.

Laspeyres index A base-weighted volume index as first devised in 1864 by the French economist Etienne Laspeyres.

Latin American Free Trade Association (LAFTA) An organization established in 1960 to coordinate the economic activities of major South American countries (and Mexico). It was superseded by the Latin American Integration Association (LAIA) in 1981.

Latin American Integration Association (LAIA) An organization established in 1981 with headquarters in Montevideo, which superseded the Latin American Free Trade Association (LAFTA). It is an economic grouping of Argentina, Bolivia, Brazil, Chile, Colombia, Ecuador, Mexico, Paraguay, Peru, Uruguay and Venezuela.

laundering A method of disguising the origin of money by moving it rapidly from one country to another. It thus becomes a complicated business to trace its origins, movements and eventual destination.

L

Counterfeit or stolen money may be laundered, although more usually laundered money represents the proceeds of crime.

Lausanne school A school of economic thought, associated with general equilibrium theory, founded in 1870 at the law faculty at Lausanne by the French economist Marie Walras (1834-1910).

law of large numbers Large groups of people behave in a more uniform way (average behaviour) than does an individual person.

law of one price When the same assets or goods are traded in different markets, their prices will not diverge (or *arbitrage* would be possible). It was first formulated by the UK economist William Jevons (1835-82).

L/C Abbreviation of *letter of credit.*

LDC Abbreviation of *less-developed country.*

leading indicator A measurable variable (such as the rate of factory construction) that moves in advance of the indicated item (such as the level of employment). *See also* **lagging indicator.**

leads and lags In international trade, the differences in timing in settling debts, perhaps causing a short-term deficit or surplus in the balance of trade. Settling early (lead) or late (lag) is generally done to take advantage of changes in exchange rates.

leakages from the circular flow of incomes Also called withdrawals, savings, tax payments, import purchases or other uses of income that do not themselves provide other incomes within the domestic economy.

lease A contract that gives temporary possession of property, sometimes in areas where prices are appreciating so rapidly that it is not in the owner's best interest to sell. Buildings are the most common subjects of a lease, although it is also possible to lease land and other possessions, such as vehicles and machinery. Long-term leases are often mortgaged, bought and sold.

leaseback An arrangement by which a property is sold on condition that it is immediately leased back to the original owner. Capital tied up in the property is thereby released for other uses.

leasehold Describing property held on a *lease.* On leasehold land, the lessee pays ground rent to the person who holds the freehold.

leasing *See* **lease.**

L

least-cost supply The assumption that a company seeking to maximize profits will use the combination of *factor inputs* that minimizes the total cost of production.

least-developed country One of the poorest countries in the world, even poorer than a *less-developed county*. The UN applies various criteria in a definition, including having a literacy rate of less than 20% and less than 10% of gross domestic product derived from manufacturing.

legal tender Currency; notes or coins that may be offered as a medium of exchange. In the UK this means any number of banknotes, £2 or £1 coins, up to £10 in 50p or 20p coins, other 'silver' (cupro-nickel) coins to the value of £5, and 'copper' (bronze) coins to the value of 20p.

lemon A colloquial term for a poor product, often one that cannot easily be distinguished from good ones. A risk-averse consumer will avoid such lemons unless their price is low enough to justify the risk.

lender A person, company or organization that makes funds (a loan) available to a borrower, often against some form security (collateral) and almost always charging interest.

lender of last resort A central bank that is prepared to lend to the banking system as a whole, including to commercial banks. In the UK the lender of last resort is the Bank of England. It must be prepared to advance money to discount houses that have insufficient funds to balance their books, preventing their bankruptcy. It therefore gives confidence to the markets and helps to prevent a damaging run on the banks. By acting as a lender of the last resort, the Bank of England is able to influence the money supply and interest rates.

Leontief paradox The fact that the USA has on average exports that are slightly more labour-intensive than its imports, despite being the most capital-rich country in the world (which would make one expect capital-rich exports). It was first observed by the Russian-born US economist Wassily Leontief (1906-).

less-developed country (LDC) A country whose levels of income and advanced technology are less than those of an industrially advanced country. It tends to depend on the *primary sector* for production and exports.

letter of credit (L/C) A letter from a bank authorizing another bank to pay the sum specified to the person named in the letter. It is also referred to as a documentary credit.

L

leverage Alternative, and mainly US, term for *gearing*.

LFS Abbreviation of *Labour Force Survey.*

liabilities A company's or person's debts. Long-term (or deferred) liabilities are usually distinguished from current liabilities, as are secured debts from unsecured debts.

liberalization Economic changes that tend to favour a free market, such as a reduction in government controls and intervention and the placing of more reliance on the laws of supply and demand.

liberal trade policy A reduction in tariffs and other controls in order to allow international trade to take place with the least amount of interference. It is a type of *liberalization.*

licence 1. A document that gives official permission to do something (such as use somebody else's patent or own a firearm), or that exempts a person from having to do something. 2. A document that proves a statutory payment has been made (eg a road fund licence or television receiving licence). 3. Formal permission to occupy or enter land. *See also* **import licence.**

licensed deposit taker A financial institution, subject to credit controls and the Banking Act 1979, that the Bank of England authorizes to conduct a banking service (although it may not call itself a bank).

licensing The practice of allowing a person or company to use a copyright or patent in return for a royalty, usually calculated as a percentage of value or a fee per unit sold.

LIFFE Abbreviation of *London International Financial Futures and Options Exchange.*

life cycle The varying pattern of consumption and income over a time period.

life-cycle hypothesis The theory that a person's present consumption depends not only on present income but also on his or her expected lifetime income, leading to lower or higher short-term consumption than present income might indicate. It was first proposed by the Italian-born US economist Franco Modigliani (1918-).

limited company (Ltd) Also called a limited liability company, a company formed from a group of people whose liability is limited to the extent of

L

the investment they have made (usually to purchase shares in the company), although occasionally limited liability is limited by guarantee to a certain amount as specified in the company's memorandum. *See also public company.*

limited liability *See limited company.*

limited partner A partner whose liability for the debts of the partnership (known as a limited partnership) is limited in law to the sum he or she invested in it. A limited partner does not generally share in the management of the firm. He or she may, however, offer advice and examine the books of account.

limit pricing A means by which a company already established in a market charges such low prices that potential competitors see them as a barrier to entry.

liquid Describing something that is readily accessible, such as assets that can be immediately realized in cash form. Money is by definition fully liquid, and cash kept in a bank is the most obvious liquid asset. Treasury bills, money at call and Post Office savings are similarly liquid.

liquid assets Assets that consist of cash or can readily be converted into cash. They are also known by various other names, such as liquid capital, quick assets and realizable assets.

liquidation The winding-up of a company, so-called because the company's assets are liquidated—converted into cash money—in order that outstanding creditors may be paid (in whole or, more usually, in part). In the USA the term is also used to denote payment of a debt.

liquidity The ease with which an asset can be converted into cash. Cash deposits in current bank accounts may be quickly withdrawn and are said to be highly liquid; money in most deposit accounts is slightly less liquid because notice must usually be given before withdrawal. Of a company, liquidity is the availability of cash (or near cash) to meet its debts and take advantage of investment opportunities.

liquidity constraint An acknowledgement that a person or company may not always be able to borrow as much money as they want, possibly because of lack of collateral or lack of creditworthiness.

liquidity preference A preference for hanging on to money (cash) rather than spending it or investing it. This may be because of a precautionary

L

motive—holding money because the financial future is uncertain; a transaction motive—holding money to pay for current spending; or a speculative motive—holding money in the hope that asset prices will fall.

liquidity trap A situation in which people prefer to hold money (cash) rather than invest in interest-bearing securities because the interest rate is so low.

listed company A company whose shares are listed on a stock exchange.

listed security A security recognized for quotation and trading on a stock exchange.

listing The flotation of a company on a stock exchange; the sum of the actions that permits securities to be traded on a stock market. The issued shares are then listed in the exchange records and their price fluctuations recorded and published.

list price The published or quoted price for goods or services. *See also discount*.

Lloyd's of London An incorporated association of insurers that specializes in marine insurance. Formally established by Act of Parliament in 1871, the Corporation developed from a group of 17th-century underwriters who met at Edward Lloyd's coffee house in London. Lloyd's supervises about 20,000 individual insurers ('names') grouped into syndicates, each of which has unlimited liability and accepts a fraction of the risk of business brought to them by one of more than 200 registered brokers. Lloyd's involvement in marine insurance currently comprises less than half the total business transacted by Lloyd's underwriters. Following disastrous losses between 1988-1994, limited liability companies are now allowed to become 'corporate names'.

LM curve *See IS curve; IS-LM model.*

loan A sum of money borrowed by one person, organization or country from another on condition that it is repaid, generally for a specified time and often at an agreed rate of interest.

loanable funds In a financial market, money that is available for lending, consisting mainly of savings. The Swedish economist Knut Wicksell (1851-1926) maintained that the interest rate depends on the supply of and demand for loanable funds.

L

loan capital Also called borrowed capital or debt capital, capital in the form of a loan that is used to finance a business, on which interest has to be paid.

loan-loss provisions Reserves held by a bank or other lending institution against loans that are not repaid by the borrower.

loan portfolio A financial institution's loans to individuals or organizations (which are therefore part—usually most— of its assets). It diversifies its portfolio to reduce risks of default (not having 'all its eggs in one basket') and because it is unlikely that a single borrower would want to borrow all the assets.

local content The part of the factor inputs to a product that originate within the producer's country. The local content may have to meet a specified level for the product to be deemed a domestically produced one (and thus qualify for movement free from tariffs in a free-trade area).

local currency The currency of a foreign country with which an exporter or trader is dealing.

local taxation A tax levied on people, businesses or their property in a particular area. The chief local taxes in the UK are business rates and council tax.

location theory The part of economics that deals with the decision-making which companies employ when choosing where to establish a business. Among the many relevant factors are nearness of raw materials, nearness of markets, nearness of other similar companies, cost of land or premises, availability of labour and availability of transport.

locomotive principle The idea that during a time of international recession it only takes one country to increase its demand for imports to stimulate economic activity in other exporting countries—acting like a locomotive to pull them out of recession. By extension, economic growth depends on growth in a leading country or leading economic sector.

Lomé Convention An agreement signed in 1975 at Lomé, Togo, by the European Community and 46 developing countries of Africa, the Caribbean and Pacific (the ACP states) by which most ACP exports were made duty-free to Community countries. Further agreements,

L

which mainly increased the extent of the *European Development Fund*, were signed in 1979, 1984 and 1990.

London Foreign Exchange Market A market that deals in sterling and various foreign currencies, using contracts that are made verbally (using telephone lines or otehr electronic means) and later confirmed in writing.

London International Financial Futures and Options Exchange (LIFFE) A financial futures market established in 1982 for dealing in options and futures contracts within the European time zone. Originally the London International Financial Futures Exchange, its name changed in 1992 when it merged with the London Traded Options Market (LTOM). A further merger in 1996 with the London Commodity Exchange (LCE) gave it unique status in the financial world.

London Stock Exchange (LSE) An organization established in London's Threadneedle Street in 1773 (hence its nickname: the Old Lady of Threadneedle Street). Today it is third in size in the world (after New York and Tokyo) but still the largest in Europe, especially since the large increase in trade in non-UK shares. All trading is done electronically using computer screens and telephones.

long-dated security A security with a redemption date of more than 15 years.

long-end Describing the part of the bond market that deals in long-term issues.

long position The position taken by a bull speculator, who acquires quantities of stock or commodities in excess of the amount contracted for, in the expectation that the price will rise and permit the surplus to be sold at a profit.

long rate The interest rate on a long-term bond, often an indication of expected inflation (or deflation).

long run Also called long term, 1. the requirement in statistical analysis and prediction that the results apply only over a lengthy period of time. 2. The period of time in which economic activities have time to complete and all variables attain their final levels. Everything could then be changed, if required. 3. A vague concept of a time period in which most variables can change and only a few do not. It can be contrasted with the equally vague *short run* and *medium run*.

L

long-run Phillips curve A graph that shows the relationship between inflation and unemployment in the long run. *See also* **Phillips curve.**

long term An alternative expression for *long run.*

long-term bond A *bond* with a long specified term to maturity.

long-term capital employed Also termed net worth, a company's long-term funds (such as the capital from the sales of shares and debentures), less any liabilities.

long-term interest rate The interest rate on government securities that have 15 or more years to maturity.

long-term unemployment Unemployment that lasts for more than a specified period (usually 6 months, 1 year or 2 years). There seems to be a tendency for job prospects to diminish as the length of unemployment increases.

Lorenz curve A graph of cumulative proportion of a variable such as income or employment against cumulative proportion of population (such as number of companies or households), which gives a measure of inequality in society.

loss A disadvantage, forfeiture of money or goods, or negative profit (the amount by which expenses of a transaction or project exceed income).

loss leader A product or service offered for sale at a substantial loss in order to attract customers. The hope is that customers who buy the loss leader will also purchase other goods or services. Under the terms of the *Resale Prices Acts 1964, 1976,* the practice is illegal if the selling price is less than the bought-in cost.

loss minimization When the condition of the market precludes *profit maximization,* a short-term strategy that a company can adopt. It is achieved by a level of output at which marginal costs equal marginal revenue.

Louvre Accord An agreement signed in 1987 by a group of industrial countries (including Canada, France, Italy, the UK, the USA and West Germany) to cooperate in setting the exchange rates of other currencies against the US dollar.

LSE Abbreviation of London *Stock Exchange.*

Ltd *See limited company.*

Lucas critique The argument that economists should not make predictions (about the effects of policy changes) on the basis that current relationships will continue to be valid in the future. It was proposed by the US economist Robert Lucas (1937-).

lump of labour The incorrect idea that because the economy requires only a certain amount of work to be done, if a given output needs fewer people to produce it unemployment is bound to rise—anything that saves labour must force up unemployment. It ignores several factors: people displaced from one economic area may be re-employed elsewhere; the relationship between wage rates and the worth of the work to a company; and the fact that advances in technology lead to higher productivity, higher wages and increased purchasing power (increasing demand).

lump-sum tax A compulsory tax that cannot be affected by actions of the taxpayer (unlike an indirect tax such as a television licence which is the same for nearly everyone no matter how much they earn or how much they paid for their television set but can still be avoided by not owning a television set). A *poll tax*, levied on every member of the population, would be a lump-sum tax.

lump system A system of payment under which workers receive a lump sum for each day's work or for the fulfilment of a daily quota. It is common in the building industry, but frowned upon because it can enable employees to avoid income tax.

luxury A good or service whose consumption varies markedly with the income of the consumer. Their consumption increases proportionally with an increase in income.

L

M

Maastricht Treaty A treaty signed in 1992 (effective 1993) by the member countries of the European Community that gave provisional agreement to closer economic and political unity (such as through the formation of the *European Monetary Union*—leading to a single currency—and a *European Central Bank*). The *Social Chapter* was part of the treaty. At the same time the Community changed its name to the European Union (EU).

macroeconomics The study of broad or aggregate economics. It concerns itself with the relationship between such major aggregates as prices, incomes, total consumption and total production, together with interest and exchange rates, savings and investment, and the use of government controls to achieve economic objectives. *See also microeconomics.*

mail order A system for buying and selling by post; the customer purchases goods or services directly from the manufacturer or distributor without the intervention of a middleman or retailer.

maintenance The practice of preserving the service potential of an asset (which is different from improvement or repair).

majority interest A shareholding that gives the holder control of a company, ie one of over 50% of the shares.

Malthusian problem The problem that if a country's population were to grow faster than output, individual incomes would fall to subsistence level. This result can be countered by falling birth rates, technical progress and, in extremis, foreign aid. The problem was first postulated in 1798 by the UK economist Thomas Malthus (1766-1834).

managed currency A currency whose exchange rate is controlled (via a central bank) by the government. The intervention is also called managed floating.

managed trade International trade that is carried out following plans agreed between the governments of the trading countries, theoretically more easy to achieve by centrally planned economies than free market economies.

management The control and supervision of a company, asset or operation; or the group of people who control and administer a company, as distinct from the workforce.

management accountant An accountant who is involved in the day-to-day running of a business, providing information upon which managers are able to base decisions. He or she assembles and processes financial information and data about quantities to enable cost control, pricing and, above all, decision making to happen. The distinction between cost accountants and management accountants is becoming increasingly blurred. *See also* **cost accountant**.

management accounting The activity of a *management accountant*.

management-utility maximization An alternative to *profit maximization* in which a company tries to maximize the satisfaction (utility) of management, by allowing it to invest in favourite projects (increasing prestige), allowing it to increase staff (increasing status), and providing expense accounts, company cars and other perquisites.

managerial theories of the firm An alternative to *profit maximization* that uses instead company objectives such as maximizing growth in assets and sales revenue, both of which tend to increase management satisfaction (utility) more than do company profits.

managing director The senior executive director of a company, junior only to the chairman, and charged with implementing decisions made by the board of directors.

Manchester school A school of economic thought, active in the UK from 1820 to 1850, that believed in laissez faire, favouring free trade with economic and political freedom.

mandatory spending Expenditure that a government organization is legally obliged to make (as opposed to *discretionary spending*).

manpower planning An alternative term for *human-resource planning*.

manufacturing cost Also called manufacturing expense or production cost, all expenses incurred by the manufacturer in the production of goods and services.

margin Part of the total cost of a product or service that represents the producer's profit, usually expressed as a percentage of revenue. Or, especially in the USA, a payment on account of a purchase which confers ownership with its attendant risks and privileges upon the buyer, but subjecting him or her to a lien on the purchase to the extent that credit is advanced to finance the full purchase price secured by the purchase.

marginal In economics, describing the difference between two figures. For example, a marginal unit is the last unit produced, or the first unit supplied, and is defined as the smallest additional amount that is economically viable to produce or buy.

marginal analysis A method used in microeconomics to study the effect of successive small changes in demand, output, prices and costs.

marginal benefit The additional benefit that accrues from increasing some activity, measured either as the addition to total benefit per unit of increase or the addition that results from a unit increase in the activity.

marginal cost The cost incurred in raising the level of output by one unit of production beyond the original target. Marginal cost calculations are used to justify going beyond the target (or, indeed, not doing so).

marginal-cost pricing A method of arriving at the selling price of a product by charging only marginal costs to it. It is seldom used except in times of intense competition.

marginal efficiency of capital (MEC) Also sometimes termed marginal efficiency of investment, the highest interest rate at which a project or investment can be expected to break even.

marginal factor cost (MFC) The additional cost that accrues to a company from using an extra unit of *factor input*.

marginal firm A company that might just decide to enter or leave an industry by a small rise or fall in profits.

marginal physical product In the short run, the extra amount of output (measured in physical terms) that results from an additional unit of *variable-factor input*, per unit of increase. It ignores the effect on price resulting from the increase in output. *See also marginal revenue product*.

marginal profit on capital The rate of return (profit) anticipated for each additional unit of capital investment.

marginal product In the short run, the extra amount of output that results from an additional unit of *variable-factor input*, per unit of increase.

marginal productivity of capital The value of the additional output resulting from using one extra unit of capital input, per unit of extra capital (and at current prices).

marginal productivity theory of wages The idea that the increased output (in terms of value) resulting from employing an additional worker controls the demand for labour. In other words, a company will not employ an extra worker unless the revenue generated is more than his or her cost.

marginal product of labour A measure of the additional output that results from employing one more worker (assuming all other factors of production do not change).

marginal propensity to consume (MPC) The proportion of any change in national income that leads to extra consumption (ie change in consumption divided by change in national income).

marginal propensity to save (MPS) The proportion of any change in national income that goes into savings (ie change in savings divided by change in national income).

marginal rate of substitution The extra amount of one product that is needed to compensate (i.e maintain the same utility to) a consumer for a decrease in the quantity of another, per unit of the decrease. Mathematically it is the ratio of the two products' *marginal utilities.*

marginal rate of tax The rate of tax paid on an increase of one unit of income. For example, if somebody pays 25% tax on income up to a limit of £20,000 and 40% thereafter, the marginal rate of tax on an income of £20,001 is 40%.

marginal rate of technical substitution The extra amount of one input that is needed to maintain constant output for a decrease in the quantity of another input, per unit of the decrease. Mathematically it is the ratio of the two products' *marginal physical products.*

marginal rate of transformation The extra amount of one output that results from a small decrease in another, per unit of the decrease. Mathematically it is the ratio of the two outputs' *marginal costs.*

marginal revenue The revenue received by a company for selling one extra unit of product.

marginal revenue product (MRP) In the short run, the extra amount of revenue that results from an additional unit of *variable-factor input*, per unit of increase. It acknowledges the effect the extra input has on increasing the amount produced and the consequent effect on the price. *See also marginal physical product.*

marginal social product The extra amount of social welfare that accrues from employing an additional unit of a *factor of production.*

marginal tax rate The extra amount of tax paid for an additional unit of value in the activity that is taxed, effectively the proportion of an employee's last unit of income that is paid in tax.

marginal utility The extra satisfaction (utility) that a person gets from a small increase in the amount of a good consumed, per unit of the increase.

marginal utility of money The extra satisfaction (utility) that a person gets from a unit increase in his or her holding of money.

marginal value product The additional value of the output that results from employing an extra unit of a factor of production.

margin requirement A deposit on a transaction equal to an agreed percentage of its value which a buyer or seller puts down (as a margin to protect against non-completion of the transaction).

market 1. A place where goods and services are bought and sold. 2. The actual or potential demand for those goods or services. 3. An abstract expression denoting any area or condition in which buyers and sellers are in contact and able to do business together.

marketable security Any security that can be traded on a *secondary market*, such as the stock exchange.

market access The availability of a national market to overseas goods and services (allowing unimpeded competition with domestic products).

market-based pricing Also called market-led pricing, the pricing of goods and services in terms of their market (as opposed to their costs).

market capitalization Also termed market valuation, the value of all the securities of a company at current market prices.

market clearing price The price for goods or services that will find buyers in a given market.

market concentration *See concentration.*

market conduct The behaviour of a company when it purchases or supplies goods and services to a market.

market economy Also called a free-market economy, a type of economy in which markets influence a major part of economic decision-making (as opposed to a *planned economy*).

market entry The entry of a new company into a market (or of a new country into a common market such as the European Union). *See also barriers to entry.*

market equilibrium The situation in a given market where, at current prices, supply and demand are the same.

market exit The withdrawal of a company from a market. *See also barriers to exit.*

market failure The result if resources are not allocated in the most efficient way to comply with supply and demand. It may lead to idle production facilities and unemployment.

market forces The forces of supply and demand, which together determine the prices of goods and services on the open market.

marketing The distribution, promotion and presentation of a product (goods or services).

marketing mix The mixture of factors that a company can employ in presenting its products for sale, including (apart from a range of products themselves and their quality) different forms of advertising, packaging and pricing.

market-maker A market principal who encourages dealing by varying the price of stock to promote its sale or purchase. The term is used especially with reference to the stock market.

market performance A measure of how well a market makes use of economic resources to meet the requirements of consumers.

market power The strength of a company (usually the dominant one) in a market, for example in being able to control production and prices without worrying about the competition. *See also* **exploitation; monopoly**.

market price The price that a consumer actually pays for a good or service in the marketplace (not necessarily the same as the price received by the seller because of indirect taxes; *see* **factor cost**).

market research A survey that is conducted to assess consumer demand. Companies carry out market research in order to maximize the efficiency of their output and to determine potential markets which may be exploited in the future. In addition, market research often suggests ways in which goods and services may be more attractively presented to the public.

market risk A part of the total risk inherent in buying stock, which depends on market movements as a whole rather than on the particular characteristics of the stock itself. For example, during a market crash, the share prices of many sound companies whose earning prospects remain unchanged may fall in line with less sound stock. This illustrates the market risk, rather than the specific risk inherent in stock market dealings.

market segmentation The classification of a market into subgroups of characteristic consumers, which can be targeted by producers and sellers.

market share The fraction of all sales in a given market (usually expressed as a percentage) that are held by one company or by one brand.

market structure The organization of a market, especially in terms of factors that affect pricing and competition (such as market *concentration*).

mark-up An adjustment of price (say, by a retailer) to allow for a profit margin. The retailer's mark-up is equal to gross profit.

Marshall-Lerner criterion A condition that must be met if a balance of payments deficit (or surplus) is to be removed by changes in exchange rate, ie by devaluation (or revaluation). It concerns the *price-elasticity of demand* for exports and imports: for an improvement in balance of payments, the price elasticities of demand for exports and imports must total more than 1. It was named after US economist Alfred Marshal (1842-1924) and Abba Lerner (1903-82).

Marxian economics A type of economics that employs the theories of the German philosopher Karl Marx (1818-83). It followed classical economics but moved it first away from agriculture towards industrial capitalism, and then predicting that eventually there would be a breakdown of the class structure in society and the elimination of private property, leading first to socialism and then to communism.

mass production A highly mechanized process of producing goods on a continuously moving production line. It works well only for large numbers of identical products.

maturity Also termed maturity date, the date, specified in advance, on which a redeemable financial instrument may be exchanged for its cash value.

MCA Abbreviation of *monetary compensatory amount.*

mean Also called arithmetic mean, an average. Of a group of figures it is the sum of all the figures divided by the number of figures in the group.

means test An assessment of a person's income and/or wealth, as carried out to establish his or her eligibility for the receipt of certain welfare benefits.

MEC Abbreviation of *marginal efficiency of capital.*

median A statistical average used as an alternative to the arithmetic *mean* when there are a few extreme values in a group of figures. It is obtained by putting the group of figures in ascending order and nominating the middle one as the median (or the average of the two middle ones if there is an even number in the group).

medium-dated gilt A gilt-edged security with a redemption term of between 5 and 15 years.

medium-dated stock Stock with a redemption term of between 5 and 15 years.

medium of exchange A property of money that allows it to be used to purchase goods and services (as opposed to exchanging goods by *barter*).

medium run A vague concept of a time period in which several variables can change and the remainder cannot. It can be contrasted with the equally vague *short run* and *long run*.

Medium-Term Financial Assistance (MTFA) Loans for two to five years by one European Union member country to another with balance of payments difficulties. There may be economic and financial conditions attached.

Medium-Term Financial Strategy (MTFS) The UK government's method, adopted in 1980 and reviewed annually, of steadily reducing the growth rate of the money supply and long-term borrowing (by the government) in order to control inflation.

member bank 1. A UK bank that is a member of a clearing system. 2. A US bank that is a member of the Federal Reserve System.

menu cost The cost to a producer resulting from price changes (usually increases), such as notifying retailers and customers, relabelling and/or repackaging products, and amending accounting systems.

mercantilism The theory that the best way of stimulating the economy and increasing the money supply is by achieving a balance-of-payments surplus, if necessary by using protectionist methods. Historically the mercantilists of 17th-century England advocated international trade, particularly exports as opposed to imports, leading at that time to an accumulation of gold by the nation.

merchandise Finished goods that are purchased by a wholesaler or retailer for resale.

merchandise account The part of the balance-of-payments accounts that deals with the export and import of merchandise (visible trade).

merchant bank An institution that specializes in raising capital, particularly for use in business or industry. It also provides banking services such as forward-rate agreements and acceptance credits.

Mercosur Also called the Southern Cone common market, a customs union set up by the Treaty of Asunción in 1991 (ratified in 1994 to take effect in 1995) between Argentina, Brazil, Paraguay and Uruguay; Bolivia and Chile became associate members in 1996. The few remaining internal tariffs were ended in 1999.

merger The fusion of two or more companies, as distinct from a takeover of one company by another. Mergers may be undertaken for various reasons, notable to improve efficiency of two complementary companies by rationalizing output and taking advantage of economies of scale, and to fight off unwanted takeover bids from other large companies. The companies involved form one new company and their respective shareholders exchange their holdings for shares in the new concern at an agreed rate.

merit goods Also called public goods or social products, goods or services generally provided by the government whose consumption is regarded as being socially beneficial (over and above the consumers' preference for them). As a result, some merit goods receive government subsidies.

MES Abbreviation of *minimum efficient scale.*

MFA Abbreviation of *Multi-Fibre Arrangement.*

MFC Abbreviation of *marginal factor cost.*

MFN Abbreviation of *most favoured nation.*

M-form organization Short for multidivisional-form, a type of company structure with decentralized management, with individual divisions or groups with their own management running their own purchasing, production and marketing activities.

microeconomics The study of the individual components of an economy in isolation. It examines the choices open to specific people, companies and industries and has been developed to enable the study of subjects such as competition, consumption, income distribution, margins and utility. *See also* **macroeconomics.**

middleman An intermediary, usually a wholesaler, retailer or broker, who acts as an agent between a buyer and a seller. Middlemen tend to push up prices by adding their own profit margin to the difference between the buying and selling prices, and it may therefore be in the interests of the buyer and seller to 'cut out the middleman' (as, for example, in mail order).

middle market price A price that is midway between the bid price and offer price on the open market. It is the price the Inland Revenue takes into account when calculating capital gains tax on share dealings.

military-industrial complex A nation's armed forces considered together with the parts of industry that supplies them.

minimum efficient scale (MES) The size of company production or output at which constant returns to scale resume after a period of beneficial economies of scale—any further increase in output does not reduce unit costs.

minimum lending rate (MLR) The minimum rate at which the Bank of England, acting in its capacity of lender of the last resort, is willing to discount bills of exchange and at which it offers short-term loans. The MLR has a direct effect on bank interest rates.

minimum wage The lowest amount a company may pay a worker, often fixed by legislation or trade union agreements.

Ministry of International Trade and Industry (MITI) A Japanese organization that corresponds to the UK *Department of Trade and Industry*.

minority interest 1. A shareholding that does not give the holder control of a company, ie less than 50% of the shares. 2. An interest held by shareholders in a subsidiary company (excluding the holding company's interest).

minority shareholder A person who holds a *minority interest* in a company.

mint An institution licensed to make coins or tokens. In the UK, the Royal Mint at Llantrisant is charged with the manufacture of British *legal tender*, but there are also several private mints that produce tokens, for example for gaming and vending machines, coins aimed at collectors, and coinage for other countries. In the USA coins are manufactured at the Bureau of the Mint.

mis-match The situation that arises when job opportunities and unemployed workers are in different locations—one reason why unemployment can exist at the same time as an unsatisfied demand for labour.

MITI Abbreviation of *Ministry of International Trade and Industry.*

mixed economy An economy in which elements of free-market economies and planned economies coexist.

mixed strategy The use of random selection to choose one option from a range of options (eg like tossing a coin or rolling a dice to make a decision). According to *game theory* it makes it impossible for an opponent to predict what a player might do.

mix of policies The idea that a government should use a mix of policies to achieve several targets (so diluting the adverse side-effects of any one of them).

MLR Abbreviation of *minimum lending rate.*

MMC Abbreviation of *Monopolies and Mergers Commission.*

mobility The extent to which any one *factor of production* can be relocated (or its use reallocated). *See mobility of capital; mobility of labour.*

mobility of capital The ability of capital (invested funds) to move between locations, such as across national borders. It allows investors to seek the best interest rates.

mobility of labour The ability of workers to move between jobs, be it different companies, different locations or different occupations. It is an aim of international organizations such as the European Union, which sees it as an aid to economic efficiency.

mode A statistical average equal to the figure that occurs most frequently in a group of figures, thereby being a measure of central tendency.

model A representation of an economic system, generally simplified so that only a few variables apply and can therefore be studied.

Modigliani-Miller theorem In a perfect capital market, the value of a company on the market is independent of the manner in which it finances its investment or distributes its profits. It was formulated by the Italian-born US economist Franco Modigliani (1918-) and the US economist Merton Miller (1923-).

modulus The absolute value of a number, irrespective of its sign (whether it is positive or negative).

monetarism A group of economic theories which state in general that the level of prices and wages in an economy is ultimately determined by the amount of money in circulation (the money supply); that variations in the amount of money (monetary growth) have no long-term effect on the level of real activity (eg output and hence unemployment); and that monetary growth can be controlled by the government in order to control price inflation.

monetary accommodation The use by a government of monetary policy to mitigate the effects of a sudden change in the supply side of the economy (eg compensating for the deflation cause by a large increase in costs by increasing the money supply).

monetary base Also termed high-powered money, all the money in circulation and at banks, including money on deposit at clearing banks and the Bank of England. It thus corresponds to M0 of the *money supply*.

monetary-base control A method used by government to control the *money supply* through its central bank (in the UK the Bank of England).

monetary compensatory amount (MCA) A temporary tax or subsidy that is meant to offset the differentials between the 'green' and real exchange rates that arise because of the European Union Common Agricultural Policy. It is being phased out.

monetary control The method used by a government to control the money supply through its central bank (in the UK the Bank of England).

monetary economy An economy that employs money as a medium of exchange and store of value.

monetary overhang The part of the money supply that people have been unable to spend and are therefore holding on to (perhaps because of shortages of desired goods and services).

monetary policy A government policy of how to regulate the money supply (and its effects on employment, industrial growth, inflation, and so on).

Monetary Policy Committee A committee of the Bank of England, established in 1997, that sets UK interest rates (formerly a function of the Treasury).

monetary sector In the UK, defined as the accepting houses, Bank of England, commercial banks, discount houses and branches of overseas banks.

monetary system The system that controls the exchange rates of a group of countries, or a system that a single country uses to control its own currency exchange while ensuring that there is enough money in circulation for internal use.

monetary union An agreement between countries in an economic union to have a common currency, fixed exchange rates and free movement of capital between countries. It is a short-term aim of the European Union.

monetary unit A country's standard currency unit.

monetization A method of financing a government's budget deficit by selling Treasury bills to the banking system in the UK, or to the Federal Reserve in the USA.

money A medium of exchange; any generally accepted token (eg coins or banknotes) that may be exchanged for—used in payment for—goods or services. It can also act as a *store of value* and as a *standard of deferred payment*.

money at call Loans that may be called in at short notice, and which therefore attract only low rates of interest.

money-demand schedule A graph that shows, at a particular level of national income, the relationship between the quantity of money demanded (*see liquidity preference* for a breakdown) and the rate of interest. *See also money-supply schedule.*

money illusion The inability of some people to realize that inflation (a general increase in prices) reduces the purchasing power of their money.

money in circulation Money that is currently invested in a financial asset or on deposit (as opposed to *inactive money*).

money laundering *See laundering.*

money market A market operated by banks and other financial institutions to facilitate the short-term (up to one year) borrowing and lending of money, and trading in financial securities; it is also sometimes known as the discount market. In the UK, the Bank of England is the lender of last resort. A wider money market includes also the markets in bullion and foreign exchange.

money multiplier A mathematical relationship between changes in the money supply and resulting changes in the national income.

money supply The total amount of money available at short notice in a given country. There are several categories of money supply, designated M0, M1, M2 and M3.

M0 is defined as notes and coins in circulation in bank tills, plus the operational balances that banks place with the Bank of England. M0 is the narrowest category and is sometimes called narrow money.

M1 is defined as notes and coin in circulation and money deposited in bank current accounts. It is the best gauge of money immediately available for exchange.

M2 is an obsolete definition of the money supply. It includes notes and coins in circulation and in bank accounts, together with funds saved in deposit accounts maintained with the clearing banks, National Giro Bank, Bank of England banking department and discount houses.

M3 is defined as M2 plus interest-bearing non-sterling deposit accounts held by British residents, and other certificates of deposit. M3 is the broadest definition of the money supply and may also be known as broad money. A subsidiary measure, £M3, excludes non-sterling deposit accounts.

money-supply schedule A graph that shows the relationship between the amount of money in circulation and the rate of interest. *See also* ***money-demand schedule***.

money wages Rates of pay expressed in terms of the current value of money (as opposed to real wages, which allows for any inflation).

Monopolies and Mergers Act 1965 The UK legislation that established the Monopolies Commission, later (1973) superseded by the *Monopolies and Mergers Commission*.

Monopolies and Mergers Commission (MMC) A UK government organization, established by the Fair Trading Act 1973, that monitors takeovers and mergers (in the public and national interest) and acts as a watchdog over monopolies and restrictive trade practices.

monopolistic competition An alternative term for *imperfect competition*.

monopoly Strictly, an industry with only one supplier. The term is also applied more widely to an industry controlled ('monopolized') by one company, which produces a sufficient proportion of the total output of that industry to effectively control supply and therefore price.

monopoly policy The policy of the government towards monopolies, as enshrined in such legislation as the *Monopolies and Mergers Act 1965*.

monopoly power The amount of control—the 'might'—that a monopoly has in a given market.

monopoly profit The extra profit a monopoly company can make in the long term (over and above the 'normal' profit in a competitive market).

monopoly tax A tax levied on the 'extra' (above-normal) profit made by a monopoly company, which has no immediate benefit to the consumer.

monopsony An industry in which there are many manufacturers but only one customer for the goods produced. By controlling demand the customer can, in theory, set the price. Monopsonies generally evolve to serve nation states; the market for warships, for example, is a virtual monopsony in that the vessels produced are purchased only by the government of the nation concerned, or by other governments that have its approval.

Monte Carlo method A way of estimating probabilities, often used to study complex economic models that defy normal analytical methods. It involves making a model with a large number of randomly chosen starting positions and following what happens by repeating some activity many times. The range of outcomes is analysed to estimate the probabilities and check for any equilibrium positions.

Montreal Protocol An international agreement, signed in 1987, to reduce the atmospheric levels of the ozone-destroying pollutants the CFCs (chlorofluorocarbons) and halon (halogenated methanes). By a 1990 amendment the use of these substances was to be phased out by 2000.

moonlighting An informal term for the practice of having two jobs, one of them generally involving work in the evening or at night.

moratorium A grant of an extended period in which to repay a loan, or a period during which the repayment schedule is suspended. Usually, it refers only to the repayment of capital, and interest payments may still be required.

Morgan Stanley Capital International World Index (MSCI Index) A world index of the prices of shares, based on more than 1,300 shares from 19 countries. It thereby covers about 60% of the share market value on stock exchanges throughout the world.

mortgage A transfer of the deeds to a property as collateral (security) for the repayment of a debt. For example, a building society that provides a loan for the purchase of a house takes legal possession of the property until the loan and interest have been repaid. The lender is the mortgagee; the borrower is the mortgagor. A mortgage is also called a legal charge.

most favoured nation (MFN) clause A clause in a trading agreement between two countries specifying that each will grant the best available tariff and quotas to the other, usually because both are signatories of the *General Agreement on Tariffs and Trade.*

MNC Abbreviation of *multinational company.*

MPC Abbreviation of *marginal propensity to consume.*

MPS Abbreviation of *marginal propensity to save.*

MRP Abbreviation of *marginal revenue product.*

MSCI Index Abbreviation of *Morgan Stanley Capital International World Index.*

MTFA Abbreviation of *Medium-Term Financial Assistance.*

MTFS Abbreviation of *Medium-Term Financial Strategy.*

MTO Abbreviation of *Multilateral Trade Organization.*

Multi-Fibre Arrangement (MFA) An international agreement, signed in 1973 by 80 nations, to use import quotas to regulate the trade in clothing and textiles. Its aim was to limit the availability of markets in Europe and North America to the poorer nations so as to protect the industries of the developed countries. The quotas are to be phased out by 2005.

Multilateral Investment Guarantee Agency An organization founded by the World Bank in 1988 to provide certain guarantees and insurance cover of non-commercial risks to private investors in developing countries.

multilateralism An indiscriminate multilateral, or international, trade, which involves the use of the proceeds of a sale in one country to fund purchases in another country.

multilateral trade The trade among all nations that import and export goods and services (with no need for any two particular countries to have balanced trade).

Multilateral Trade Organization (MTO) An organization, established in 1993 as part of the *General Agreement on Tariffs and Trade,* which enforces the agreed rules for international trade.

multinational Concerning more than one nation, particularly with regard to the dealings of large companies.

multinational company (MNC) Also called a multinational corporation or multinational enterprise (MNE), a company that has facilities such as those for production and marketing in various countries other than its country of origin.

multi-plant firm A company that has two or more plants at different locations, either as branches or subsidiaries. For example, transport costs for a bulky product may be lower using several small branches around the country that one large plant at a single location.

multiple equilibrium Two economic equilibrium positions that occur simultaneously, such as a high-income, high-spending boom and a low-income, low-spending slump.

multiple exchange rate A variable currency exchange rate that some countries quote, often giving a more favourable rate to importers of wanted goods and to tourists.

multiplier A mathematical formula that relates a change in spending to the consequent overall (and often disproportionate) change in another parameter, such as output or national income.

multiplier-accelerator model An economic model that interrelates the effect of the multiplier (in which an increase in investment results in an increase in output) and the accelerator (in which an increase in output results in an increase in investment). This can lead to a boom, which is inevitably followed by a slump, creating the normal *trade cycle.*

multi-product firm A company that produces more than one kind of product that may also be of different construction. Most companies are in this category although for simplicity much of economic theory deals only with single-product companies.

mutual company A company or organization owned by its depositors or members but which does not issue stocks or shares; profits belong to the members. In the UK, many insurance companies and (formerly) building societies have this status. The conversion of status of such organizations to incorporation as a limited company (which can issue shares) is termed demutualization.

mutual fund An alternative US term for a *unit trust*.

mutual interdependence A market situation in which each company adopts a competitive strategy that tries to anticipate what its rivals will do (eg with respect to advertising, prices and so on).

N

NAC Abbreviation of *National Advisory Council on International Monetary and Financial Policies.*

NAFTA Abbreviation of *North American Free Trade Agreement.*

NAIRU Abbreviation of *nonaccelerating inflation rate of unemployment.*

NAO Abbreviation of *National Audit Office.*

narrow-band Describing a currency whose exchange rate is allowed to float within set limits (typically 2.5% above and below the central rate), which if exceeded bring about central bank intervention.

Nash equilibrium In *game theory*, a non-cooperation situation in which everybody is pursuing his or her best possible strategy given the strategies of all other players. It was first described by the US mathematician John Nash (1928-).

National Advisory Council on International Monetary and Financial Policies (NAC) A US government organization that coordinates the participation of the USA in international financial institutions and practices associated with them. Members of the council are drawn from the Treasury, the Federal Reserve, banks, commerce and trade.

National Audit Office (NAO) An organization established in the UK in 1983 that audits the accounts of government departments and checks on their financial effectiveness.

national average earnings index A measure of UK inflation based on changes in the levels of earned income.

National Bureau of Economic Research (NBER) A private US organization established in 1920 to promote and supply analytical data about the US economy.

national debt Debts owed by the UK government both at home and abroad, ie the sum of government borrowing, including such things as National Savings, Treasury bills, and government bonds. The US equivalent is called the Federal Debt.

National Economic Development Council (NEDC or Neddie) A UK government organization, established in 1962, that patrolled general industrial development and encouraged economic growth, whose responsibilities were split among various sub-committees (Little Neddies) in 1964. It became part of the British Technology Group in 1981.

national income 1. Also termed factor income, the total of all money received in a particular period by households in return for their supplying *factor inputs* to companies. 2. Any of various income totals, such as *gross domestic product, gross national product* or *national product.*

national income and expenditure accounts The statistics about a country's economy (consumption, income, investment, and so on) over a period, usually a year. *See national income (2).*

National Institute of Economic and Social Research (NIESR) A UK non-profit making organization, established in 1938, that works with the Treasury in trying to predict future economic trends (today using computer models).

nationalization A government policy whereby industries previously in private ownership are bought by the state and subsequently controlled by the government. *See also privatization.*

nationalized industry An industry that is owned by the state and controlled by the government, which was previously in private ownership.

National Loans Fund An account opened by the UK government in 1968 for handling the national debt and domestic lending.

national plan A long-term plan for an economy's development, such as the five-year plans once favoured by the former Soviet Union and other centrally-planned economies.

national product The value of the total production from enterprises owned by a country's residents, no matter where they operate. Compare with *domestic product.*

National Trade Data Bank (NTDB) A bank of data on international economic and export information, as supplied by 19 different US agencies.

N

natural economy An economy in which barter is the most common form of exchange.

natural growth rate The national income growth rate that just keeps a constant unemployment rate.

natural monopoly A type of monopoly that arises where such is the scale of business operations that is sensible to have only one supplier of the service (such as nationalized or privatized energy and water utilities).

natural rate of interest An interest rate at which the demand for and supply of loans is equal.

natural unemployment rate Another term for *nonaccelerating inflation rate of unemployment.*

natural resources Basic raw materials and land (including agricultural produce) as inputs to a production process. They may be renewable (such as timber and fish), non-renewable (such as minerals and fossil fuels) or non-expendable (such as a mountain landscape). Together with capital and labour they make up the three *factors of production.*

natural wastage A method of reducing the work force of an organization without resorting to enforced redundancies. As far as possible, the employer does not replace employees who die, retire or resign.

NAV Abbreviation of *net asset value.*

NBER Abbreviation of *National Bureau of Economic Research.*

NBV Abbreviation of *net book value.*

near money A liquid asset that can be transferred immediately (such as a bill of exchange or cheque), although not as liquid as cash. It is also known as quasi-money.

necessary condition A factor that *must* be present for a particular objective to be achieved, as opposed to a sufficient condition, which has merely to be adequate for the objective.

necessity In contrast to a *luxury*, a good or service that (at a given price) rises in consumption proportionately less than a rise in income.

NEDC Abbreviation of *National Economic Development Council.*

Neddie *See National Economic Development Council.*

negative equity An asset that is currently worth less than the money borrowed to pay for it. An all-too-common example is a house whose current market price is less than the remaining value of the *mortgage* taken out to buy it.

negative income tax (NIT) A system of taxation by which those earning less than a specific income receive tax credits to bring their income in line with a guaranteed minimum income.

negative interest A charge made by a bank or other financial institution for holding funds for a certain time.

neoclassical economics The school of economic thought that towards the end of the 19th century superseded *classical economics*. It analyses how companies (and people), making use of the *price mechanism*, can make decisions to maximize their own objectives and thus achieve permanent market equilibrium. Its theories are largely based on the teachings of the US economist Alfred Marshall (1842-1924).

neoclassical synthesis The principal view in macroeconomics during the 1960s that represented a compromise between of Keynesian and classical elements.

neoKeynsian Describing the economic theories that more-or-less support the views of Keynes (*see* *Keynesian*) and have developed from them.

net That which remains after all deductions and charges have been made. *See also* *gross*.

net assets The difference between a company's assets and its liabilities (sometimes termed owners' equity).

net asset value (NAV) The value of a company's shares determined by dividing its net assets by the number of issued shares. It is seldom the same as the market value.

net book value (NBV) Also called depreciated cost or value, the value of an asset on a company's books minus any depreciation since purchase or revaluation.

net domestic product The value of *gross domestic product* after a figure for capital consumption has been deducted.

net economic welfare A wider measure of economic welfare than merely income per head that it includes, for example, such things as the value of looking after children, the sick and the elderly.

N

net exports The amount of exports minus the amount of imports (by category or value).

net foreign assets The value of residents' assets located overseas minus those owned by non-residents but located here (ie the foreign holdings of domestic assets).

net income For a given accounting period, the amount by which all revenues and gains exceed all expenses and losses. It is also called net gain.

net investment Gross investment capital minus *capital consumption* (such as depreciation).

net national product The value of residents' income resulting from factors of production (gross national product) minus capital consumption; the income may accrue overseas or at home.

net present value (NPV) In a discounted cash flow, the present value of cash outflows from a company less the present value of cash inflows. The worth of a future project can be assessed by discounting all future cashflows to the present to see if a desired rate of return would be achieved. A negative NPV would indicate that the project is not viable.

net profit The income that remains after deducting all expenses.

net realizable value (NRV) The amount that could be obtained for an asset (less direct selling costs). Or the sales value of a company's stock (less cost of sales). Both may be less that actual cost.

net tangible assets A company's *tangible assets* minus its current (not total) liabilities.

net wealth A person's wealth (total gross assets) minus any debts. A similar quantity for a company is called *net worth*.

network externality An *external economy* that results from being connected to other people (such as by the Internet).

net worth Also called long-term capital employed, the value of a company after liabilities have been deducted from the true market value of its assets.

net yield The yield (dividend or interest) on a financial security after deduction of income tax, generally expressed as a percentage of their price.

N

neutrality of money The controversial idea that the money supply growth rate does not really affect the economy (only price levels). *See also supemeutrality of money.*

neutral taxes Taxes that do not affect incentives and therefore result in inefficiency. There seem to be few of these, except a *lump-sum tax* or a *poll tax.*

new classical economics The school of macroeconomic thought which assumes that rational expectations are held by all economic decision-makers and that equilibrium growth is coupled to the natural unemployment rate. Thus only unanticipated government policies can have a long-term impact on the economy.

New International Economic Order (NIEO) Proposals, originating with the United Nations in 1974, which maintain that economic imbalances between developing and developed countries can be corrected only by changes in the way countries can borrow money and carry out international trade. There is little evidence so far that they are anything more than proposals.

new issue An issue of shares by a company that is seeking a listing on a stock exchange for the first time. The term may also apply to the issue of equities or loan stock by an existing listed company in order to raise additional capital.

newly industrialized country (NIC) A developing country that has recently established manufacturing industries in a move away from reliance only on agriculture, the extraction of minerals, and other primary activities. Economically, it lies midway between a developing country and an advanced country.

new protectionism The use of export restraints, import licenses, local content requirements and other such measures to restrict international trade. *See protectionism.*

New York Stock Exchange (NYSE) The biggest stock exchange in the world, established in 1792, which trades in stocks, shares, bonds, warrants, rights and options. More than 2,000 companies and 5,000 securities are listed. Situated in Wall Street, it is colloquially called Big Board (after the huge illuminated display of share prices on the floor of the exchange).

N

NIC Abbreviation of *newly industrialized country.*

NIEO Abbreviation of *New International Economic Order.*

NIESR Abbreviation of *National Institute of Economic and Social Research.*

NIT Abbreviation of *negative income tax.*

no arbitrage The idea that it is impossible (or very difficult) to resell a particular good or service, thus allowing the seller to charge different prices to different consumers (*see price discrimination*).

nominal anchor A commodity, such as gold or silver, to which general prices can be pegged. A fixed exchange rate with a respected hard currency can also act as a nominal anchor.

nominal exchange rate A currency's exchange rate in terms of current prices (and ignoring any inflationary effects).

nominal gross domestic product The *gross domestic product* expressed in terms of current prices.

nominal interest rate A rate of interest without an allowance for inflation.

nominal partner A partner who lends his or her name to a firm, but who has invested no capital and does not take an active part in the partnership. Her or she remains liable for the partnership's debts.

nominal price The minimal price assigned to an item so that a transaction may be accounted for.

nominal rate of protection The proportional increase in price of an import resulting from a tariff, which is a measure of the *protection* gained by a domestic manufacturer of the same good or service.

nominal value An alternative term for *face value.*

nominal variable Any economic variable that is measured in terms of money, such as prices and wages.

nominal yield The return on a financial security expressed as a percentage of its face or nominal value (as opposed to its market price).

nominee shareholder Usually an institution that acquires shares in a company on behalf of somebody else (the beneficial owner). This enables the true shareholder's identity to be concealed and is often used when a person wishes to build up his or her shareholding prior to a takeover bid.

nonaccelerating inflation rate of unemployment (NAIRU) The rate of unemployment as it would be in an economy that has a constant inflation rate.

nondiscretionary competition policy A policy that stipulates certain (unbreachable) standards of market conduct and structure as a way of controlling monopolies.

nondurable good A good that is used up with only one use, such as a bottle of wine (a consumer good) or a blasting explosive (a capital good).

non-executive director A member of a company's board of directors who plays no active part in the day-to-day running of the company. He or she may attend board meetings and offer advice. Non-executive (or outside) directors are often well-known public figures whose appointment lends cachet to a company, or whose presence on the board is valued for their expertise, impartiality or wide-ranging contacts.

non-inflationary growth Economic growth that is not accompanied by a rise in prices.

non-marketable debt Also termed a non-marketable security, a debt instrument for which there is no secondary market. Such securities include National Savings Certificates, Premium Bonds, certificates of deposit, official funds in perpetual or terminable annuities, and the whole of the external national debt.

non-marketable security An alternative term for *non-marketable debt.*

non-marketed economic activity An economic activity that produces goods or services that are not sold through a market. Such activities include things that people do for themselves or their families or which charities and other voluntary organizations give away for free.

non-monetary job characteristics The various properties of a job excluding pay or salary. They include holidays, hours of work, location, promotion opportunities, training and working conditions.

non-performing asset The part of a company's capital that is currently yielding no return, and on which none is expected. Fixed assets are generally classified as non-performing.

N

non-performing loan A loan whose interest payments are very overdue (usually taken to be 90 or more days in the USA).

non-price competition Any type of competition in business except that involving pricing (such as advertising and packaging).

non-profit making organization (NPO) A company or organization that has a legal obligation not to make a profit. The term is most usually applied to registered charities.

non-satiation The idea that consumers can always find something more to spend money on if their income (and spending power) increases.

non-systematic risk The risk involved in a group of activities where there is little correlation between the variations in the results—no one factor affects all of them in a similar way (as it does with a *systematic risk*).

non-tariff barrier A hidden trade barrier, often achieved through regulations that are difficult for importers to comply with.

non-tradables Also termed non-tradable products, goods and services that cannot be traded between countries (because of their intrinsic nature, not because of regulations).

nontraded product *See non-tradables.*

non-voting share A share that carries no voting rights. Such shares are issued to raise additional capital for a company, while permitting existing shareholders to retain control. They are often known as A-shares and generally rank pari passu with voting shares in respect of other rights.

normal goods Goods whose sales increase as people's spending power increases (as opposed to inferior goods, whose sales increase when spending power decreases).

normal profit A profit that is sufficient for a company to stay in business.

normative economics The study of how an economy ought to be run (rather than how it is actually run, which is the role of *positive economics*). It may involve ethical considerations and value judgements, as well as ideas about equity (fairness) in society.

North American Free Trade Agreement (NAFTA) An agreement for the establishment of a free trade area established in 1989 between Canada and the USA, with Mexico joining in 1992 (coming into force in 1994).

N

NPO Abbreviation of *non-profit making organization.*

NPV Abbreviation of *net present value.*

NRV Abbreviation of *net realizable value.*

NTB Abbreviation of *non-tariff barrier.*

NTDB Abbreviation of *National Trade Data Bank.*

numeraire A good or currency that is used as an international value standard for other goods (eg the Ecu in the European Monetary System and the US dollar in the petroleum trade).

NYSE Abbreviation of *New York Stock Exchange.*

N

O

obsolescence The loss of the value of something when it becomes out of date. In accounting, obsolescence refers to an asset that has to be written off, not through deterioration but when its continued use would be uneconomic. For example, a piece of machinery may be superseded by a new, faster version; it is therefore uneconomic for the company to continue to use it, and the asset becomes obsolete.

OECD Abbreviation of *Organization for Economic Cooperation and Development.*

OEIC Abbreviation of *open-ended investment company.*

off-balance-sheet finance A type of company finance such that some or all of it (and associated assets) do not appear on the company's balance sheet. Although legally allowable, the practice can give a very distorted view of a company's financial status.

offer curve Also termed contract curve, a graph that shows the theoretical relationship between a country's ability to export and import goods and services—indicating how willing other countries would be to trade with it at prevailing prices.

offer for sale An offer by a company to sell its shares to an issuing house, which then publishes a prospectus and sells shares to the public.

offer-for-sale by tender An offer by a company to sell its shares to people who tender for them, at a price above a stated minimum.

Office of Fair Trading (OFT) A UK government organization, established after the Fair Trading Act 1973, which encourages fair competition among UK businesses. It investigates anti-competitive and restrictive practices, and whether takeover bids should be referred to the Monopolies and Mergers Commission.

Office of Management and Budget (OMB) A US presidential office that draws up the annual federal budget to present to Congress, and thereafter controls how it is administered.

Official List Formally the *Stock Exchange Daily Official List* (SEDOL), the official publication of the London Stock Exchange which appears daily at 5.30 p.m. detailing price movements and dividend information for almost all the securities quoted on the exchange.

offshore fund An investment scheme operated from a *tax haven,* by which investors may benefit from the haven's tax privileges without leaving their home country.

OFT Abbreviation of *Office of Fair Trading.*

oil crisis A sudden large rise in the price of oil or a sudden fall in its availability.

oil embargo A refusal to export oil (to a given country, for political reasons).

Okun's law During a time when an economy is changing cyclically, the figure for actual output divided by potential output rises proportionately more than unemployment falls. It was formulated in 1968 by the US economist Arthur Okun (1928-80).

oligopoly A market in which there are many buyers but few sellers. Such conditions give the producer or seller a certain amount of control over price, but leave him or her especially vulnerable to the actions of competitors.

oligopsony A market in which there are only a few buyers and many small suppliers. In such conditions the buyer can often negotiate price discounts and extended credit.

OMB Abbreviation of *Office of Management and Budget.*

OMV Abbreviation of *open-market value.*

oncost An additional expense, such as that incurred from employing extra staff (wages oncost) or from storing goods (storage oncost). The term has also been used a synonym of overheads.

opaque policy measures Policies that are concealed with regard to who makes them, what they consist of and what they cost (as opposed to *transparent policy measures*).

OPEC Abbreviation of *Organization of Petroleum Exporting Countries.*

open economy An economy that takes (a major) part in unrestricted international trade.

open-ended fund An alternative term for a US *unit trust.*

open-ended investment company (OEIC) An open-ended fund listed at a single unit share price on a stock exchange, common in the USA.

opening price The price of a share or commodity at the beginning of a day's business on a stock exchange. This may differ from the previous evening's closing price, generally because the price has been adjusted to take into account events that have occurred overnight and the performance of other exchanges.

open-market operations The intervention by a central bank to control the amount of money in circulation or to stabilize interest rates (eg by the large-scale purchase of securities).

open-market value (OMV) An asset's value regarded as the amount that somebody would be willing to pay for it.

open outcry A trading method for commodities or securities in which dealers shout out buy or sell offers on the main floor of the exchange. Potential buyers or sellers also shout, and eventually one of each type get together to make a trade.

open position An exposed position of a speculator who has bought or sold without making any hedging transactions, and who therefore gambled that the market will rise or fall as he or she predicted.

operating margin A company's *operating profit* expressed as a proportion of price or operating costs.

operating profit or loss A profit or loss made by a company through its main activity, calculated by taking operating costs away from trading profit (or adding operating expenses to its trading loss). It excludes interest on loans, returns on other investments, or any other extraordinary items.

operating ratio A measure of a company's efficiency, such as the creditor/debtor ratio, labour turnover ratio or stock/sales ratio.

operational research (OR) The application of mathematical techniques to determine, for example, how the various activities within an industry may be regulated to coexist with maximum efficiency.

opportunism When a contract has been agreed, an attempt by one party to change the terms to his or her advantage (in the knowledge that the other party is committed).

opportunity cost The revenue foregone by using an asset for one purpose rather than another. For example, a company owning a building which it uses as storage space could rent it to someone else. That rent is the opportunity cost of the building.

optimal-growth theory The part of economics that seeks to find the growth level that gives the greatest benefit to society.

optimization Choosing from among possible economic resources those that give the 'best' result for the welfare of society as a whole.

optimum savings The proportion of income that should be saved or invested to give the best combination of current consumption and future growth.

optimum tariff The export tariff that results in the best benefit to society by balancing the improved terms of trade against the resulting reduction in quantities traded.

option An investor may pay a premium in return for the option to buy (a call option) or sell (a put option) a certain number of securities at an agreed price (known as the exercise price), on or before a particular date. The dealer may exercise his or her option at any time within the specified period and normally does so at an advantageous time depending on market prices. Otherwise the dealer may allow the option to lapse.

OR Abbreviation of *operational research.*

order book The total of outstanding orders from customers, usually in a given period of time.

order-driven Describing an economy, industry or trading on a stock market that reacts in relation to the flow of incoming orders.

ordinal utility The relative satisfaction (utility) that a consumer gets from a product. The actual satisfaction cannot be measured quantitatively and so the consumer rates products in order of their utility (1st choice is the most satisfying, then 2nd choice, 3rd, and so on).

ordinary resolution A resolution passed by a company's shareholders at a meeting (usually the annual general meeting), generally by a majority of those present unless the articles of association say otherwise.

ordinary shares Company shares whose holders are the owners of the company. They are entitled to a dividend (at the discretion of the directors) after other preferential payments have been made. Ordinary shares are sometimes classed as either voting or non-voting shares, and are often also known as equities.

organic growth Also called internal growth, a company's expansion that derives from within the organization as opposed to external growth (eg that resulting from a merger).

organizational slack Underutilized resources within an organization, sometimes useful in an emergency to meet a sudden increase in demand.

Organization for Economic Cooperation and Development (OECD) An international organization established in 1961, mainly to coordinate aid to underdeveloped countries. Its members include the European countries, Australia, Canada, Japan, New Zealand and the USA.

Organization of Petroleum Exporting Countries (OPEC) An organization of African, Middle Eastern and South American oil-producing countries which acts as a cartel to control the international price of crude oil. Its influence, greatest in the 1970s, waned somewhat with discoveries of offshore fields of oil and gas in North America and western Europe.

organization theory A branch of economics that deals with the (usually decentralized) making of decisions within a large organization.

organized labour The part of the workforce (labour) that belongs to a trade union, which negotiates on its behalf with management.

original income A person's or household's income before payment of taxes or receipt of benefits or other transfer payments.

output The amount produced (goods or services) by a company, single person or a machine.

output effect The effect on the quantity of an input used that results from an increase in output (at constant input prices), bearing in mind that some production processes employ more than one input.

output gap The difference between an economy's theoretical maximum activity and the actual level, expressed as a percentage.

output method A way of determining domestic product in terms of the outputs of various economy sectors (as opposed to the *expenditure method*).

output per hour worked Formerly called output per man hour, output measured per unit of labour input.

outside money *See inside money.*

over-capacity working The situation in a company or industry that is producing more than its normal capacity (perhaps by working extra hours, extra shifts, during holidays, and so on).

overdraft When a bank customer withdraws more money from the bank account than is actually deposited with the bank, the excess is a bank overdraft. An overdraft facility must normally be agreed with the bank in question and interest on it is charged on a day-to-day basis. It attracts high interest rates and ideally is used only for short-term borrowing. An unauthorized overdraft attracts even higher rates of interest.

overfull employment An employment level that causes an excess demand for labour because the available labour force cannot fill all the job vacancies. It results in price increases and accelerates inflation.

overhead costs Also called overheads, the costs incurred in the everyday running of a business and not variable according to its output. Also known as indirect costs, fixed costs or supplementary costs, or 'burden' in the USA, overhead costs include heating, lighting and energy costs, administration, insurance, rent and rates. Cost of sales and research and development costs are also usually included.

overheating Describing an unhealthy economic situation in which bank borrowing, balance of payment deficit, prices and wages are all rising.

overlapping generations In an economic model the assumption that people live for more than one time period but also live for only a certain time, so that in each period there are some 'new' people that were not there previously and some 'old' people who will not be there in the next period.

overmanning The employment of more labour than is needed for a particular production process (but *see organizational slack*).

overseas bank From a UK standpoint, a foreign bank that has a branch or branches in the UK.

overshooting Describing price trends on a currency market that continue to rise above levels anticipated by analysts.

overstimulation An increase in the level of effective demand (resulting from a government's monetary policies) that accelerates inflation or creates balance-of-payments deficits.

oversubscription The situation that arises in a sale of shares by application and allotment where the number of shares applied for exceeds the number of shares available. The distribution is then often made using a ballot.

over-the-counter (OTC) market A market on which securities not listed on any stock exchange may be bought and sold. In practice, the OTC market is operated by a limited number of market-makers, often on the basis of matched bargains.

overtime Work done by agreement in extra hours over and above the normal working week, usually paid for at higher rates of wages.

overtrading A potentially dangerous (financially) situation in which a company tries to take on more business than its working capital will allow.

overutilized capacity Production output levels that are higher than those at which short-run average cost is minimized.

over-valued currency A currency that trades on foreign exchange markets at a price that makes exports uncompetitive, usually leading to a balance of trade deficit.

own brand Also called own label, a large retailer's private brand name for goods that would normally be sold, at a higher price, under another well-known brand name (often obtained from the same manufacturer or supplier).

ownership The basic right to possess something. It should not be confused with possession, for whereas a person may own something, he or she may still lose possession of it (eg to a bailee or a thief).

P

Paasche index Also termed current-weighted index, a volume index (usually of prices) that employs weighed values of current statistics rather than figures form earlier periods. It was devised by the German economist Hermann Paasche.

packaging The cost (including design, printing etc.) of the package that protects a product and presents it at point of sale.

package of policies Several policy measures introduced at the same time in order that their individual side-effects will be less disturbing than those produced by an energetically-pursued single policy change.

paid-in capital In the USA, owners' equity in a company, ie the total amount invested during and since its incorporation. It is equivalent to *paid-up capital* in the UK.

paid-up capital That part of a company's *called-up capital* that has so far been paid by shareholders.

P & L *See profit and loss account.*

paper profit An apparent increase in the value of an asset or investment, not realizable until it is sold.

par Equal to the face value, or to the current rate of exchange.

paradox of thrift The observation that an increase in the expected proportion of incomes people want to save (propensity to save) may not increase the economy's national income, because savings reduce consumption and lessen aggregate demand.

paradox of value The observation that the price (value) of a good depends on its scarcity rather than on it utility (usefulness)—consider the usually cited extreme example of diamonds and water.

parallel imports Imports that are taken into a country and sold at a lower price than the one that normally prevails there (because they are cheaper in the country of origin).

parallel money markets The markets in certificates of deposit, Eurocurrency, local authority loans and other short-term financial

P

securities (excepting bills of exchange, bonds and Treasury bills traded on the discount market).

Pareto optimality The situation in an economy in which no change can increase anybody's welfare without reducing somebody else's. It was first described in 1906 by the Italian economist Vilfredo Pareto (1848-1923).

partial equilibrium analysis In studying the effects of changes to some part of the economy, such as a market, the deliberate omission of the effects these changes might have in some other part of the economy. *See also general equilibrium.*

participation rate An alternative term for *activity rate*.

partnership A formal business association, in the UK normally formed between two to twenty partners. The partners are jointly liable for the debts of the partnership, so that if one partner dies or decamps, the remaining partners are responsible for any debts.

partnership at will Partners are normally bound by a formal agreement; if not, the partnership is termed a partnership at will, and may be broken at any time by any partner.

part-time employment Long-term employment that entails an employee putting in less than a full working week.

par value An alternative term for *face value* or nominal value.

patent An authorization that grants the addressee the sole right to make, use or sell an invention for a specified period of time. Applicants for a patent must establish the novelty of their inventions.

Patent Office A UK government organization that grants patents and oversees the registration of trademarks, industrial designs and other types of intellectual property.

paternalism A view that advocates regulations should be introduced into society for people's 'own good', even if these regulations disagree with the people's own preferences.

pawnbroker A licensed dealer who lends money secured against goods, called a pledge, and issues a formal receipt for them. Loans are normally made for a period of six months and seven days and, if not repaid in that time (with interest), the pawnbroker is entitled to sell the pawned goods.

P

pay The money given to an employee in return for performing work. Salaries, wages and overtime are payment for a specific amount of time spent at a job; bonuses, piecework and profit-sharing schemes are payment for results.

payback period The time that elapses before a new project's cash inflows equal its cash outflows. In the USA it is also called the payoff or payout period.

pay control The part of a prices and incomes policy that attempts to control wages, usually by limiting wage increases. Imposing a complete standstill on wage rates is termed a pay freeze.

pay freeze *See pay control.*

payment in kind A payment, generally of wages, made in goods or services rather than in money. Payment of total wages in kind was made illegal in the UK in the 19th century, but part-payment in kind still occurs (for example, luncheon vouchers and the use of a company car are payments in kind).

payments union An agreement between two or more nations to combine their reserves of foreign exchange, thus making internal trade straightforward and reducing the total reserve that each member country needs to hold.

payroll A list of people employed (usually full-time) by a company and of the amount that each is due to be paid.

payroll tax A tax on a business undertaking levied in relation to the number of people employed, or as a percentage of the total wages bill. It is sometimes used to control the relative elasticities of the supply and demand for labour. Its imposition deters companies from employing more workers than they currently require.

peace dividend Extra resources made available by cuts in defence spending (as happened following better relations between the former Eastern bloc countries and Western nations).

peak-load pricing Charging increased prices for unstorable products (such as electricity or a telephone service) when demand is at its peak, because the capacity for such output has to be maintained (and paid for) even at times of low demand.

PEG Abbreviation of *price-earnings growth factor.*

pendular arbitration A type of arbitration in which the arbiter is allowed to accept only the position of one side or the other (and cannot recommend a compromise), thus encouraging reasonable rather than exaggerated demands by each side.

penetration price A relatively low price charged for a new product in order to gain access to a market or in order to increase sales (and hence market share) of an existing product.

pension A regular payment, made weekly, monthly or annually after a person retires from full-time employment, generally for the rest of the pensioner's life.

P/E ratio *See price-earnings ratio.*

per capita income A country's national income divided by its population (just the adult population, the total population or the adult equivalent population, which counts children as 'fractions' of an adult).

per capita real GDP A country's real gross domestic product divided by its population (defined as under *per capita income*).

perfect capital mobility A hypothetical situation in which there is completely free movement of capital between countries which does not occur because of various controls and the perceived risks of lending or investing overseas.

perfect competition Also called pure competition, an idealized situation in a market in which all rival products are the same (so the buyers have no preference), there are many small buyers and sellers (so that none can on its own control price) who all try to maximize profit and can leave or join the market whenever they like, and buyers pay only the lowest price.

perfect market A market in which there is *perfect competition.*

perfect oligopoly An *oligopoly* in which the goods being produced by each seller are of exactly the same type.

perfect substitute A good or service than is identical in use to another good or service (their *elasticity of substitution* is infinitely large).

performance-related pay (PRP) A salary increase or bonus awarded to an employee in recognition of good performance at work.

peril point According to the US Tariff Commission, the point at which any further lowering of tariffs would reduce import prices to such an extent that the survival of domestic industry would be threatened.

P

periphery A sparsely populated outer region of a country with poor communications and infrastructure, as opposed to the densely populated core which does have such facilities.

permanent income The level of spending (ie consumption) that somebody can maintain indefinitely, even if his or her income varies from time to time.

perpetual inventory An alternative term for *continuous inventory.*

per se illegality Under a *nondiscretional competition policy,* a ban on restrictive trade agreements, mergers and other aspects of market conduct and structure.

personal disposable income A person's income after deduction of taxes (and, in the UK, National Insurance contributions).

personal distribution of income The distribution of national income among different people, measured either after or before the deduction of taxes and the addition of benefits or other transfer payments. *See also functional income distribution.*

personal income distribution *See personal distribution of income.*

personal loan Generally an unsecured loan made (usually by a bank but now increasingly by registered brokers) to a private individual. This form of loan is generally fairly modest and intended for some specific purpose, such as the purchase of a car.

personal preference A person's 'taste' for such things as goods and services (consumption) and work.

personal savings ratio The part of a person's or household's disposable income that is saved divided by the total disposable income.

personal sector The part of the *private sector* of the economy that deals with the transactions of individuals, households, charities, unincorporated businesses and so on, as opposed to the *corporate sector* and government sector.

personal selling A way of selling that involves face-to-face contact between a salesperson and a prospective customer.

PESC Abbreviation of *Public Expenditure Survey Committee.*

peso problem The tendency for rates of interest to remain high in countries that have a history of high inflation.

petrocurrency Money (usually US dollars) paid to the exporters of petroleum in exchange for their product. After the OPEC countries markedly increased prices, the amount of petrocurrency in circulation exceeded the oil-exporting countries' economies to absorb it. As a result, much of it was invested in the world's financial markets, where it helped to offset the trade deficits caused by the OPEC price rises.

petrodollars Petrocurrency denominated in dollars.

PFI Abbreviation of *private finance initiative.*

Phillips curve A graph showing the relationship between unemployment and the rate of wage changes (wage inflation) and thus, by extension, prices. It confirms that low unemployment tends to drive up wages and thereby increase inflation. It was formulated in 1958 by the UK economist Alban Phillips (1914-75). See *stagflation.*

physical capital A company's capital that takes the form of physical goods, such as work in progress and stock (inventory). See also *financial capital; human capital.*

physical control A direct control imposed on consumption or production, such as rationing and import licenses or quotas.

physiocracy An early school of economic thought that regarded land as the only source of income and wealth (and should therefore be subject to tax). It also advocated free trade and laissez-faire. It arose in France during the 18th century and was championed by the work of French economist François Quensay (1694-1774).

piece-rate A method of paying a worker in accordance with the number of items (pieces of work) that he or she produces; the sum paid per piece is the piece-rate. Sometimes a bonus is also paid for production in excess of a pre-set target.

piecework Work that is paid for per unit of output (instead of per hour of time worked). See *piece-rate.*

Pigou effect The idea that unemployment can be prevented by flexibility in prices and wages—low prices and wages will eventually lead to full employment. It was put forward in the late 1920s by the UK economist Arthur Pigou (1877-1959).

P

Pink Book The informal name of *United Kingdom Balance of Payments*, published annually by the Central Statistical Office.

Pink Sheet A daily US publication, by the National Quotation Bureau, that lists bid and offer prices of brokers who deal in American Depositary Receipts (ADRs) and over-the-counter stocks (OTCs).

placing The process of issuing shares through an intermediary, usually a stockbroker or syndicate. The intermediary 'places' the shares with clients, frequently institutional investors, or with members of the public. A certain proportion of any share quoted on the London Stock Exchange must be made available to the public through the Exchange.

planned economy An economy in which some or all economic activity is planned and undertaken by the state, directly or indirectly, irrespective of the market forces of supply and demand, and without private enterprise.

planned investment The sum that people, companies and government organizations plan to invest, which often differs from actual investment for various unforeseen reasons.

planned savings The sum that people, companies and government organizations plan to save, which often differs from actual investment for various unforeseen reasons.

player In *game theory*, a person, company or government that chooses various strategies to take part in the situation modelled by the game.

plc or PLC Abbreviation of *public limited company.*

ploughed-back profit An alternative term for *retained profit.*

point elasticity An exact measure of how supply or demand alters with changes in another variable such as incomes and prices. It is equal to the percentage change in, say, demand divided by the percentage change in, say, prices.

polarization Under the terms of the UK Financial Services Act, a regulation that does not allow financial intermediaries to act as advisers about financial products and at the same time sell their own products. They must act either as independent advisers, recommending the best product for their client from all those available, or as tied agents, selling only their own products— ie they must polarize.

P

policy coordination The idea that if different countries collaborated in setting their national monetary and fiscal policy better results would accrue.

policy ineffectiveness theorem In an economy with flexible prices and wages, only *unanticipated* government policy to increase demand will effect employment and output.

policy instrument Any policy that is under the control of the fiscal or monetary authorities, such as changes in rates of taxation or the money supply.

political economy The former name of the subject now almost invariably called economics.

political union An agreement among nations to create a trading bloc with no trade, monetary or taxation barriers between the members.

poll tax A tax charged to every adult in a community, generally as a means of raising revenue for local government. The term was also applied to the defunct community charge in the UK (now replaced by council tax).

pollution Any harmful substance (eg industrial waste, infection, poison, smoke and fumes or source of radioactivity) or even noise that damages the environment or people's enjoyment of it.

pollution control Any way of preventing or reducing pollution, such as a tax on an activity that causes pollution (the 'pollutor pays' principle).

popular capitalism Capitalism that has reached a large number of a country's population, through increased personal investment, growth in small businesses, proliferation of profit-sharing schemes, and so on.

population 1. The number of people who live in a specified area. It may be defined as the adult population, the total population or the adult equivalent population, which counts children as 'fractions' of an adult. 2. In statistics, any data that has been counted or is based on sampling.

population trap A situation in which a country's rate of economic expansion cannot keep up with its increasing population.

portfolio A selection of securities held by a person or institution. Portfolios generally include a wide variety of stocks and bonds to spread the risk of investment, and the contents of the portfolio are generally

P

managed—that is, continually adjusted in order to maximize income or growth.

portfolio theory The study of how an investor can maximize his or her return, or minimize the risk, from a varied portfolio of securities.

positional goods Goods that are always scarce and whose production cannot be increased (eg antiques).

positive economics The study of economic events and ideas than can, at least in theory, actually happen (as opposed to those that 'ought' to happen, which are studied in *normative economics*).

potential competition All competition, from possible as well as from existing rivals.

potential entrant A company that can and will enter a market if the conditions are right. *See also barriers to entry.*

potential gross national product At any given time, the maximum real output of a nation's economy that is possible by using all of its factor inputs (such as capital and labour).

potential output The output that an individual company could produce by using all of its factor inputs (such as capital, labour and production technology).

pound The standard currency units of Cyprus (divided into 100 cents); Egypt, Lebanon, Sudan and Syria (divided into 100 piastres); and the Falkland Islands, Gibraltar and the UK (divided into 100 pence).

pound sterling The standard currency unit of the UK, so called to distinguish it from other currencies called the pound.

poverty The situation of people who cannot afford an adequate standard of living. It may be defined in relative terms (eg belonging to the poorest 5% of the population) or in absolute terms (eg earning less than half the minimum age).

poverty line An income that is just sufficient to avoid poor people form fulfilling an absolute definition of *poverty*. *See subsistence level.*

poverty trap A situation in which the benefits and taxation system make it difficult for poor people to escape from *poverty*. For instance an unemployed worker may be better off on benefits than if he or she were in a job.

P

PPI Abbreviation of *Producer Price Index.*

PPP Abbreviation of *purchasing power parity.*

precautionary demand for money The demand for money that people hold for emergencies (unforeseen expenditure). *See also speculative demand for money; transactions demand for money.*

precautionary motive The reason for holding on to money for emergencies (unforeseen expenditure).

predatory dumping The selling of an exported product on a foreign market at less than market value, to beat local competition. Once competition is eliminated, the price generally rises.

predatory pricing The policy of setting a price for a product at less than market value to drive out competition (and deter new entrants to the market).

predetermined endogenous variable In a dynamic economic system, a variable that originates within the system as a result of previous events.

preferences Consumers' choices of products to buy.

preference shares Also known as preferred stock, preference shares offer the shareholder preferential claims to dividends, usually at a fixed rate, and a prior claim to ordinary shareholders on the company's assets in the event of liquidation. The market price for the preference shares tends to be more stable than that of ordinary shares. Preference shareholders may not vote at meetings of ordinary shareholders. Preference shares fall into five categories: cumulative, non-cumulative, redeemable, participating and convertible. They are known as preferred stock in the USA.

preference/similarity theory A theory that attempts to explain the international trade in manufactured goods in terms of consumers' preferences and desire for variety. For example, a country may export goods (such as vacuum cleaners) and import the same goods (of a different make) from another country.

premium In general, any price, payment or bonus valued higher than the norm. More specifically, it is the difference in price between the offer price of a new share issue and the price at which it begins trading, if the latter exceeds the former. The term is also used to describe the positive difference between the face value and redemption value of any stock or bond.

P

present discounted value The present value of money that is due to be paid some time in the future. Mathematically it is given by $A(1 + r)^{-t}$, where A is the sum to be received, r is the interest rate per period and t is the number of periods (into the future).

present value An assessment of the current net cost or value of future expenditure or benefit. Most frequently it is used to measure return on capital investment.

pre-tax profit Profit calculated before allowance is made for tax (such as corporation tax and capital gains tax).

price The cost of purchasing a unit of goods or services. Very broadly, prices are generally set by the manufacturer and retailer, taking into account all fixed costs and variable costs and allowing for a profit margin.

price ceiling An upper limit of a product's price, as set by the government.

price competition A type of rivalry between suppliers that involves cutting prices to win over new customers. In extreme and aggressive form it is termed a price war.

price control A method of controlling inflation or allocation of resources in a centrally-planned economy by pegging prices within specified limits. Market forces make it difficult to control prices in this way in the long term, and the method is normally used only for short-term crisis management.

price discrimination The practice of charging different prices for the same product to different buyers (ie charging more to people whom the seller thinks can afford it, and charging less to people with less purchasing power, for example children's fares and admission charges).

price-earnings growth factor (PEG) The ratio of the predicted *price-earnings ratio (P/E ratio)* of a share to is anticipated growth rate in *earnings per share*, devised to help in choosing investments (the higher, the better).

price-earnings ratio (P/E ratio) The current market price of a company's ordinary shares divided by the *earnings per share* (the higher, the better).

P

price effect The effect that a change in price has on the demand for a good or service, usually a reduction in demand if the price change is an increase (except for an *inferior good*).

price-elastic Describing a good or service that sells in proportionately smaller quantities compared to the proportionate increase in its price; ie a price increase has a more serious effect on sales than expected. *See price elasticity.*

price elasticity A measure of the way in which a change in the price of a good or service affects the numbers sold. It is defined as the percentage change in numbers sold divided by the percentage change in price. The value of this ratio is greater than 1 for things that are *price elastic*, and less than 1 for those that are *price inelastic.*

price-elasticity of demand A measure of how demand reacts to a change in price, equal to the percentage change in demand divided by the percentage increase in price.

price-elasticity of supply A measure of how supply reacts to a change in price, equal to the percentage change in the quantity supplied divided by the percentage increase in price.

price fixing Collusion between suppliers to agree a common price for a good or service they all supply; it is illegal in many countries. *See also collusion; cartel.*

price floor The lowest price than can be charged for a product, as set by the government.

price index A series of numbers that represent average prices over a period of time, relative to a base (usually 100 or 1000) assigned to the first period. *See also share index.*

price inelastic Describing a good or service that sells in proportionately larger quantities compared to the proportionate rise in its price; ie a price increase has less serious effect on sales than expected. *See price elasticity.*

price leader Also called price-maker, a product that can dictate the price within its market (because of its perceived value), which rival products have to undersell.

price level An economy's general level of prices, usually as measured by an index such as the *Retail Price Index.*

P

price-maker An alternative term for *price leader*.

price mechanism The operation of the laws of supply and demand, which determine prices.

price parallelism The tendency for suppliers in an oligopoly market to charge the same prices, resulting either from *price fixing* or a wish to avoid profit-reducing *price competition*.

price reform A movement towards a system in which opportunity costs determine prices (market economy) from one in which prices are controlled (centrally-planned economy).

price regulation A system in which a supplier's prices are not allowed rise above a certain level, as applied by the government to many UK public utilities (such as providers of electricity, gas and water), mainly to prevent abuse by a monopolist.

prices and incomes policy A government policy for controlling prices and wages as a means of checking inflation.

price-sensitive Describing goods or services whose sales are greatly affected by a change in price; similar to *price elastic*.

price squeeze A type of restrictive trade practice that can arise when a supplier of raw materials manufactures finished goods as well as supplying other manufacturers. By charging high prices to the other manufacturers, the supplier can sell the product at a lower price (and thereby capture much of the market).

price stability An anti-inflationary measure involving the maintenance in an economy of a steady general level of prices over a period of time.

price support A way the government supports farmers' incomes by fixing the prices of their products above the normal market price (and buying any unsold surplus). *See also* **Common Agricultural Policy**.

price system The market mechanism that causes an excess demand to increase prices and an excess of supply to decrease them. It thus influences the decisions of producers about what (and how much) to produce and how to produce it.

price-taker A company whose products are not readily distinguished from the competition, whose prices it must therefore undercut in order to obtain a market share.

P

price theory The part of microeconomics that studies the determination of market prices and the quantities of goods and services dealt in that market.

price volatility The extent to which prices fluctuate over time in any market.

price war *See price competition.*

pricing policy The way in which a company determines the prices of its products, in practice often using a method such as *cost-plus pricing* (although in theory *marginal-cost pricing* in a perfect market).

primary sector The part of the economy that deals with raw material extraction and agricultural production; fisheries are also included.

prime costs The combined cost of direct expenses, direct labour and direct materials, as assigned to a product.

prime lending rate The preferential interest rate charged in the USA for short-term loans made to people or organizations with a high credit rating. It is approximately equivalent to the banker's base rate in the UK.

prime rate An alternative term for prime lending rate.

principal In finance, the original sum invested or lent, as distinct from any profits or interest involved. A principal is also a person who gives instructions to an agent.

principal-agent problem The difficulty of getting an agent to act in the best interests of the principle rather than out of self-interest. One solution is to have a very detailed, enforceable contract between the two parties; usually, mutual trust is the solution.

principles of taxation The three different ways of applying taxation, listed in this Dictionary under *ability-to-pay*, *benefits-received* and *redistribution-of-income*.

prior charge The prior claim over ordinary shareholders that holders of debentures and preference shareholders have on a company's profits or repayments of capital.

prisoners' dilemma A fundamental idea in *game theory*, a situation that demonstrates the disadvantage of being unable to reach a binding agreement with other players; it shows that the best individual behaviour is different from the best group behaviour. It postulates that two prisoners must individually decide whether or not to confess to being jointly involved in a crime without knowing what the other will say—and the penalty will be less if you confess and the other prisoner does not confess. The actual options, and penalties, are as follows: if you both confess, you both get 4 years in prison; if neither confesses you both get 2 years; if your partner in crime confesses and you do not, you will get 10 years and he will go free; if you confess and he does not, you go free and he gets 10 years. Acting individually, it seems 'logical' that you will do best to confess and settle for a prison term of 4 years. But in fact if you both remain silent you get only 2 years. Moral: you do better to act unselfishly and to cooperate.

private company A privately-owned company whose shareholders' liability may be limited or unlimited. See *private limited company*.

private cost The cost to a company for using *factor inputs* to produce an output. It includes implicit costs (for inputs such as the use of premises owned by the company) and explicit costs (for inputs such as capital and labour bought in from outside the company). See also *real cost*.

private enterprise An undertaking by an individual or private group working without significant support from the state.

private finance initiative (PFI) A programme of construction projects in the private sector to which the UK government contributes some of the finance.

private products The goods and services that individual consumers buy for their own personal use (thus making them unavailable to anyone else).

private limited company A company with a share capital of at least £50,000 whose shares are not available to the general public through the medium of a stock exchange (ie it is unlisted), and whose members do not exceed 50 in number. The shareholders' liability is limited the value of their shareholding. See also *public limited company (plc)*.

private net product An alternative term for *net national product* (to differentiate it from *social net product*).

private property 1. In economics, assets that form part of the personal wealth of their owner. 2. In law, something that belongs exclusively to a certain person or organization (as opposed to public property, which belongs to the government).

private sector That part of the business activity of a country that is financed and controlled by individuals or private companies (ie mainly shareholders and institutional investors).

private-sector balance Within the *private sector* of the economy, the difference between savings and investment.

privatization The practice of offering shares in previously state-owned industries or enterprises for sale to the general public. British Aerospace, British Rail and British Telecom are privatized companies in the UK. It may also be called denationalization.

process innovation A new (and cheaper) method for making an existing product. *See also product innovation.*

procurement The purchase of goods and services by the government.

producer Also termed a supplier, a company or government organization that produces goods and services, known in economics as a producing unit.

producer goods Also termed intermediate goods, commodities and goods (such as fuel) that are *factor inputs* in the production of other goods and services (ie they are not supplied directly to consumers).

Producer Price Index (PPI) A measure of inflation based on price changes of finished goods (as they leave the factory).

producer's surplus The extra income a supplier receives over and above the minimum he or she would be willing to accept to keep up the same level of supply.

product development The processes involved when a company creates a new product (for new or existing markets), usually to maintain its competitive position in a market.

product differentiation The extent to which a product is perceived as being different from its rivals by potential purchasers. A product with little differentiation has to be sold at a lower price than its rivals in order to obtain market share.

product diversification A decision to begin manufacturing new products, usually by *horizontal* or *vertical diversification*. The main purpose is to lessen the risk of commercial failure caused by a sudden fall in demand for a particular product. Diversification is also attractive to companies that are dependent on seasonal or cyclical business.

product innovation A new or improved product that is made using existing production processes. *See also* ***process innovation.***

production Broadly, the practice of manufacturing goods or providing services for sale. It may be measured in units of production, labour cost, or the time (machine or man hours) taken to produce them.

production cost An alternative term for ***manufacturing cost.***

production externality Any external effect of production that has no direct effect on the person or company doing the production (such as noise or pollution).

production function A mathematical relationship between a company's or nation's output and the factors of production (inputs) employed to produce it.

production possibility boundary Also termed transformation curve, a diagram that shows the maximum possible output of one good or service by efficiently using available resources (the outputs of others)— a way of illustrating scarcity in terms of a company, industry or country.

production subsidy A government payment to domestic producers of particular goods and services, paid as a certain sum per unit produced.

productive efficiency The efficiency of a market, using current technology, to produce current products at the minimum long-term cost. It occurs when there is a long-term balance of supply and demand in the market for the outputs of plants of optimum size.

productivity A measure equal to the output of any of the factors of production (land, labour and capital) per unit of input. It may be enhanced by the improvement of any one of these three factors, most usually by the introduction of new technology or an incentive scheme. Productivity of land is generally measured in output per hectare or acre, that of labour in output per working hour, and that of capital as a percentage per annum.

product liability The liability of a manufacturer *or* seller for damage caused by a product.

product life cycle A sequence in the production and sales of a product over its lifetime, generally taken to occur in five stages: development, introduction, growth, maturity and decline. Cashflow does not usually become positive until towards the end of the growth phase, with sales maximized at the middle of maturity.

product market A market in which goods and services are sold at prices determined by the laws of supply and demand.

product mix The mixture of products supplied by a company, ideally consisting of some mature products, some products in their growth stage and some newly-introduced products (*see product life cycle*).

profit The surplus money, after all expenses have been paid, generated by a company or enterprise in the course of one accounting period.

profitability A measure of a company's record of producing revenue that exceeds its expenditure.

profit and loss account (P & L) An annual summary of a company's financial operations, required by law to be submitted to the UK Registrar of Companies by every trading company over a certain size (*see small company*). The profit and loss account has three sections: the trading account, the profit and loss account and the appropriation account. The profit and loss section takes the (gross) profit or loss figure from the trading account, and after accounting for income not concerned with trading and expenses such as those incurred in administration, deducts tax from the final net profit or loss figure.

profit centre The part of an organization that creates revenue and to which costs can be assigned. *See also cost centre.*

profit margin Sales less all expenses (outgoings), usually expressed as a percentage of net sales or as simple net profit. Company policy generally specifies some profit margin below which it would be hardly worthwhile producing goods. *See also gross margin; net margin.*

profit maximization The principle in accounting that operations should be presented in such a way as to make net income as large as possible.

profit motive A company's (or anybody's) objective to make a profit—to ensure that income is greater than costs.

profit-related pay A method of paying employees a basic salary/wage plus a percentage of the company's profits.

P

profit-sharing The distribution of some or all of a company's profits to its employees as a bonus. The distribution may be in the form of cash or shares.

profit-taking The act of selling stock and taking a profit on the transaction, instead of waiting for a better price. It occurs when dealers believe that the market will not improve much more, at least in the short term.

progressive tax A tax that increases as its base (eg, income) increases. *See also regressive tax.*

progress payment On a large time-consuming contract, such as a big construction project, a payment made for work done at various pre-defined stages towards completion. In this sense it is also known as payment on account.

promissory note A document that states that a person promises to pay a certain sum of money on a certain date. It is also known as a note of hand.

propensity to consume A fraction given by personal consumption divided by disposable income. *See also average propensity to consume.*

propensity to import A fraction given by the total value of imports divided by national income.

propensity to save A fraction given by personal savings divided by disposable income. *See also average propensity to save.*

propensity to tax A fraction given by total tax revenue divided by national income.

property Legally, property is divided into real and personal property. Real property may be defined as land and buildings held freehold. Personal property consists of other personal possessions. More specifically, property is sometimes defined as something that appreciates in value or yields income.

property company A company that develops, invests in or trades property (buildings).

property income Sometimes also termed unearned income, income that comes from owning property of any kind, including dividends (on shares), rents (on buildings) and interest (on investments). *See also unearned income.*

P

property lending The making available of funds to purchase property, generally using a legal charge on the property as collateral (ie a *mortgage*). *See also* **negative equity**.

property portfolio A collection of properties that are owned by a property company for development or as an investment for rental income.

proportional tax A tax that is levied at a constant rate (percentage) no matter how much income is being taxed.

prospectus A document that describes a proposal, such as that issued to prospective shareholders by a company that intends to make a public issue of shares, giving details of past and present performance and of prospects.

PRP Abbreviation of *performance-related pay*.

protection A way of cutting down imports by imposing quotas, tariffs and other import restrictions. Its justification is to raise employment and profits in domestic industries (*see* **protectionism**).

protectionism A policy based on self-interest, for example one that shields an industry against foreign competition, usually by the imposition of selective or general quotas and tariffs.

PSBR Abbreviation of *Public Sector Borrowing Requirement*.

PSDR Abbreviation of *Public Sector Debt Repayment*.

PSFD Abbreviation of *Public Sector Financial Deficit*.

PSNB Abbreviation of *Public Sector Net Borrowing*.

PSNCR Abbreviation of *Public Sector Net Cash Requirement*.

public choice theory The part of economics that deals with the ways in which society should make decisions to maximize social welfare. It involves deciding what *public goods* to supply (in terms of quality, quantity and type) and how they should be paid for.

public company A company that is limited by guarantee or shares, which has more than £50,000 of share capital and is referred to as a public company in its memorandum of association. It must be registered at Companies House and carry the words 'public limited company' or the abbreviation 'PLC' or 'plc' after its name. Its shares are available to the general public through a stock exchange.

P

public corporation A formal term for a *nationalized industry.*

public debt The *national debt* and other debts incurred by the government (such as money owed to it by local authorities and nationalized industries).

public enterprise A *nationalized industry* or other economic activity of a state-controlled or state-owned enterprise.

public expenditure The spending on goods and services by public corporations and by central and local government.

Public Expenditure Survey Committee (PESC) A UK government organization that reviews planned expenditure (both short-term and long-term) in the run up to the annual Public Expenditure White Paper.

public finance The money for *public expenditure* raised by government borrowing and taxation.

public goods The goods and services that all people in society can use, such as defence, law and order and public amenities such as museums and art galleries, mostly provided by the government (and financed through taxation) but sometimes also by charities and voluntary organizations.

public interest The 'general good' of society, as opposed to the benefits that accrue to private people or companies that make economic decisions.

public limited company (plc, PLC) *See public company.*

public ownership The ownership of a business enterprise by the government or some government-controlled organization. *See nationalization.*

public sector That part of the business activity of a country that is financed and controlled by the central and local government. State public sector industries are often known as *nationalized industries.*

Public Sector Borrowing Requirement (PSBR) The difference between the government's expenditure and its revenue. The term has been replaced by *Public Sector Net Cash Requirement.*

Public Sector Debt Repayment (PSDR) The amount of past borrowings owed by the government that it can afford to repay in a given period (derived from a *budget surplus*).

P

Public Sector Financial Deficit (PSFD) The amount by which public-sector spending exceeds government revenue from taxes and other receipts (such as those from the sale of government-owned property).

Public Sector Net Borrowing (PSNB) The amount of current public spending and investment, minus total public revenue.

Public Sector Net Cash Requirement (PSNCR) The *Public Sector Net Borrowing* together with the funding requirements of financial transactions (such as lending to the public sector). It is generally financed mainly by issuing gilt-edged securities (gilts) and other long-term loans. It was formerly known as the Public Sector Borrowing Requirement.

public utility An industry that supplies essential public services, often as a monopolist. Such utilities include electricity supply, gas supply, postal services, telephones, water supply and some transport services.

public works Construction projects that the government pays for, including bridges, government buildings, hospitals, publicly-owned homes, roads, and schools. *See also pump priming.*

pump priming Small amounts of government spending, financed by borrowing not taxes, in an attempt to stimulate the economy by increasing aggregate demand (and thus reducing unemployment). A favourite target of such spending is *public works*.

punishment strategy In *game theory*, the response of an injured player which is to take temporary or permanent action that punishes the player who caused the injury and deters him or her from doing it again.

purchasing power A person's or company's ability to buy goods and services. An organization with high purchasing power (such as a supermarket chain) can often negotiate lower prices with suppliers.

purchasing power parity (PPP) The idea that in the long run, under a floating exchange rate regime, currency exchange rates are determined by the amount of goods and services that each can purchase.

purchasing power parity exchange rate An exchange rate that is based on the relative prices of the same group of goods in two countries, thus taking into account relative local purchasing power.

pure competition An alternative term for *perfect competition*.

pure floating exchange rate Also called a clean floating exchange rate, a floating exchange rate that is determined by the market with no intervention from governments or central banks. Any such intervention makes it a 'dirty' floating exchange rate.

put option An option to sell shares, commodities or financial futures at an agreed price on or before an agreed future date.

P

Q

QR Abbreviation of *quantity restriction.*

q theory A theory of investment which states that a company should not invest unless the ratio of the value of its shares to the market value of its physical assets is greater than 1. This ratio is known as Tobin's q after the US economist James Tobin (1918-).

qualification of accounts An auditors' report that a company's accounts do not give a true and fair view of its affairs, for the reasons specified.

quality control In a production process, the checking of the quality of a product (or representative samples of it).

quality ladder In a company's development of a product, the trend to continually improve the quality of the product over time.

quango An abbreviation of quasi-autonomous non-governmental organization, which in the UK covers many semi-permanent public bodies set up to investigate certain cases or to deal with special problems. Examples are the Advisory and Conciliation and Arbitration Service (ACAS), the Economic and Social Research Council (ESRC) and the National Economic Development Council (NEDC).

quantity demanded The amount of a good or service that consumers purchase at a given price in a given time.

quantity discount Also termed quantity rebate, a reduction in purchase price granted because of the large amount of goods or services being purchased.

quantity equation A relationship between price levels and the *quantity of money,* usually stating that the quantity of money multiplied by the velocity of circulation equals the price level multiplied by the volume of transactions. In practice this generally reduces to price level is proportional to money supply. It is also known as the Fisher equation after the US economist Irving Fisher (1867-1947).

quantity of money The amount of money in circulation (for the various definitions *see money supply*).

quantity rebate *See quantity discount.*

quantity supplied The amount of a good or service that suppliers offer for sale at a given price in a given time.

quantity restriction (QR) A limit of the amount of goods that can be imported or exported; a quota.

quantity theory of money The theory that in any economy the general price level is directly proportional to the quantity of money (money supply), and nothing else. *See quantity equation.*

quantity traded The amount of a good or service that is sold or purchased, generally determined in a given market by the effects of supply and demand.

quasi-rent A payment for the short-run use of a *factor of production* (rather like rent paid for the use of land or buildings).

quota An amount of something (eg goods) allowed to one person, company or country, normally fixed by a body in authority. Some countries impose import quotas on the quantity of certain goods that may be imported.

quotation 1. A cost estimate submitted by a contractor; a tender. 2. The current market price of a commodity or security, as stated by a dealer or market-maker. 3. The appearance of a company's shares on the Official List of the stock exchange.

quotation spread The difference between the offer price and the bid price on a security. It is also known as the bid-offer spread.

quoted company A company that has received a listing on a stock exchange.

quote-driven Describing a market (such as a stock market) that reacts in terms of prices to the quotations of market-makers rather than to the number and flow of incoming orders.

Q

R

R & D Abbreviation of *research and development.*

random sample A sample of a population (in the statistical sense) that is chosen in such a way that each member of the population has the same chance of being included.

random walk A theory of stock movements developed in the 1950s and 1960s, which states that share prices move in a random way, and so their movements up or down cannot be predicted.

RAROC Abbreviation of *risk-adjusted return on capital.*

rateable value The value of a property for the purpose of calculating *rates,* based on an estimate of the rent the property would command (the annual value) on the open market with vacant possession.

rate of exchange Also called exchange rate, the rate at which various currencies are exchanged for each other.

rate of interest *See interest.*

rate of return The amount of money made on an investment (in the form of interest or dividend), normally expresses as a percentage of the amount invested. The revenue a company receives for investing resources in some commercial activity is also known as its rate of return.

rate-of-return regulation The imposition by the government on a monopoly supplier (such as a public utility) of a maximum allowable profit level.

rate of technical substitution (RTS) The increase in the output of one product that can result from reducing the production of another by one unit, equal to the ratio of their *marginal products.*

rates In the UK, a local government tax levied on householders and occupiers of commercial premises to pay for local works and services, expressed as a certain amount in the pound of *rateable value.* For private property, rates have been replaced by council tax, which is payable by the occupant.

R

rational expectations The idea that people and companies should make decisions about the future using *all* currently available information in an unbiased way.

rationalization The reorganization of a company or industry so as to more efficiently use resources or to increase profits. It may involve such measures as closing small costly plants and centralizing production, and increasing profitability by reducing overheads and labour costs.

rationing A way of allocating a good or service for which the demand exceeds the supply. The scarce commodity is allocated physically rather than allowing market forces to operate (which would rapidly drive up the price).

raw materials Any materials purchased for and employed directly in a production process. Raw materials, such as chemicals, sheet metal and timber, are generally at a low level of finish compared to the manufactured product that results from their consumption.

real balance effect The way that changes in the real value of money balances result in changes in demand. When prices rise (inflation) the real value of holdings of money falls, reducing its purchasing power and leading to a reduction in demand. Conversely, when prices fall (deflation) the real value of cash holdings rises, increasing purchasing power and consumption.

real balances The real purchasing power of a balance of money (the amount of real goods and services it would buy), equal to the ratio of the money supply to a price index.

real business cycle The idea that fluctuations in the activity of an economy (the *business cycle*) result from random shocks in production processes, rather than from fluctuations in demand. Such shocks may include breakthrough technical developments, natural disasters and wars or insurrection.

real cost The actual resources consumed in the production of a good or service (or the *opportunity cost* in terms of foregone alternatives). Unless a tax or subsidy applies to the inputs, it equals the *private cost*.

real exchange rate The value of one country's real goods and services divided by the value of another country's—ie, the rate at which they can be interchanged.

R

real gross domestic product The gross domestic product expressed in real terms (by dividing the gross domestic product by a price index such as the GDP deflator).

real gross national product The gross national product expressed in real terms (by dividing the gross national product by a price index such as the GDP deflator).

realignment of exchange rates From 1979 under the European Monetary System, a series of exchange-rate changes. Countries with high inflation and balance-of-payments deficits had the relative par values of their currencies lowered, whereas those of countries with low inflation and a balance-of-payments surplus were raised.

real income Also termed real wage, money income stated in real prices, obtained by dividing income by a price index such as the Retail Price Index.

real interest rate An interest rate after taking into account the effects of inflation. For example, if an investment pays 5% interest and inflation is running at 4%, the real interest rate is only 1%.

real national income The national income divided by an appropriate price index to indicate the real affordable spending level.

real price The price of a good, service or security stated in constant price terms, to take inflation into account. *See real value.*

real terms The value of goods or services arrived at by allowing for current price level fluctuations. *See real value.*

real value The value of something when compared to fluctuations in price indices, as occur during times of inflation or deflation. For example, the real value of a 10% wage increase at a time of 5% inflation is only 5%, because the cash represented by the 10% increase will purchase only 5% more goods.

real variable An economic variable stated in physical units (such as the tonnage of coal mined), as opposed to monetary variables (in money terms) and pure numbers (with no units).

real wage *See real income.*

receiver An official into whose hands a company with financial difficulties is placed to ensure that, as far as possible, creditors are paid.

R

receivership A company's state when a *receiver* is called in.

recession The stage in a trade cycle in which the decline in economic activity accelerates, causing investment values to fall, companies to have to deal with adverse trading conditions, and unemployment to rise and so income and expenditure to fall. A recession may end in a *depression* unless there is a recovery.

reciprocity A reduction in import duties, quotas or tariffs in exchange for similar concessions from another country. Other similar mutual arrangements (such as the setting up of financial institutions in two countries) are also termed reciprocity.

Recognized Investment Exchange (RIE) A market that has been authorized by the UK Securities and Investment Board to carry out investment business. Its individual members must also be authorized, in accord with the Financial Services Act.

recommended retail price (RRP) The retail price of a product as suggested by its manufacturer (which is seldom legally enforceable, although some manufacturers have other ways of getting retailers to comply with their wishes). The RRP is often specified on the packaging to indicate to customers that the retailer is not overcharging and to allow a comparison to be made between the prices of competing brands.

recovery An upturn in the financial position of a company, a market or the economy in general.

recycling The sorting of waste products so that they can be reused. The term was also used in the mid-1970s for the practice of banks of taking surplus funds from OPEC countries and investing them elsewhere (so that the recipients could spend it with OPEC).

redeemable (financial) security A security (stocks or bonds) that is repayable at par value at a specified date or dates (or in the event of something specified happening).

redemption The repayment of an outstanding loan or debenture stock by the borrower.

redemption date Also termed maturity, the date on which a loan or debenture is to be repaid. Redemption dates (plural) are those on a stock which is redeemable at par. In the case of UK Treasury stocks, the precise date of repayment is decided by the government.

redemption value Also termed maturity value, the price at which a security is redeemed at its redemption (maturity) date.

redemption yield Also termed yield to maturity, for securities with a fixed *redemption date*, the yield taking into account capital gain upon redemption plus the dividend, related to the market price of the security.

redeployment The moving of a factor of production to a different location or purpose. If the factor is labour, it can result in redundancy because no alternative jobs are available for surplus workers.

rediscounting The buying of negotiable securities such as bills of exchange, bonds and Treasury bills (which will have been discounted at the time of original purchase) before they reach their redemption (maturity) dates.

redistributive tax A tax that is intended to divert wealth from richer households (through income tax and inheritance tax) to poorer ones (through benefits and tax allowances). It generally includes high marginal rates of tax on large incomes.

red-lining A practice among some US lenders, illegal in some states, whereby declining neighbourhoods and Third World countries are blacklisted for mortgages and loans.

reducing-balance depreciation An alternative term for *decreasing-balance depreciation*.

redundancy The ending of employment through no fault of the employee, usually because a job no longer exists. In the UK a redundant employee who worked full time may have a legal right to compensation.

reflation Government action that attempts to boost a country's economy. It is done by increasing the money supply, usually by reducing interest rates and taxation.

refusal to supply The refusal by a producer to supply his or her product to everyone who asks for it, perhaps as a desire to avoid 'low-quality' distributors or those who stock rival products. It may also be a means of setting up *exclusive dealing* and *tie-in sales*.

regional aid Central government help for regions of high unemployment or generally low incomes. *See enterprise zone*.

R

regional policy Government policy designed to improve regions of high unemployment or generally low incomes and bring them nearer to the levels in the rest of the country, mainly by stimulating investment in the depressed regions. *See enterprise zone.*

registered company A joint-stock company that in the UK is registered with the *Registrar of Companies.*

Register of Companies A list of UK companies kept at Companies House in Cardiff, detailing registered addresses and names of directors.

Registrar of Companies A person who keeps a record at Companies House in Cardiff of all UK joint-stock companies. The registrar also holds their memorandums of association and copies of the annual report and accounts.

Registrar of Friendly Societies A person who keeps a record of all UK friendly societies and oversees their activities on behalf of the Department of Trade and Industry.

regression analysis A measurement of the average change in one variable quantity resulting from unit increase in one or more other variable quantities.

regressive tax A tax that is levied as a smaller proportion of income the greater the income is. Even a fixed tax (such as the duty of petrol) can effectively be regressive because it represents a smaller proportion of a high-income earner than of a low-income earner.

regulation 1. A rule or order than people or companies have to obey. 2. The control and supervision of economic activities by the government, *quangos* or other regulatory organizations (*see self-regulatory organization*). *See also deregulation.*

regulatory agency A government department, quango, self-regulatory organization or other body that formulates and enforces *regulations.*

regulatory capture The situation that arises when regulators champion the interests of the industry or organization they are supposed to regulate.

relative-income hypothesis The idea that a person's or country's position in the income hierarchy affects attitudes to consumption (spending) and saving. A rich member of a poor community has a very diffferent attitude from that of a poor member of a rich community—the former will tend to spend a lower proportion of income than the latter

R

relative prices The comparison of prices among real goods and services ('item A has twice the cost of item B') as opposed to absolute money prices.

reneging Going back on a bargain, contract, deal or promise. *See opportunism.*

renewable energy Energy whose production does not consume irreplaceable resources (unlike the energy produced by burning fossil fuels). Examples include solar energy, tidal energy and wind energy.

renewable resource A resource that can be used continually without its being consumed (because it is replaced or exists in infinite quantities). For example, water as used in tidal power or hydroelectricity generation is a renewable resource.

rent Also called rental payment, money paid for the occupation or use of something for a period of time (such as a building, factory, office, car or television set). *See also* **lease.**

rent back To sell property (offices, factory space, etc.) on the understanding that the new owner will lease back the property to its original owner. It is a way of raising capital by realizing property assets without having to vacate the premises.

rent control The government regulation of rents on homes, usually by capping increases or setting the amount of rent.

rentier A person whose chief income is in the form of interest from guilt-edged securities and other financial investments.

rent-seeking Looking to improve one's financial position at the cost of somebody else, such as when a company management puts more effort into increasing its share of turnover that in improving turnover as a whole, or in seeking government subsidies rather than increasing productivity.

repeated game In *game theory*, a game that players expect to be repeated many times in the same form. A player can therefore learn about other players' strategies and use the information to change his or her own strategy (unexpectedly) in future games.

replacement cost For a given asset, the current market price of another similar asset (as opposed to historic cost, which was what was paid for it originally).

R

replacement investment The investment needed to replace a company's equipment that has become obsolete or worn out.

replacement ratio An unemployed worker's income (in the form of benefit) divided by his or her income when working. The lower this is, the greater is the incentive to seek work.

repo Abbreviation of repossession, or of *repurchase agreement.*

representative firm A hypothetical economics concept of a 'typical' company, arrived at by assuming that an industry is made up of a number of companies of the same size.

repressed inflation *See suppressed inflation.*

repurchase agreement (repo) A transaction between a bond dealer and a bank. The dealer sells government securities while at the same time agreeing to buy them back at a specified time at a price high enough to allow the bank a profit margin. In this way, the repro may be looked upon as a form of loan.

reputational policy A policy that depends on the policy-maker's reputation for keeping his or her promises. In other words, do you believe the government when it says that it will reduce inflation by gradually reducing the money supply over a prolonged period? The policy will not work if the government is not trusted to keep its promise.

required rate of return The minimum *rate of return* that is needed in order to justify a company investment (ie for it to be profitable).

resale price maintenance (RPM) A practice whereby a supplier refuses to sell goods to a retailer unless the retailer agrees to sell them at a certain price, or above a minimum price. Resale price maintenance may be applied to prevent retailers from using the product as a *loss leader*. In the UK, it is allowable under the Resale Prices Act 1976 if the supplier can prove to the Office of Fair Trading that it is in the interests of the consumer, as in the case of books and some pharmaceuticals.

Resale Prices Acts 1964, 1976 UK legislation enacted to control *resale price maintenance*, making it illegal except in certain special circumstances.

rescheduling of debt A method used by a company or even a country with financial problems, in which existing loans are converted into others with a more remote repayment date (or instalment dates), sometimes insisted on by the lender and backed by a third-party guarantee.

research and development (R & D) An activity that aims to discover or invent new products or services. It covers pure scientific and technical research, applied research, product improvement and technological innovation.

reserve Also called reserves, the part of a company's undistributed capital (excluding share capital) resulting from retained profits or the issue of shares at above nominal value.

reserve assets A bank's short-term or current assets that can easily be converted to cash, which it holds for such things as day-to-day cash withdrawals. In the UK they have to be kept at a minimum level specified by the Bank of England.

reserve asset ratio Also called liquidity ratio or reserve requirement, the fraction of a bank's total assets (deposits and other liabilities) that it maintains in the form of *reserve assets*, in some countries specified by the monetary authorities to ensure banks' solvency or to limit bank lending. *See also* **bank multiplier**.

reserve currency A foreign currency held by a central bank in order to fund foreign trade.

reserve requirement *See reserve asset ratio.*

reserves *See reserve.*

reserve tranche For a member of the International Monetary Fund, the first 25% of its quota which is unconditionally available if necessary.

Resolution Trust Corporation (RTC) A US federal organization established in 1989 and responsible to the Federal Deposit Insurance Corporation that winds up **thrift and loans** that have gone bankrupt.

resource allocation The allocation of an economy's (scarce) factors of production among available alternatives. *See* **efficient resource allocation**.

resources Anything that can act as an input to an economy, including capital goods, human resources and natural resources. Some economists limit the definition to scarce factors of production.

R

Restrictive Practices Court (RPC) A UK court established in 1956 to apply the Restrictive Trade Practices Act 1956 to trade agreements. From 1964 it was also responsible for applying the Resale Prices Act 1964.

restrictive trade agreement *See restrictive trade practice.*

restrictive trade practice Also called restrictive trade agreement, an agreement made between two companies that aims to make restrictions regarding the supply of their goods, on such things as price, quantities, processes, geographical area, and so on. On the whole, restrictive practices are assumed by the law to be against the general public interest and are illegal in the UK unless approved by the Office of Fair Trading.

Restrictive Trade Practices Acts 1956, 1968, 1976 UK legislation that controls *restrictive trade practices* between rival producers.

retail The sale of goods or services to the general public, or describing the sector of the service industries that is concerned with selling (also called the retail trade).

retailer A shop or store that sells goods to the general public.

retail outlet A location or facility from which consumers can buy products. Examples include a shop, supermarket, mail-order house, vending machine and Internet web site.

retail price The price at which goods or services are actually sold through a retailer (higher than the wholesale price because of the retailer's mark-up).

Retail Price Index (RPI) An analysis of trends in retail prices, expressed as an index number and used to evaluate changes in retail prices with reference to inflation (and thus a measure of the cost of living). It is usually related to a 'basket' of particular goods and services. In the USA it is called the Consumer Price Index (CPI). In the UK it has three variants: the headline rate, including all items of expenditure; the underlying rate, which excludes mortgage interest payments; and the core rate, which excludes mortgage interest, indirect taxes (such as value-added tax) and council tax.

retail sales The fraction of the total spending on consumption derived from *retail outlets*.

retained earnings That part of a company's post-tax earnings not distributed to shareholders, and thus retained by the company to finance its day-to-day activities and any future expansion. Retained earnings are added to *reserve* and thus appear on the company's balance sheet. They are also called retentions, retained income, retained profits or ploughed-back profits.

retained profits Alternative term for *retained earnings.*

return on capital employed (ROCE) Also called return on capital (ROC), a measure of how well a company's capital is used, equal to 100 times the trading profit (before tax and interest) divided by the average capital employed.

returns to scale The relationship between a product's output and the amount of factor inputs used to produce it. They are increasing if output rises proportionately more than inputs and decreasing if output rises proportionately less than inputs.

revaluation 1. A practice by means of which a company puts a new value on its fixed assets, because nominal values and real values of such assets as property and machines have changed significantly 2. An increase in the overall value of the currency of a country.

revealed preference An indirect method of expressing consumer preferences for particular products, assuming a rational choice is made based only on product prices and consumer income (spending power). For example if product X is preferred to product Y, and Y is preferred to Z, it can be assumed that X is preferred to Z.

revenue The money received from any transaction or sale (including interest on investments); income. A government's revenue comes mainly from taxes. *The* Revenue is short for **Inland Revenue.**

revenue tariff A type of tariff that is introduced mainly to raise revenue for the government, as opposed to a protective tariff imposed to reduce competition for domestic producers.

reverse takeover The purchase of control of a public company by a smaller, private company. This is often done in order that the private company may obtain a listing on a stock exchange.

reverse yield gap A situation in which low-risk assets provide greater returns that high-risk assets.

R

revised sequence The idea that the goods and services available to consumers are determined actively by suppliers, rather than the conventional view that suppliers passively react to the demands of consumers.

revolving credit *See revolving loan.*

revolving fund A fund that is automatically renewed at the start of each period (or as soon as it is depleted, such as a *petty cash* fund).

revolving loan A loan that is automatically renewed at the start of each period (or as soon as the sum is repaid). For example, a bank may arrange to lend a customer a certain amount each month. It will prevent borrowing above that limit once it is reached, but allow borrowing to go on at the start of the next month. The arrangement is also known as revolving credit. In the USA it is known as a *revolver*.

Ricardian equivalence The idea that the effect of government spending on the savings behaviour of individuals is the same no matter if it is financed by borrowing or by taxes, because money borrowed now will have to be repaid in the future and so taxes will have to rise. It was first formulated by the UK economist David Ricardo (1772-1823).

Ricardo effect When during an economic boom the prices of goods rise more quickly than wages do, investors tend not to invest in companies that make capital goods because of their relatively long production times. Producers with a shorter turnover time will be a more profitable investment. It was first formulated by the UK economist David Ricardo (1772-1823).

RIE Abbreviation of *Recognized Investment Exchange.*

rights issue The practice of offering existing shareholders the opportunity to buy more shares (ie subscribe more capital), in order that a company may raise additional capital. Rights issues act as a protection for the shareholder, in that the total number of shares issued increases without decreasing the percentage holding of each shareholder.

ring-fence To allocate government or local government money for a specific purpose—the money is 'spoken for' in any planning activity.

risk The amount a buyer or seller potentially stands to lose by a transaction. There are various identifiable risks in financial trading, including credit risk, exchange rate risk, interest rate risk and political risk. People who do not (want to) take risks are described as risk-averse.

risk-adjusted return on capital (RAROC) A way of taking risk into account when comparing the returns on different investments—returns on risky investments are adjusted downwards.

risk analysis An analysis of the potential gains or losses from a financial transaction, such as an investment. Where there is a range of possible outcomes, their respective probabilities can be estimated.

risk assessment The measuring of economic risk and the calculation of the benefits and costs resulting from reducing that risk. It may show that sometimes the risk reduction is not worth its cost.

risk-averse *See risk.*

risk-bearing Describing the person who has or who shares the loss if an investment or project goes wrong, from the shareholders and creditors of a company to the sole-trader in a one-man business.

risk capital The capital invested long-term in a company, or a security, that presents a risk (ie the possibility of a loss or, indeed, a gain). The term is also used as an alternative to *venture capital*.

risk-free security An investment that is free (or virtually free) from risk, such as government securities, especially if they are indexed (eg to the Retail Price Index).

risk pooling The combining of two or more unrelated risky investments or projects in the hope that returns from some will counteract any losses from others. *See also portfolio.*

risk premium In the currency markets, the difference between the forward exchange rate and the expected future spot rate.

risk sharing The shifting of all or part of a risk from one party to another, for example by issuing shares to finance a risky project (when the risk is shared by the new shareholders).

ROCE Abbreviation of *return on capital employed.*

rolling over The practice of carrying over loans or other debts into the future rather than paying them at the due date, by arrangement with the lender (usually for an additional fee).

R

royalty A sum paid to an inventor, originator or author, or the owner of something from which a product can be made (such as an oilfield), and calculated as a proportion of the income received from the sale of the product.

RPC Abbreviation of *Restrictive Practices Court.*

RPI Abbreviation of *Retail Price Index.*

RPM Abbreviation of *resale price maintenance.*

RRP Abbreviation of *recommended retail price.*

RTC Abbreviation of *Resolution Trust Corporation.*

RTS Abbreviation of *rate of technical substitution.*

rules-based policy A policy that follows recognized rules (and is therefore predictable) as opposed to a *discretionary policy* (which is not).

rules of origin In a *free-trade area*, rules that define which goods can be imported duty-free.

running costs Also called running expenses, direct expenses or variable costs, the costs incurred in the day-to-day running of a business and which vary with the quantity of output. They include costs incurred in the purchase of the factors of production (such as raw materials and labour) and in the marketing, advertising and distribution of goods.

running yield An alternative term for *earnings yield* or flat yield.

Rybcznski theorem If only one factor of production is increased, there will be a rise in the output of a product that uses it intensively and a fall in the output of companies using other factors of production (which have not increased).

R

S

salary Money paid to an employee, normally expressed as so much per year (per annum, p.a.), but usually paid monthly by cheque or directly into the employee's bank account. *See also* **wages.**

sales promotion Together with merchandising, the various methods employed by companies to increase sales. They include advertising, coupons (with a money value or discounting the next purchase), reduced price combination packs ('3 for the price of 2'), point-of-sale displays, and so on.

sales revenue The income from selling goods or services.

sales-revenue maximization A company policy to maximize the income from sales (subject to making a specified minimum profit), rather than the more usual profit maximization.

sales tax A tax imposed on goods or services at the point of sale, such as value-added tax (VAT) in the UK.

S & L *See Savings and loan association.*

S & P *See Standard and Poor.*

satisficing A policy that tries to achieve 'enough' (ie a minimum acceptable level) of something without going for the maximum possible, although other things may simultaneously be maximized. For example a company may be satisficing profit while trying to maximize market share or sales.

saturation point The level above which the take-up of a good or service is not likely to increase. For instance 75 mobile phones per hundred of the population may be saturation point, and further sales of mobile phones will be replacements or result from an increase in the total population. Obviously, manufacturers of mobile phones would like to see the saturation point in the upper 90s per hundred.

savings Money (income) set aside and not spent, often invested in a way that pays interest or makes a profit (although it can just be hidden under the mattress). There is no formal distinction between savings and investment, although most people regard saving as 'putting by'

S

regular small sums. Savers generally seek a 'safer' investment than an ordinary investor, who may be prepared to take more risk. In corporate terms, savings are retained profits. *See also* **investment.**

savings and loan association (S & L) The US equivalent of a UK building society in which people invest personal savings and often earn interest. Often notice of withdrawal must be given.

savings function A function that shows the relationship between savings and such factors as age, assets, status and, particularly, income. Plotted as a graph, it is called a savings schedule.

savings ratio The proportion of income that is saved, for an individual equal to total disposable income divided by the amount saved. Similar ratios can be calculated for companies (where savings equal retained profits).

savings schedule *See savings function.*

Say's law Supply creates its own demand, ie producing an output creates income such as profits and wages that equals the output and is just sufficient to buy it. It was first proposed in the 1820s by the French businessman and later economist Jean-Baptise Say (1767-1832).

scarce currency clause Under the rules of the International Monetary Fund, a currency can be declared scarce if the fund runs out of it. Member countries modify their trade policies to discriminate against goods from the country with the scarce currency.

scarcity A situation in which the demand for a good, services or resource far exceeds the supply. *See* **rationing; resource allocation.**

scenario In economics, an account of how an economy would evolve based on certain assumptions about how it might work. Alternative scenarios can be drawn up by varying the assumptions.

Scheduled Territories Also known as the Sterling Area, a pre-1979 term for areas where sterling was the official currency (and so there were no exchange control restrictions). In the end it consisted only of Great Britain, the Channel Islands and the Isle of Man.

Schengen Treaty An agreement, signed in 1990 in Schengen, Luxembourg, between Belgium, France, Germany (as it was to become), Luxembourg and the Netherlands, to do away with border controls and customs at their common borders, to give police the right

S

of pursuit across borders, and to specify entering nationalities that would need visas. Austria, Greece, Italy, Portugal and Spain later also joined the agreement.

scrip issue Also called bonus issue or capitalization issue, extra shares issued to existing shareholders free of charge. It is done by transferring reserves into the company's share account. In this way, the company increases its capitalization while at the same time reducing its share price and increasing the number of shares on the market.

SD Abbreviation of *standard deviation.*

SDR Abbreviation of *Special Drawing Rights.*

search unemployment A type of unemployment that occurs when somebody who is unemployed looks for any acceptable offer of a job (but not just any job).

seasonal adjustment A method of removing (often misleading) seasonal variations from data in order to expose the underlying trend.

seasonal unemployment A type of unemployment caused by seasonal fall-off in demand for workers because of the nature of the occupation (for example, the agricultural industry needs crop pickers only at harvest time).

SEC Abbreviation of *Securities and Exchange Commission.*

secondary benefits Extra benefits that arise indirectly from the direct primary benefits of a project. For example, although the primary benefit of a new bypass is the speeding of traffic flow and a reduction in congestion, secondary benefits include less noise and atmospheric pollution in the town that is bypassed.

secondary market A market in securities that have been listed for some time, rather than in new issues. Secondary market trading occurs on a stock exchange.

second-best Describing an economy that cannot optimize the allocation of resources perhaps because of an external factor such as pollution, ie some optimum conditions are satisfied but others through necessity are not.

second-degree price discrimination A type of price discrimination in which consumers are offered a choice of contracts and associated

S

prices. For example, advance or group bookings may command lower prices. *See also first-degree price discrimination; third-degree price discrimination.*

sector A defined part of an economy, such as the corporate sector (consisting of companies), the private sector (consisting of unincorporated businesses and individual people) and the public sector (the state), or the primary sector (extraction and farming), secondary sector (manufacturing) and tertiary sector (services).

secular stagnation A long period of time in which the economy remains in the depression stage of the *business cycle*, characterized by low demand when compared with the available capacity to produce. Contributory factors include falling investment, high exchange rates (limiting exports) and high savings (reducing consumer spending).

secular trend Over a long time period, an upward or downward movement in an economic variable (ignoring the effects of seasonal variation and the business cycle).

secured loan A loan secured by specified assets (collateral) that revert to the lender if the loan is not repaid. It generally attracts lower interest than an unsecured loan.

securities *See security.*

Securities and Exchange Commission (SEC) A government organization founded in 1934 that regulated the securities market (brokers and stock exchanges) in the USA. It also controls auditing practices and the financial reporting of companies.

Securities and Futures Authority (SFA) A self-regulatory organization (SRO) established in the UK in 1991 to regulate the conduct of people who deal in debentures, futures, options and shares. It was formed by combining the functions The Securities Association (TSA) and the Association of Futures Brokers and Dealers (AFBD).

Securities and Investments Board (SIB) A UK financial watchdog, set up in 1986 by the Department of Trade and Industry to oversee the UK's deregulated financial markets. The US equivalent is the *Securities and Exchange Commission.*

securitization A tendency of companies to use security markets to raise finance rather than the more traditional financial intermediaries such as banks.

S

security Anything (usually property) pledged as collateral against a loan, or the document that sets out the terms of such collateral. A security is also any financial instrument that is traded on a stock exchange and that yields an income. It represents a loan that will be repaid at some time in the future. Such securities include bills of exchange, bonds, debentures, gilt-edged securities, options, shares, stocks and unit trusts (but not insurance policies).

segmented market A market in which contact between different suppliers or consumers is limited, so that different prices may be charged or paid for similar products.

seigniorage Originally, the profit that the ruler of a country made from issuing currency, now applied to the government's ability to obtain revenue by issuing new money.

Select Committee on Estimates A group in the UK Parliament (House of Commons) that examines proposed government spending to make sure that public money is spent wisely.

self-employment Being in business on one's own account. The self-employed include those who run their businesses, either alone or in partnership, and professional people such as doctors and lawyers.

self-financing Describing a company or organization that is funded without the need to borrow or issue shares. It is generally financed by capital provided by the founders.

self-financing ratio The investment funds from a company's undistributed profit divided by its total investment funds.

self-fulfilling expectation An expectation that makes somebody behave in such a way as to cause the thing expected, applied particularly to financial markets. For example, if investors expect prices to fall they postpone purchases but bring sales forward, creating an excess on the market and causing prices to fall.

self-liquidating asset An asset that has a predetermined lifetime and liquidates itself at the end of that period. For example, in the investment trust sector, a closed-end fund with a stock exchange listing is self-liquidating.

self-regulatory organization Sometimes called a self-regulating organization, a non-governmental organization in the UK, set up under

S

the Financial Services Act 1986, that governs a particular area of business activity, laying down codes of practice and protecting consumers and investors. There have been various mergers among the original SROs until there are currently four: the Financial Intermediaries, Managers and Brokers Regulatory Organization (FIMBRA), the Investment Management Regulatory Organization (IMRO), the Life Assurance and Unit Trust Regulatory Organization (LAUTRO) and the Securities and Futures Authority (SFA).

self-sufficiency The ability of a person, community or even a country to restrict consumption to home-produced products.

seller concentration In a particular market, the number and relative sizes of the suppliers. Many sellers and many buyers creates perfect competition; few sellers and many buyers is an oligolpoly; and one seller with many buyers is a monopoly.

seller's market A market that is more favourable to sellers than to buyers. Such a market often arises when demand is greater than supply.

selling cost The extra expenditure required to increase sales of a product.

selling price Broadly, the cash price a buyer must pay for securities, goods or services.

separation of ownership from control The situation in which a company's owners (usually shareholders) take no active part in its management (usually the function of the board of directors).

serial correlation An alternative term for *autocorrelation.*

service Something provided, usually for a fee, that may not be classed as manufacturing or production in any form (such as legal advice, agency services, banking, brokerage, financial advice and insurance).

service economy The total output of the services, or tertiary, sector of an economy. It is also an economy that is based on services rather than manufacturing industries.

service flows The services provided by durable goods—those that last for many years, such as freezers and furniture.

service industry Businesses engaged in the service, or tertiary, sector of an economy, such as a bank, shop or restaurant.

service sector Also called tertiary sector, the part of the economy that consists of services.

settlement The act of paying in full for goods or services received, or of repaying a debt or loan.

settlement risk The risk in securities trading that after one party to a deal delivers securities or pays cash while the other side delays payment or delivery.

shadow price The price attributed to a good, service or resource that does not have a normal market (to determine price) or because prices are grossly distorted in any market that does exist, perhaps because of scarcity or rationing. It corresponds to the true *opportunity cost* to the economy.

shakeout When a market cannot support the number of suppliers it has attracted, many of the less profitable suppliers leave the market, with only the more healthy operators remaining. In the USA, this process of 'natural selection' is known as a shakeout.

share *See shares.*

share capital The capital raised by a company through an issue of shares.

share economy The aggregate value of companies quoted on a stock exchange. In the UK it is known as 'Quoted UK plc'. It is also an economy in which many people are shareholders.

shareholder Person who holds shares in a company (and is thereby one of its owners).

shareholders' capital employed The original share capital invested in a company together with any reserves (such as retained profits).

share index An index that shows the average change in value of a number of individual shares. Share indexes therefore give an overall guide to movements in the financial markets. Examples include the Financial Times Stock Exchange 100 Index (FOOTSIE), the Nikkei-Dow Average and the Dow Jones Industrial Average.

share issue A method of raising capital used by a limited company, which may issues shares valued at a fraction of the company's total value. The shares are generally placed on the market by a stockbroker acting on behalf of the company in question and may, in most cases, be purchased by financial institutions, other companies and members of the public.

share option A UK scheme that gives employees the option to buy shares

S

in their company at attractive prices (normally well below market price) at a specific future date. It therefore constitutes a type of profit-sharing scheme.

share premium On a new issue of shares, a premium charged on the nominal value of the shares if it seems that the real value is likely to be much higher.

share price The price at which a share is bought or sold, bearing in mind that the bid (buying) price is less than the offer (selling) price to a market-maker. The mid-market price, as quoted in the financial press, is the mean of the two.

share price index See *share index*.

share register Also known as register of members, a register of shareholders that is held by a company (and viewable at its registered office), giving names, addresses, details of shareholding, and so on.

shares Forms of security that represent a shareholder's stake in a company. Income on shares is in the form of a dividend rather than interest, and is declared depending on the company's financial performance over a year. In the USA shares are known as common stock.

shell company A company that does not produce anything in the usual sense, but exists only in name. Shell companies may be set up and sold to people who are unfamiliar with the procedure for doing this (for their convenience), or may be remnants of a defunct company that has been sold on to somebody else. They may also be set up for use at some future time, or to operate as the holder of shares.

sheltered monopoly A monopoly that has some form of protection against competition, such as tariffs to restrict competition from overseas or laws that prevent competitors from entering the market.

Sherman Act One of the fundamental US Antitrust Laws, the pioneer federal statute in this field (passed 2 July 1890), and a cornerstone in the legal expression of public policy against restraint of trade and monopoly or attempts to monopolize.

shift system A method of getting more production from a process by employing two (or three) times the normal number of workers who work two (or three) consecutive shifts of, say, 8 hours and keep production going for 16 (or 24) hours.

S

shift work Work at non-standard hours (such as the night shift, often 8 p.m. to 4 a.m.). Unsociable hours may be compensated for with higher rates of pay. *See* **shift system.**

shock A totally unexpected event that significantly effects an economy, such as a breakthrough technical development, natural disasters or war.

shop A location that consumers visit to purchase goods and, occasionally, services; a common type of **retail outlet.**

shortage A situation in which the demand for a good or service is greater than the available supply. *See* **rationing; resource allocation.**

short-dated security A fixed-interest security that has a redemption date of less than five years.

short position In the position of having sold more commodities or securities than one owns.

short run A vague concept of a time period in which only a few variables can change and most cannot. It can be contrasted with the equally vague **medium run** and **long run.**

short-run capital movement The movement of capital (usually liquid assets) between countries that can be reversed quickly if necessary. A common cause is speculators taking advantage of favourable exchange rate differences.

short-termism A policy of favouring short-term investments that yield immediate profit, rather than (possibly more secure) long-term investments.

short-term monetary support (STMS) A European Monetary System intervention mechanism by means of which a country with balance of payments difficulties gets its central bank to borrow (for three months) from other members' central banks. An extension to the agreed term is called a rallonge.

short-time working A reduction in the number of hours a worker is employed for to reduce output and lower labour costs, as an alternative to laying off workers (who then become unemployed).

shutdown price A selling price that is so low that at this or any price below it a company would prefer to close down production rather than continue.

S

SIB Abbreviation of *Securities and Investment Board.*

SIC Abbreviation of *Standard Industrial Classification.*

Silicon Valley The popular name for the district around San Jose, California, which is home to many hi-tech industries, particularly in computers, information technology and telecommunications.

simple interest A rate of interest calculated by keeping interest that has already accrued separate from the capital sum. Thus, when calculating the next interest payment, the capital sum only (excluding the interest already accrued) enters the calculation. In mathematical terms, simple interest equals $Atr/100$, where A is the amount invested or borrowed, t is the time in years and r is the interest rate as a percentage per annum. *See also* **compound interest.**

simulation The employment of quantitative models to imitate how an economy works, generally using a computer. It can study in numerical terms the effects of changes in economic variables or policies.

single currency An objective of the European Monetary System, as defined by the 1991 Maastricht Treaty, under which a single central bank would issue currency that could be used anywhere in the EU. The target date for its implementation, 1999, had already passed when most member states finally adopted the euro in January 2002 (Denmark, Norway, Sweden and the UK were exceptions).

Single European Act 1986 Legislation enacted in each member state of the European Union that aimed to establish a single market throughout the Union by 1992 by removing remaining obstacles to free movement (of people, capital, goods and services) across borders. This '1992 Initiative', as it became known, has still not been fully implemented.

single market *See Single European Act 1986.*

sinking fund A sum of money set aside for a specific purpose and invested so that it provides the required amount at the right time.

SITC Abbreviation of *Standard International Trade Classification.*

skilled work The type of work that can be done well only by somebody with the proper training and experience (or both). It generally commands higher wages and securer employment than unskilled work.

skimming the market The policy of setting the price of a new product so high that only enthusiasts or trend-setters will buy it.

skimming price A high price that yields high profit (*see* **skimming the market**).

slack Underutilized or unused resources *See* **organizational slack**.

sleeping partner A partner who invests capital in a firm but takes no active part in its management. He or she does, however, remain liable for the partnership's debts.

slump A period of time during which the economy is poor, with high levels of unemployment and reduced economic activity.

Slutsky equation A relationship that shows how a change in demand brought about by a change in price can be allocated between the income effect and the substitution effect.

small company A company that meets various criteria and is thereby permitted in the UK to issue less detailed annual reports to shareholders and file abbreviated accounts with Companies House. Its turnover has to be less than £2.8 million, its balance-sheet total less than £1.4 million and its number of employees less than 50. If its turnover is less than £90,000 and balance-sheet total less than £1.4 million, it is exempt from a statutory audit of its accounts.

Smoot-Hawley Tariff Act US legislation of 1930 that introduced protectionist tariffs, probably—along with similar measures in Europe—contributing to the subsequent depression.

social accounting The country's *national income and expenditure accounts* presented in such a way as to reveal transactions between the various sectors of the economy.

social benefit The total increase in society's welfare that results from some economic activity, equal to the benefit to the person or company introducing it as well as the resulting benefit to society.

social capital The total of all productive assets in a society. They include those that produce non-marketable products (such as education) as well as those that result in marketable outputs (and which make profits).

Social Chapter Part of the social charter agreed by EU member states under the terms of the 1993 Maastricht Treaty (except for the UK). It deals mainly with employment protection and other similar social issues.

S

social charter A raft of measures agreed by members of the EU under the terms of the 1993 Maastricht Treaty intended to harmonize social legislation (particularly that relating to employment) throughout the Union.

social cost The total cost to society of some economic activity, including the direct cost to the person or company performing it as well as any resulting cost to society (which cannot seek compensation).

social grade An alternative term for *socioeconomic group.*

socialism An economic system in which resources and the means of production are owned collectively, usually through the state. In an ideal socialist society, goods and services are produced for consumption rather than profit; there is no competition among producers; levels of investment, production and prices are set by the state; and wealth is distributed equitably. *See also* **capitalism; communism.**

social net product The difference between the *social benefit* and *social cost* of an economic activity.

social opportunity cost In using resources to produce a particular good, the amount of other goods that have to be done without because those resources have been consumed and are no longer available.

social overhead capital The types of capital goods that benefit everybody and cannot be closely associated with any particular production activity. Examples include the infrastructure (roads etc.), hospitals and schools.

social ownership The ownership of some or all of a countries industries by the state (on behalf of society in general).

social products An alternative term for **merit goods** or **public goods.**

socioeconomic group Also called social grade, a method of classifying people (and by inference their families) in one of six bands according to occupation, much used in economics and marketing. The grades are:

A top professionals and company directors

B senior managers

C1 clerical workers

C2 skilled workers

D semi-skilled or unskilled workers

E people dependent on the state

S

soft budget constraint A spending limit imposed on a public organization which knows that exceeding it will not result in serious consequences.

soft currency A currency of which there is a surplus on the market and which is therefore relatively cheap.

soft landing A successful result from trying to check inflation by applying just the right measures to reduce excess demand without undermining business confidence. *See also* **hard landing**.

soft loan A loan that carries an unusually low rate of interest, often advanced as a form of foreign aid.

sole proprietorship A non-company business owned by one person (ie not limited for liability).

sole trader A person who trades on his or her own behalf and has not registered as a business. In the financial world, a sole trader is 1. somebody who is involved in buying and selling securities short-term, for his or her own account; 2. somebody who specializes in buying and selling securities on behalf of a broker or dealer, usually working as an employee; 3. a person who buys and sells contracts in financial futures without a hedge in the appropriate cash market.

Solow growth model An economic model that concentrates on how advances in technology, as well as increases in investment and population, affect the growth of total gross domestic product. It was devised in 1970 by the US economist Robert Solow (1924-).

Solow residual The part of national income growth that cannot be attributed to growth in capital (denoted by profits) and labour (denoted by wages), which according to Solow results from advances in technology. The idea was developed by the US economist Robert Solow (1924-).

solvency The state of a person or company that is cash positive, and able to pay all bills as they fall due; ie its assets are more than its liabilities. Its converse is insolvency.

sound money Money that, through the government's monetary policy, stabilizes real purchasing power.

source and disposition of funds Also termed sources and uses of funds, a company statement outlining how it has raised funds and used then in a particular period.

S

sources of capital The sources from which companies and government organizations get their funds. They include borrowing from banks, government funding, issues of bonds and debentures, private savings, retained company profits, and sales of shares.

Southern Cone common market *See Mercosur.*

sovereign debt The debt of an independent nation's government, for which there is no legal redress—you cannot take a government to court.

spare capacity Equipment and/or labour that is not currently needed. It may be retained to meet a sudden demand or to cover for broken-down equipment or absent labour. *See also **excess capacity; organizational slack.***

special deposit An extra deposit, over and above the usual minimum reserve requirement, that a bank may have to make at the central bank. It may be imposed to control the money supply by limiting bank lending (and reducing bank profits). *See also **corset.***

Special Drawing Rights (SDR) A form of credit extended by the International Monetary Fund to its member countries as an addition to the credit they already hold. SDRs do not represent actual money, they are simply a form of credit, but they do not have to be repaid to the IMF and thus form a permanent addition to the reserves of each member country. Originally they were allocated in proportion to a country's subscription to the IMF, but since then additional allocations have been made. At first SDRs were valued in relation to the value of gold, but have since been valued in relation to the member country's own currency. SDRs may be exchanged between member countries or between those countries and the IMF.

specialization A situation in which a person or company concentrates on producing one particular good or service, and obtains other goods and services from other producers. It makes best use of specific skills and scarce resources; it is a type of ***division of labour.***

specie points For two currencies on the ***gold standard,*** the limits between which their exchange rates were allowed to fluctuate.

specific tax A tax that is levied at a fixed rate per physical unit of the thing being taxed (irrespective of its price). UK examples include the cost of a firearms certificate and a television receiving licence. *See also **ad valorem tax; value-added tax.***

S

speculation Broadly, the practice of making investments or going into a business that involves risk with the expectation that a profit can (theoretically) be made. The term is sometimes used with pejorative undertones to apply to investment for short-term gain and equates it with gambling. It has been said that the difference between speculation and gambling is in the expertise and experience of the speculator.

speculative demand for money The demand for money balances that are held in liquid form in order to be able to take immediate advantage of any favourable good deals on the financial market. It is inversely related to the current rate of interest.

speculative motive The reason why people and companies hold money balances (to avoid possible losses or capital gains). *See speculative demand for money.*

spill-over effect The awareness of a product in a country where it is not marketed, resulting from advertising in a neighbouring country (whose media may cross the national boundary).

sponsor An alternative description of an *issuing house* for a new issue of securities.

spot market A market in which the goods sold are available for immediate delivery. It is also known as the non-contract market.

spot price A price quoted for goods available for immediate delivery, usually higher than the forward price because it takes into account all costs except delivery.

spread Broadly, the difference between two (or sometimes more) prices, rates or values, such as the bid and offer prices on a market.

SRO Abbreviation of *self-regulatory organization.*

stability and growth pact An agreement signed in Dublin in 1996 among European Union countries that members of the Economic and Monetary Union (EMU) would strictly adhere to rules concerning balance of payments deficits.

stabilization Following a disturbance to a system, changing its behaviour so that it returns to—or more rapidly returns to—a state of equilibrium.

stabilization policy A once-popular set of government policies designed

S

to reduce fluctuations in the economy, particularly in national income. Examples included reducing demand to counteract inflation or increasing demand to combat unemployment. Today it has been replaced by the *Medium-Term Financial Strategy*, which is a non-stabilization policy.

stabilizer Something that acts to keep, eg, the economy or prices, stable. Also known as a built-in stabilizer, it is also the part of a system that stabilizes it to keep fluctuations to a minimum without direct intervention.

Stackelberg duopoly A type of *duopoly* in which one company leads and the other follows. The leader acts strategically, anticipating the follower's reactions, and the follower acts non-strategically, just following the leader with no anticipation.

stag A person who buys new issues of shares in the hope that he or she will be able to make a fast profit by selling them soon after trading opens on a stock exchange. With the UK privatization programme of the later 1980s, the number of stags increased.

stages of economic growth The phases that some economies have gone through historically, such as the five stages represented by Hunter-gathering, Animal hunting, Agriculture, Manufacturing industry and Service industry.

stagflation A mainly US term for a combination of high inflation and economic stagnation.

stagnation An economic situation in which there is little or no change in income levels or production methods.

stakeholder A person or group that, because of its involvement, has a direct interest in an organization's performance, such as employees and investors.

stamp duty A duty levied on the completion of certain transfer documents. For example, stamp duty is paid in the UK (on property over a certain value) when a person signs property transfer documents.

Standard and Poor (S & P) Ratings A classification of US securities in terms of risk, varying from AAA (Triple A), the highest, to DDD (in default).

standard deviation (SD) A statistical measure of dispersion (the spread of

S

a series of values around their mean) equal to the square root of the mean of the squared deviations.

Standard Industrial Classification (SIC) A method of classifying business, manufacturing and all commercial activity for statistical purposes. *See industrial classification.*

standard international trade classification (SITC) An international trade classification system adopted by the United Nations in 1950.

standardization The use or production of components that are identical and therefore fully interchangeable, a necessity for successful mass production (and the subsequent repair of such goods).

standardized commodity A commodity with interchangeable units produced to the same specification so that they can be traded on forward markets and future markets.

standard of deferred payment One of the properties of money which allows people making deals to specify values for future payments and receipts. *See also store of value.*

standard of living A measure of people's ability to purchase the goods and services they want.

standby arrangement A conditional arrangement, extending up to 3 years, that guarantees an International Monetary Fund member a specified amount of credit.

standby letter of credit (LC) A contractual arrangement guaranteeing economic or financial performance involving three parties: the 'issuer' (bank), 'account party' (bank customer) and 'beneficiary'. The bank guarantees that the account party will perform on a contract between the account party and the beneficiary. *See also letter of credit.*

staple commodity Also called primary commodity, a country's most important product (such as oil in some Middle Eastern countries).

state enterprise An undertaking initiated and controlled by the government, generally for the benefit – direct or indirect – of all its citizens, for example a nationalized industry.

statement of account A document issued by a creditor (to a debtor) detailing transactions to date and any balance still due.

state trading enterprise (STE) A government-established organization

S

that produces, exports and/or imports certain products (with various exclusive or special trading privileges).

static equilibrium An equilibrium whose contributing variables do not change over time (as opposed to *dynamic equilibrium*).

statistics 1. The branch of mathematics that deals with the collection of numerical data and its analysis. 2. The numerical data collected for analysis by statistical methods.

statutory company A UK company set up by Act of Parliament to produce essential services such as the provision of power and water.

statutory monopoly A monopoly that cannot legally have any rivals (such as the former status of the UK Post Office).

STE Abbreviation of *state trading enterprise.*

steady state In an economy, a condition in which all aggregates are the same: gross domestic product is constant, investment is zero, population growth is zero and there is no technical development. The labour force remains the same because those who retire are replaced by new entrants.

steady-state growth In an economy, a situation in which all aggregates grow at a constant rate (*see steady state*). If they grow proportionately at the *same* rate it is known as *balanced growth.*

sterilization In economics, the methods employed by the central bank to prevent the domestic money supply from being affected by balance-of-payments deficits or surpluses. It can sterilize cash outflow (to maintain the money supply) by buying securities and sterilize cash inflow (to decrease the money supply) by selling securities.

sterling See *pound sterling.*

sterling area See *scheduled territories.*

sterling bloc Countries of the British Commonwealth that fixed the exchange rate of sterling to favour trade within the bloc. See *scheduled territories.*

sticky wages Wage rates that do not quickly react to changes in the market. Employers are reluctant to increase wages at a time of temporary labour shortage (because of the difficulty of restoring them

S

to their former level) and workers are reluctant to accept a real reduction in wages (ie a wage increase that is less than the rate of inflation).

STMS Abbreviation of *short-term monetary support.*

stochastic Dependent only on chance; random. The outcome of a stochastic process is unpredictable because it involves a random element.

stock 1. A fixed-term security denominated in units of £100. 2. Generally in the USA, and sometimes in the UK, an alternative term for ordinary share. 3. The raw materials or manufactured goods held by a manufacturer, wholesaler, retailer or end-user (also known as stock-in-trade or inventory).

stock appreciation An increase in the worth of a company's stock (inventory), generally because of inflation.

stockbroker Formal name agency broker, somebody who gives advice and buys and sells stocks and shares on a stock exchange on behalf of clients.

stock control The processes used to make sure that the ordering, delivery and handling of a company's or retailer's stock is done efficiently.

stock dividend The issuing of a company's stock instead of a dividend. *See scrip issue.*

stock exchange Essentially a place where securities, stocks and shares are bought and sold. *See London Stock Exchange.*

stock exchange listing A company's inclusion among those that have their shares traded on a stock exchange.

stockholding cost Also termed inventory cost, the cost to a company of holding stocks of raw materials and finished goods, to meet any sudden demand for either. *See just-in-time.*

stock market An organized market in securities, stocks and shares; a stock exchange.

stock option A UK term for an option to apply for or take a company's shares.

stockpiling The building up of levels of stock (inventory), perhaps before launching a new product or in anticipation of a retail sale.

S

stocks *See stock.*

stock split A US term for a free bonus issue of shares to shareholders in some proportion to their existing holding, which has the effect of increasing the number of shares held but not the stake in the company.

stocktaking The task of counting (and often valuing) the stock-in-trade of an organization, such as a manufacturing company, wholesaler, retailer or end-user. The stock valuation appears in a company's financial records at the end of an accounting period. Some organizations carry out continuous stocktaking, often with the aid of a computer program.

stock valuation Also called inventory evaluation, another term for *stocktaking.*

Stolper-Samuelson theorem A theorem about the effects of trade between industries on the distribution of income in an economy. It states that such trade lowers real income from a country's scarce factor, which is heavily imported, and raises real income from a factor that is plentiful and heavily exported. It was postulated by the US economist Paul Samuelson (1915-).

stop-go cycle A government attempt to stabilize the economy by alternately stimulating aggregate demand and then trying to reduce it, but which in fact tends to enlarge the movements of the business cycle.

store of value One of the properties of money which allows people to hold it to fund some future purchase without losing purchasing power in the meantime. *See also* **standard of deferred payment.**

straight-line depreciation A method of calculating the rate of *depreciation* of an asset. A fixed proportion of the total original value of the asset is written off in each accounting period, making allowance for its current resale value either as a useful asset or as scrap (salvage value). Thus the depreciation at any one time is the asset's original cost less net residual value, divided by its predicted lifetime (in years).

strategic entry deterrence Any action taken by a company to dissuade competitors from entering its market, such as large **sunk costs** or attractively priced long-term customer contracts.

strategic trade policy A trade policy that is designed to make other countries alter their trade policies (to the advantage of the country which started it).

S

strategic trade retaliation A trade restriction that is imposed in retaliation to one made by another country and to dissuade it from making any more.

strengthening of a currency An increase in one currency's price in terms of another, usually because of an in crease in the demand for it.

strike price Also called striking price and exercise price, the price at which an option for the purchase or sale of a security is exercised.

structural budget deficit The amount of government borrowing if there were no recession or boom (an *output gap* of zero).

structural impediments initiative An agreement signed between Japan and the USA in 1990 with the intention of reducing the USA's balance-of-trade deficit with Japan.

structural transformation A large-scale change in a country's economy, such as a major shift of resources from the primary (agricultural) sector to the secondary (industrial) sector. A change from a planned economy to a market-based one would also be considered to be a structural transformation.

structural unemployment An unusually high level of unemployment caused by the change from a labour-intensive to a capital-intensive (often hi-tech) economy.

stylized facts Very broad generalizations; unprovable assumptions about real situations that claim to be true.

subcontractor A person or company that makes part of or all of a final product on behalf of another company. Some manufacturing contracts specifically do not permit the use of subcontractors.

subsidiarity The idea that policy decisions should be made at the lowest level consistent with their being effective (as opposed to the idea of centralized decision-making).

subsidiary A company that has more than 50% of its voting shares owned by another company (which is known as the parent or holding company).

subsidized credit Borrowing that is made available at favourable rates of interest (below current market rates). It is inefficient economically if the favourable rate is less than the rate of inflation (tantamount to a negative real interest rate).

S

subsidy A sum paid (by government) to companies in certain industries to enable them to sell their goods or services at a price close to the prevailing market price. A subsidy is also used to provide financial support to a commercial or quasi-commercial activity that would otherwise not be viable in narrow profit-and-loss terms, usually in order to sustain broader economic and social benefits.

subsistence level The minimum consumption level or income on which people can survive, well below the *poverty line.*

subsistence wage The lowest wage on which a worker can survive.

substitute Also called substitute product, any good or service that can be effectively used instead of another—a price rise in one increases the demand for the other.

substitute product *See substitute.*

substitution The switching from one good or service to another when the price of one of them rises. *See substitute.*

sufficient condition A factor that is adequate enough for a particular objective to be achieved, as opposed to a necessary condition, which must be present for the objective.

sunk cost A cost (usually of purchasing an asset) that has been incurred and can be accounted for as an asset even though its value is irrecoverable (eg the costs of earthworks for a building project). In this sense it is a type of historical cost.

superneutrality of money The idea that a change in an economy's money stock can affect only the rate of inflation and no other variable. *See neutrality of money.*

supernormal profits Profits that are more than usual for the industry concerned.

supply The provision of goods or services, or the amount of these available on the market.

supply and demand The two market forces that in microeconomic theory determine the prices of goods, services or investment instruments. If supply is low and demand high, prices increase. Conversely, if demand is low and supply high, prices fall (unless price controls are in operation).

S

supply curve A graph that shows, for a particular industry, how much companies will supply at every possible price.

supply schedule A table that list the various possible prices of a product along with how much of it can be supplied at each price.

supply services In the UK government's accounts (and budget), as approved by Parliament, an annual estimate of expenditures on such things as defence, education, the National Health Service, and so on.

supply-side economics A school of economics that developed in the USA in the late 1970s and early 1980s, emphasizing supply instead of demand in economic analysis, and particularly the disincentive effects of high taxes on productivity, investment and growth.

supply-side policy An economic policy that attempts to increase the total supply available by such measures as improving efficiency by reducing restrictive practices, improving productivity through better worker training, and so on.

surplus value The extra output that workers can produce over and above their needs.

supporting a currency The practice of actively buying securities or foreign exchange by an 'official' in order to stop their market value from falling. This most often happens when a central bank buys its own securities to stop the price falling and thus forestall a rise in interest rates.

support ratio The inverse of the *dependency ratio.*

suppressed inflation An inflationary trend that has been slowed down or completely halted, usually by extensive government intervention in the economy. It is also known as repressed inflation.

surcharge An extra charge imposed on certain goods, such as an added tax on imported goods (when it may be referred to as surtax).

surtax A higher rate of income tax formerly levied in the UK on high incomes, abolished in 1973. *See also* **surcharge.**

sustainable income That part of distributable income that a company can expect to earn in the next accounting period if it continues at its present level of activity.

S

sustained yield Using any natural resource, the output level that can be obtained continuously without jeopardizing future productivity. It can be achieved by replanting forests and restocking fisheries, for example.

swap A financial transaction in which assets are exchanged by two people.

syndicate A group of people who come together to work for a common aim, for example managing the issue of a security or underwriting risks for Lloyd's of London.

syndicated credit Credit, such as a large bank loan, made by a group of banks to a single borrower.

syndicated loan See *syndicated credit*.

synergy The additional benefits to be gained by the combination of hitherto separate activities. It is sometimes colloquially expressed as '2 + 2 = 5', and cited to justify the takeover or merger of companies with complementary or mutually reinforcing activities or resources.

systematic risk The risk that difficulties in any one financial market or institution may spread and cause problems for the whole system.

S

T

Taft-Hartley Act The common name of the US Labor-Management Relations Act 1947, which restricted trade union activities and banned the closed shop.

takeover The buying of a proportion of another company's shares so that the purchaser gains control of the company or its assets. *See also merger*.

takeover bid An offer by one company to buy a majority of the shares of another, thereby gaining control of the target company. It is often shortened to 'bid'.

Take-Over Panel A London Stock Exchange body responsible for seeing that the City Code on Takeovers and Mergers is observed by parties wishing to make a takeover bid.

take-up rate Among people who are entitled to a state benefit, the fraction that actually claims it (usually well below 100%).

tangible assets Literally, assets that may be touched, such as buildings or stock; they are also called tangibles. They may be contrasted with intangible (or invisible) assets, such as a company's goodwill or the expertise of its staff.

tap When the UK government makes a new issue on the gilt-edged security (gilt) market, it is very rarely fully subscribed. The remaining gilts in the issue are gradually released by the government broker and this action is known as a tap.

tap issue An issue of government securities direct to government departments rather than onto the open market. *See also **tender issue***.

target An objective towards which somebody or an organization is working. In corporate finance, 'the target' is a company that is the object of a takeover bid.

targeting Attempting to ensure that only particular groups receive state benefits rather than anybody who applies for them, by such methods as a *means test* or by providing *benefits in kind* rather than as cash.

target price The theoretical selling price set annually for farm produce under the Common Agricultural Policy of the European Commission. It may be achieved by purchasing goods at the *intervention* price.

target zone The range defined by the preferred upper and lower limits of a country's exchange rate.

tariff Generally, a list of charges made in return for goods or services. 1. More specifically, it is the list of dutiable goods and duty payable, issued by (in the UK) Her Majesty's Customs. 2. A system of charges in which a certain rate is payable up to a certain point (eg a certain quantity of goods) and then the rate changes beyond that point.

tatonnement A process that explains how a perfect market achieves equilibrium from any previous disequilibrium no matter the way by which prices change. At first, buyers and sellers make their own prices. Then if supply and demand are in balance in one area the prices are left alone; where there is insufficient demand, prices are reduced; and where there is excess demand, prices are increased. The process continues until all markets are in balance, and then (and only then) trading begins. The idea was first suggested by the French mathematical economist Marie Walras (1834-1910).

tax The money paid to central or local government to finance its expenditure and implement its financial policy. Various kinds of taxes are collected by the Inland Revenue in the UK (the Internal Revenue Service in the USA), HM Customs and Excise (in which case the tax is known as *duty*) and local government authorities. *See also rates; value-added tax (VAT).*

taxable income The income on which taxes are levied. It is calculated by deducting personal allowances (and any other tax-deductible expenses) from gross income.

tax allowance The deduction from gross income to give *taxable income*.

tax and price index (TPI) An index introduced in 1979 to compare levels of taxation with retail prices and relate them to average wage levels. The TPI is used to calculate the real spending power of the nation.

tax assessment A calculation of a person's income tax liability made by the Inland Revenue on the basis of a tax return. (If actual income figures are not available it may be estimated.) Alternatively, using self-assessment a person may calculate his or her own liability for income tax, but must still make a tax return to the Inland Revenue.

T

taxation The imposition and subsequent collection of tax.

taxation schedule A graph that illustrates the relationship between the receipts from taxation and the level or national expenditure or income.

tax avoidance The legal avoidance of or reduction in income tax, achieved by arranging one's financial affairs so as to take advantage all possible concessions. Such a device is also termed a tax shelter in the USA. Tax avoidance should not be confused with tax evasion (which is illegal).

tax base The form of income upon which tax is calculated. For example, the tax base for income tax is a person's taxable income, for corporation tax a company's profits.

tax-based income policy A policy of using higher taxes as an attempt to reduce inflation. The reasoning is that companies will make smaller increases in wages and prices if sudden rises in income attract very high taxes.

tax bracket The percentage of a person's income that he or she pays in tax depends on the level of income. Incomes are divided into brackets (ranges) for the purpose of calculating tax. The term is also applied to people in that bracket.

tax burden The total amount of taxes paid by a country's population, including corporation tax, excise duty, income tax and value-added tax, plus the cost of collecting them, generally expressed as a fraction of gross national product.

tax evasion The evasion of tax liabilities by providing false information to the Inland Revenue. It is a criminal offence in the UK. *See also **tax** avoidance*.

tax exile A person who lives abroad in order to minimize liability for tax.

tax expenditure The cost to the government of giving tax relief and making tax allowances. It is a way of using the tax system to increase incomes without the government appearing to spend any money.

tax haven A country (such as the Bahamas, the Cayman Islands, Liechtenstein and Monaco) that has liberal tax and banking regulations. In some instances it benefits companies to set up their registered offices in such a country, to avoid paying taxes in their own country.

T

tax holiday The period during which a start-up company need not pay taxes.

tax rebate Also called a tax refund, the repayment of tax that has already been paid (usually because it was assessed too high).

tax relief Concessions made to taxpayers in respect of certain liabilities (such as, at one time, mortgages).

tax return A document submitted to (in the UK) the Inland Revenue annually, stating a person's earnings and expenses for the year and used to calculate a person's tax liabilities.

tax revenue The government's income from taxes, both direct (such as income tax) and indirect (such as value-added tax).

tax shelter An investment instrument that does not attract tax. In the USA, the term is also used for *tax avoidance*. *See also* *tax haven*.

tax tolerance A population's willingness to endure high (or even higher) taxes, in little evidence in most countries in recent years.

tax wedge The difference between the extra money a worker gets for extra work and its cost to the employer (because the employer has to pay additional insurance contributions and so on).

tax year Another term for *fiscal year*.

tax yield The amount of money a tax actually raises (equal to the tax base times the tax rate minus the cost of collecting it).

technical efficiency For a production process, obtaining the largest possible output attainable from a particular set of inputs.

technical insolvency A situation in which a company's losses outweigh its share capital (ie it has negative assets), perhaps because of the cost of fighting a takeover battle.

technological gap theory An economic theory that attributes long-term change in the pattern of international trade to advances in technology and the innovations that accompany them. There is a time gap between the introduction and export of a new product by one (technically advanced) country and its home production by other countries.

T

technological unemployment A type of unemployment that results from technological advances in production methods (such as automation, which increases individual productivity but requires fewer workers).

technology gap The difference between the production techniques of two countries.

tender Generally, an offer to supply goods or services at a certain price and under certain conditions. A tender is usually submitted in response to an invitation to do so, normally in competition with other potential suppliers.

tender offer An offer for sale by tender. In the USA, it is an offer made to the shareholders of a public company to buy their holding at a certain price, normally above the current market price. This may be done by a company in order to effect a takeover.

tender issue The Bank of England's method of issuing Treasury bills in which the bills go to the highest bidder (usually a discount house) for a specified quantity of bills. See also *tap issue*.

term loan A fixed loan made for a specified number of years, unlike a demand loan which a borrower may be asked to repay at any time.

terms of trade An indication of a county's trading prospects, based on a comparison of its import prices and export prices.

term structure of interest rates The relation between the interest rate paid on a security and the unexpired time to its maturity (redemption date).

test discount rate In a UK nationalized industry, the real rate of return needed to justify investment in a commercial project.

tertiary sector A major part of a developed country's economy, concerned with service businesses. It is thus synonymous with the service industry.

test market A small defined geographical area in which a new product is launched to test its sales potential.

Thatcherism The economic policies of the UK government when Margaret Thatcher was Prime Minister between 1979 and 1990. They were characterized by deregulation and privatization of industry, the encouragement of competition, the use of monetary policy to combat inflation and a lessening of trade union power.

T

theory of consumer behaviour The economic theory that deals with the ways in which consumers allocate income when purchasing goods and services, based broadly on the assumption that consumers try to maximize satisfaction (utility).

theory of demand The economic theory that deals with the ways in which market demand (and supply) affects the prices and quantities traded of specific goods and services.

theory of markets The economic theory that deals with the ways in which scarce factors of production are shared among various markets for products, particularly as it affects prices.

theory of supply The economic theory that deals with the factors that affect market supply and ways in which supply (and demand) affects prices and quantities traded of specific goods and services.

theory of the firm The economic theory that deals with how companies use factor inputs to produce outputs of goods and services, and the decision-making involved in deciding prices and levels of production (assuming profit maximization is the chief aim).

third-degree price discrimination A type of price discrimination in which different categories of consumers are charged different prices (eg lower prices for students and retired people). *See also **first-degree price discrimination; second-degree price discrimination.***

third world A collective term for less developed and poor countries.

threshold The limit or point at which something changes.

threshold agreement An agreement between an employer and employees (or the representative trade union) that wages will increase only if the rate of inflation reaches or exceeds a certain level, the threshold.

thrift US shorthand for thrift and loans.

thrift and loans Financial institutions in the USA that are backed by an insurance fund and oriented towards the customer. They are also known as industrial banks. *See also **savings and loan association.***

tied aid Financial aid to a less developed country that is conditional on its being spent on products from the donor country.

tied loan A loan made by one country to another on condition that the money concerned is spent on the lending nation. Tied loans are a common form of foreign aid because they create employment and have no effect on the lending country's balance of payments.

tie-in sales The situation in which the supplier of a product requires the buyer to purchase also one or more other products—the tied products. It is a type of restrictive trade practice.

tight fiscal policy A fiscal policy that is intended to reduce demand, using such measures as lower government spending or higher taxes.

tight monetary policy A monetary policy that is intended to reduce demand, using such measures as making borrowing more difficult. *See* tight money.

tight money Money that is available only at a high rate of interest. It is created when the authorities reduce the money supply in an attempt to curtail the level of activity within the economy; funds therefore become scarce and thus attract higher interest rates.

time deposit Cash deposited in a bank and earning interest (as opposed to a non-interest earning demand deposit).

time discounting The practice of valuing future income or payments at a lower level that on the same income or payments occurring now. *See time preference.*

time horizon The longest time in the future that is considered in making current investment and other economic decisions.

time inconsistency A 'change of mind' that occurs some time in the future after the occurrence of some particular event. Governments have a reputation for not keeping their promises in this way.

time preference A theory of interest which suggests that interest is the price paid by the borrower for immediate consumption, and is compensation to the lender, who loses the opportunity to use the articles or money lent for his or her own purposes. Therefore, time preference is a person's preference for current rather than future consumption, or *vice versa*.

times covered The number of times profits exceed payments of interest, and therefore a measure of a company's ability to service a debt. It is also called income gearing.

T

time-series data Information about a single factor—person, company or even nation—that relates to a succession of periods of time, as opposed to cross-section data which comprises information about a number of factors in the same period of time.

Tobin's q *See q theory.*

Tobin tax A tax on dealings in foreign exchange, named after its proposer, the US economist James Tobin (1918-).

token coin A coin whose exchange value is more than the value of the metal from which it is made. Some gambling and vending machines take token coins.

Tokyo Round A round of international trade negotiations (the seventh) that began in 1973 and finished in 1979, in association with the General Agreement on Tariffs and Trade. Agreement was reached on the use of *countervailing duties*, a reduction of a third in the developed countries' tariffs, and on various other aspects of import controls.

total cost The total of all expenditure incurred in an accounting period, often divided into fixed cost and variable cost.

total domestic expenditure The total amount spent by a country's residents on *final products* (ie excluding *intermediate products* but including imports) plus general government final consumption.

total final expenditure The total *domestic expenditure* plus exports.

total physical product The total short-run output obtained using various quantities of variable-factor input.

total revenue For a company, the overall price obtained for a certain product multiplied by its quantity.

total utility For an individual, the overall satisfaction (utility) he or she obtains from the consumption of a certain amount of a product (in a given time).

tournament theory The idea that reward can be related to an economic agent's relative, rather than absolute, performance. As a result, the agents compete with each other, rather like competitors in a tournament.

TPI Abbreviation of *tax and price index.*

trade The business of buying and selling in general. In the USA, a trade may be another term for a bargain or deal.

tradeable Describing any good or service that can (at least in theory) be traded on the international market.

trade agreement An agreement between two or more countries or two groups of countries regarding general terms of trade.

trade association An organization that represents the interest of companies within a particular industry, especially in discussions with government.

trade balance An alternative term for *balance of trade.*

trade barrier Something that restricts or discourages trade, such as high levels of import duty or low import quotas.

trade creation The increase in international trade that follows the formation of a customs union or free trade area (with its abolition of trade barriers such as tariffs and quotas).

trade credit The credit one company or business gives to another, usually in the form of time to pay for goods or services supplied. *See also* **trade diversion.**

trade cycle The irregular pattern of movement in employment and prices, ie economic activity, which tends to go up (boom) and down (slump) cyclically.

trade debt A debt incurred by a company during the normal course of business as the result of non-payment of bills.

trade debtor A company or person who owes money for goods or services received.

trade deficit An excess of a county's imports over exports, resulting in a negative balance of payments.

trade discount A discount offered to trade customers, ie to customers who are likely to place large and regular orders. A trade discount therefore recognizes the value of the customer concerned.

trade diversion After the formation of a customs union or free trade area (with its abolition of trade barriers such as tariffs and quotas), the trade between members that replaces trade with non-members. *See also* **trade creation.**

T

trade gap In an adverse balance of trade, the difference between the values of imports and exports.

trade integration The setting up of free trade between countries by means of a free trade area, a customs union, a common market or—the most comprehensive—an economic union.

trade investment An investment in capital goods related to existing business, or in a new business in an established sector.

trade liberalization The removal of restrictions on international trade. *See trade creation; trade diversion; trade integration.*

trademark A logo or name (trade name) used to distinguish one manufacturer's product from another's. Registered trademarks may not be used by another manufacturer in the country of registration.

tradeoff The exchanging one thing for another. Goods may be traded off against each other, but so may many other things, such as the terms of an agreement.

trade sanctions The banning or severe limitation of trade between two countries imposed by one of them as a punitive action against the other.

trade war A retaliatory action, such as an embargo, by one government against another that has imposed tariff barriers against its exports.

trade-weighted index An index number, such as a price index, weighted in proportion to the share that other countries have in a country's trade, generally used to work out the effective exchange rate with those countries.

trading currency The currency used on an invoice for international trade. It can be that of one of the trading countries or even of a third country (such as US dollars).

transaction cost The cost incurred by certain transactions, such as sales and purchases.

transactions demand for money The practice by people or companies of holding money as cash or in highly liquid form to fund short-term future expenditure.

transactions in external assets and liabilities An account that lists sales and purchases of overseas assets by UK citizens and sales and purchases of UK assets by foreigners. It constitutes the capital account of the balance of payments.

transactions motive The motive behind the *transactions demand for money.*

transfer costs The total opportunity costs of transferring raw materials or finished goods between locations, including administration and handling as well as actual transport.

transfer deed A document that proves the sale of a property or registered stock. To make the transfer official, the seller must sign the deed. In the case of registered stock, the document is also known as a stock transfer deed or transfer form.

transfer earnings The amount a factor of production has to earn before it is worth transferring it to its next best use. Any earnings in excess of this is *economic rent.*

transfer payment A payment made by the UK government that is not in return for goods or services, such as state pensions and unemployment benefit.

transfer price Within a group of companies, the price at which goods or services are sold by one subsidiary to another.

transformation curve A graph of the total amount of one good or service that could be produced by reducing production of a second one and moving the resources so saved to the first.

transitional unemployment A type of unemployment that results from a major shake-up in the organization of an economy (such as after a war or after a change to a market economy from a centrally-planned one). Less-skilled workers are likely to remain unemployed while new job opportunities are being created.

transitivity If product combination X is preferred to product combination Y, and Y is preferred to combination Z, the principle of transitivity states that X will be preferred to Z.

transmission mechanism The ways in which changes in interest rates, prices or money supply work their way through the economy and have an effect of aggregate demand and, possibly, exchange rates.

transparent policy measures Government policies that can be seen in

T

action with regard to who makes them, what they consist of and what they cost (as opposed to *opaque policy measures*).

transplant A good or service, previously imported, that is now made in the country that once imported it (eg cars made in South America by US companies or in the UK by Japanese companies).

transport cost The cost of moving things between locations. Such costs are higher for perishable, fragile or bulky goods.

Treasury The government department that deals with national finance and government funding, and is responsible for the execution of the government's financial policy. Some large companies also have treasury departments.

Treasury bill 1. In the UK, a government bill of exchange issued in £5,000 denominations to discount houses at a discount on its face value and repayable on a certain date (usually 91 days hence). 2. In the USA, often abbreviated to T-bill, it is a short-term bill of exchange issued by the US Treasury in $10,000 denominations.

Treaty of Rome A treaty signed in 1951 that established the European Economic Community (EEC), which has now become the European Union (EU).

trend A direction of movement in prices (or another parameter), which may be measured over periods of time, and possibly extrapolated into the future.

trend growth An economy's long-term sustainable growth, assuming a constant level of inflation.

trickle-down theory A theory according to which the money put into the pockets of those who are already rich through government policy is thought to seep down into the hands of those who are less well off. Trickle-down is thought by some economists to be a more effective method of redistributing wealth than are *transfer payments*.

triple-A rating In the rating of US stocks and bonds, the highest rating a stock may achieve.

trough The lowest level of activity or real incomes in a *trade cycle*.

true and fair view A view of a company's affairs that an auditor of its accounts is required to take in giving an opinion.

T

trust 1. A group of companies that join forces to create a cartel, or in some cases a monopoly. In the later sense it is more often used in the USA, eg in the term anti-trust law. 2. A sum of money or property placed in the care of a group of trustees, to be managed (although not necessarily invested) for the benefit of an individual or an organization such as a charity. 3. In the securities industry, an investment operation that is managed by a group of trustees on behalf of other people, such as a unit trust.

turnkey contract A contract, found especially in the computer and construction industries, in which a supplier provides a complete customized package to a client (who has merely to 'turn the key' and take over the package).

turnover The gross value of all sales made by a company during an accounting period; total sales revenue. The term is also used for the rate at which stock or some other asset is turned over (the turnover rate).

turnover tax A type of sales tax that is levied at each stage along the distribution chain. Value-added tax (VAT) is an example.

two-gap model The idea that a less developed country's development is hampered by two gaps—one between export revenue and the imports required for development and one between domestic savings and the required level of investment.

two-part tariff A system of charges comprising two elements. In some cases, a fixed sum is supplemented by a variable sum (eg a taxi driver may make a fixed charge and then add a certain amount depending on the time of day and the time the journey has taken, or the distance travelled).

T

U

UA Abbreviation of *unit of account.*

UDEAC Abbreviation of *Central African Customs and Economic Union.*

U-form organization Short for unitary-form, describing a company structure that has centralized management with undermanagers for various functions (such as finance, production and marketing). *See also M-form organization.*

unanticipated inflation Future inflation that takes companies, consumers and workers (through trade unions) by surprise because, unlike *anticipated inflation*, it is not expected.

unavoidable cost Cost that has to be met no matter what course of action is taken. *See also avoidable cost.*

unbundling A colloquial term for *asset-stripping.*

uncalled capital Money owed to a company on partly-paid shares. It exists as a reserve to be called upon at any time by the directors of a company.

uncertainty An event whose outcome can only be estimated, as opposed to *risk.*

uncompetitive Describing any economic activity that does not make a profit, generally because the price of a good or service is too high.

UNCTAD Abbreviation of *United Nations Conference on Trade and Development.*

undated security Also called irredeemable security, a fixed-interest security that has no redemption date attached.

undercapitalization The financial situation of a company that does not have enough capital to take it through the initial burn-out period immediately after start-up.

underground economy That part of a country's economy controlled by organized crime. It is better controlled and more concentrated than the *black economy.*

underlying rate of inflation The rate of inflation determined by the Retail
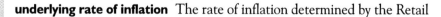

Price Index and ignoring the effect of mortgage interest rates (RPIX), as opposed to the headline rate of inflation which does include mortgages.

undersubscription The situation that occurs when there are fewer applicants for a new issue of shares than there are shares on offer. *See also underwriting.*

undervalued currency A currency that has been oversold, ie its value has fallen below market value usually because of government intervention to make its country's export prices more competitive.

underwriting 1. Activity of a person or organization (often a merchant bank) that takes up a proportion of the risk of something, eg an underwriter may take up the shares of an issue that are not taken up by the public, in return for a commission. For the issuer, the underwriter represents a guarantee that the whole issue sill be subscribed. 2. The process of assessing proposals and/or risks for insurance.

undistributable reserves Company reserves that may not be distributed (as dividend to shareholders), including the capital redemption reserve, most unrealized profits, share capital and the share premium account.

undistributed earnings Also called undistributed profit, an alternative term for *retained income.*

UNDP Abbreviation of *United Nations Development Programme.*

unearned income Any income not derived from work or fees of office (such as dividends on shares and interest on investments). It is liable for income tax in the UK, at the same rate as earned income. In the USA, the term denotes advances received from customers (ie, money received before goods or services are delivered), also called deferred credit or unearned revenue.

unemployment In economic terms, not using all the available labour resources, leading to a level of production that is less than it could be. In personal terms, the state of being out of a job (when willing and able to have one). Economists have many terms for the various forms of unemployment (*see* under the following adjectives in this Dictionary: *classical, concealed, cyclical, demographic, disguised, frictional, involuntary, Keynesian, long-term, search, seasonal, structural, technological, transitional* and *voluntary*).

unemployment rate The proportion of the labour force that is without a job (but willing and able to work), expressed as a percentage.

unemployment trap The situation that arises when unemployment benefit lessens the desire to find work.

unfair competition A claim by a company that its rivals are employing practices with which it cannot (or is unwilling to) compete.

unified budget A government budget that includes both spending plans (expenditure) and proposals for taxation (revenue), as employed since 1990 by the UK government.

uniform business rate A UK tax, set nationally but levied at a local level on businesses, to pay for services such as street cleaning and refuse collection.

unitary taxation A system in some US states whereby a company is liable to pay tax not only on gains made from operating within that state but also on revenue generated elsewhere.

unit cost The cost of producing one item. It is calculated by taking the total cost of production and dividing it by the number of units produced. It is used mainly in determining the price that should be charged for a product. A unit cost may also be assigned to sales (as the cost of selling one item).

unit elasticity A situation in which a change in one economic variable is matched by an equal change in another.

United Nations Conference on Trade and Development (UNCTAD) A multinational organization founded in 1964 under the auspices of the United Nations to represent less developed countries and press for more aid to, investment in and trade with these countries.

United Nations Development Programme (UNDP) A multinational organization established under the auspices of the United Nations to provide soft loans and technical help to less developed countries.

United Nations Monetary and Financial Conference 1944 Also called the Bretton Woods Conference (after its location at Bretton Woods, New Hampshire, USA), a conference that considered post-World War II international financial relations and established the International Monetary Fund and the International Bank for Reconstruction and Development (World Bank).

unit of account (UA) A standard unit used in statements about the financial activities of international financial organizations, such as the European currency unit (ECU) used by the European Monetary System and therefore not necessarily a tangible unit.

unit trust A trust into which investors may buy by acquiring units. The capital collected in this way is invested in various securities in a wide range of markets. Contributors to unit trusts benefit from the diverse nature of the portfolio built up, and from the expertise of a fund manager.

universal agent An agent with unlimited authority to close contracts on behalf of the principal. *See also* **special agent.**

unlimited company A company that consists of members who are all liable for the total of the company's debts. *See* **limited company.**

unlimited liability The liability of the members of an unlimited company, or of the general partners in a partnership, or of the sole proprietor of a sole proprietorship. *See* **limited liability.**

Unlisted Securities Market (USM) A former market for shares that do not fulfil the requirements for a full quotation on the London Stock Exchange, or that do not wish to be quoted, but which do fulfil certain less stringent requirements. It closed in 1996 to be replaced by the *Alternative Investment Market.*

unofficial economy The economic activities that do not comply with legal and tax rules, ranging from paid occasional help (eg with gardening) to large-scale trafficking in drugs. *See also* **black economy; grey economy.**

unrequited exports Exports that are used in the settlement of previous debts and so have no corresponding inward flow of goods or money in payment.

unsecured loan Also called an unsecured debt, a loan made without any security such as a charge on the assets of the borrower.

untied aid Financial aid to other countries 'with no strings attached'—it can be spent on goods and services from anywhere (unlike *tied aid*).

upward-sloping demand curve A *demand curve* that shows that demand increases as price rises, as opposed to the normal situation in which the curve slopes downwards (demand decreases as price rises). *See also Giffen good.*

urban economics The part of economics that deals with highly populated areas, including their special problems (eg congestion and pollution).

Uruguay Round The eighth round of trade talks under the *General Agreement of Tariffs and Trade* (GATT) held in 1986 (and continuing until 1994) at Punta del Este, Uruguay. Among its achievements were the *Multi-Fibre Arrangement* and a new *General Agreement on Trade in Services.*

USM Abbreviation of *Unlisted Securities Market.*

US Trade Representative A US organization, part of the Executive Office of the President, which conducts trade talks and decides US trade policy.

usury Moneylending at an (undefined) excessive rate of interest, not in itself illegal.

util A proposed but still hypothetical unit for measuring utility (in the economic sense of satisfaction or individual welfare).

utilitarianism The idea that organizations, governments and indeed societies should be rated in terms of how well they provide for people's welfare—'the greatest good for the greatest number'. It was championed by the UK philosopher Jeremy Bentham (1748-1832).

utility 1. The satisfaction, or individual welfare, that a person derives from consuming a food or service. 2. An industry that provides basic necessities such as power or a clean water supply, also termed a *public utility.*

utility function A relationship between utility and the quantities of goods and services a person consumes (an increasing function). There are also other functions relating utility to income, labour (work choice), prices and wages. For example quantities of goods and services consumed are made proportional to their prices.

utility maximization A way of explaining consumers' choices in terms of their utility functions, which they try to maximize.

U-turn A sudden reversal of a decision or policy, such as a government's economic policy when it is overtaken by events (or when it fails).

V

vacancy rate The number of unfilled jobs among those available expressed as a percentage of the total available workforce.

value A term that is not as precise as it may seem. The value of something is the price a buyer is prepared to pay for it, but this can fluctuate according to all sorts of variables, for example whether it is a buyer's market or a seller's market, to what use the buyer will be putting the item, and so on. Usually the term is qualified, to minimize possible confusion.

value added The difference between the price a company or industry pays for its materials and the price at which it sells finished goods. For example, a used-car dealer may acquire a car, recondition the engine and repaint the body. When the dealer sells the car, the added value is the value of these operations as reflected in the new (higher) selling price of the car.

value-added tax (VAT) A form of indirect taxation in which the producer, seller and consumer pay a percentage of the value added to the product or service. For example, if a manufacturer buys raw materials at £10 per unit and sells each unit of product for £20, the value added is £10. The manufacturer is required to pay a percentage of the £20 in VAT, and can claim back the VAT paid on the £10-worth of materials. VAT in the UK is 17.5 per cent for most things (since April 1991), although some goods and services are exempt and some zero-rated.

value-for-money audit An audit of a non-profit making organization, such as a charity or government department, to check that it working efficiently and giving value for money.

value in exchange The value of something as form of exchange, rather than as an object of use. For example, precious stones are worth virtually nothing in terms of real value in use but because they are rare and desirable, they command a high price. *See also* **value in use**.

value in use The value of something to the person using it, which may be different to the sale value of the object. For example, a machine may be valuable to its owner because it produces goods for sale, whereas it may be valueless in itself, perhaps because it cannot be moved. In accounting terms, an asset's value in use can be calculated by discounting the future cashflows that would accrue from its continued use. *See also value in exchange.*

value judgement An opinion of how good (or bad) something is that cannot be tested quantitatively (ie made a matter of fact). *See normative economics.*

value paradox An object or commodity may be valuable in terms of exchange, but totally worthless in terms of use. Equally, a thing may be extremely valuable in use but is inexpensive to acquire. For example, salt or water are very useful commodities, but are fairly cheap. Most precious stones may be said to be totally useless, but are expensive to buy because they are so rare. The value paradox is this apparently illogical assignment of value. *See also value in use; value in exchange.*

value-subtracting industry An industry in which value added is negative—the value of the output is less than that of the inputs. This may happen if it is highly subsidized or if real current prices are not employed (as happened in some state-owned enerprises in former centrally-planned economies).

variable cost Also called direct cost, an expense that varies with the level of activity, such as costs incurred in production that vary depending on the quantity of output.

variable factor input A factor input that can be easily varied in the short term to meet the requirement for increased or decreased production. The facility with which one factor input can replace another is termed variable factor proportions.

variety The number of different products in a company's product range, differentiated by brand name, price or specification.

VAT Abbreviation of *value-added tax.*

VCTS Abbreviation of *Venture Capital Trust Scheme.*

Veblen effect The idea that consumers' demand for a particular good increases as price increases (*see upward-sloping demand curve*) because of *conspicuous consumption*. It was put forward by the US economist Thorstein Veblen (1857-1929).

velocity of circulation A measure of total transactions (eg national income such as gross domestic product, GDP) divided by the money supply, equivalent to the number of times each money unit has been used to purchase the GDP—the speed at which money circulates.

venture capital Also known as risk capital, capital invested in a venture (usually a young company, often in high-technology areas) that presents a risk.

Venture Capital Trust Scheme (VCTS) A scheme established in 1993 that gives incentives (such as tax-free dividends) to corporate investors in unquoted companies.

VER Abbreviation of *voluntary export restraint.*

vertical diversification Diversification into industries or businesses at different stages of production to the diversifying company. *See also horizontal diversification.*

vertical integration The amalgamation of companies involved in different stages of production in the same industry, for example to form one company capable of extracting raw materials, using them to produce goods and then distributing and selling the manufactured product.

vertical merger A merger between two companies, one of which is a major supplier of the other (they operate at different stages of production).

vertical restraints Conditions or restrictions placed on a buyer by a seller (or vice versa), such as *tie-in sales* and *resale price maintenance.*

very long run A time period that is long enough for new production methods (resulting from innovation and invention) to be generally adopted.

visible balance An alternative term for *balance of trade.*

visible exports Also known as visibles, goods sold to foreign buyers and shipped abroad. The difference between the value of visible exports and visible imports is the balance of trade.

visible imports Tangible products that are imported; imports of goods rather than of services.

visibles A short term for visible exports.

visible trade The trade in *visible exports* and *visible imports.*

volatility A measure of the stability of a particular financial instrument. If, say, a share price or a market index moves often and oscillates wildly, it is said to be volatile.

volume index A measure of consumption or production based on a weighted average of the consumption or production of a representative 'basket' of goods and services. *See Laspeyres index; Paasche index.*

voluntary exchange A type of exchange in which each of the two parties is completely free to choose not to trade. If the exchange takes place, both parties gain (or neither loses).

voluntary export restraint (VER) Also called voluntary export restriction, a limitation on certain types of exports from one country to another (or group of countries) in order to forestall the imposition of import quotas or other restrictions by importing countries. It is often preceded by a voluntary restraint agreement, stating that this is what the exporting country intends to do.

voluntary group A wholesaler that supplies a group of (small) retailers, who receive favourable prices in return for placing a certain amount of business with the wholesaler. The voluntary group, in turn, gets price discounts from manufacturers because of its purchasing power.

voluntary liquidation Also termed voluntary winding-up, the liquidation of a company that has decided to cease trading, rather than one that has gone bankrupt.

voluntary unemployment A type of unemployment that results when workers refuse to take jobs because the wages are too low (perhaps compared to unemployment benefit available).

voting rights The rights of a shareholder to vote at a company's annual general meeting (AGM). This right depends on which type of shares are held; generally, ordinary shares carry voting rights whereas debentures do not. The articles of association and the company's prospectus detail which shares carry voting rights and which do not.

voting shares Company shares that carry *voting rights.*

voucher A document (such as a receipt or invoice) that supports or proves entries in a book of prime entry. A voucher is also the name given to a paper given in place of money (such as a gift voucher or a luncheon voucher).

V

W

wage differential The difference between levels of wages, caused by many variables, such as occupation, industry, sex and age of employee, geographical location, experience and qualification of the employee, and so on.

wage drift The difference between actual wages received (including commission, bonuses, overtime etc.) and the nationally agreed *wage rate.*

wage economy 1. An economy in which most of the peoples' income is from wages. 2. An informal term for the earned income in an economy.

wage freeze A situation in which wages are fixed for a certain period of time, either by government authority on a national level or by agreement within a single company or industry.

wage-price spiral A self-sustaining form of inflation. If a producer is forced to increase wages, he or she must increase the price of the product to cover the increased wages cost, which in turn leads to new wage demands by workers. It is also termed an *inflationary spiral.*

wage rate The wage paid for the normal number of working hours (exclusive of bonuses and before tax). Higher rates may be paid for overtime, unsocial hours, weekend working, and so on.

wage restraint A voluntary agreement between government and trade unions that wage increases will be modest in an attempt to combat inflation. It is generally a more acceptable policy that a *wage freeze.*

wages A payment made to a worker, normally at a fixed rate per hour, day or week (and usually paid weekly). *See also salary; wage rate.*

wage stickiness The reluctance of wages to fall when there is an excess of supply in the labour market.

Wall Street The brief name for the New York Stock Exchange (which is located in Wall Street, Manhattan). Sometimes the name is further abbreviated to *The Street.*

Walras's law In an economy where people do not save (ie they spend all their money), the total value of goods demanded equals the total value of goods supplied. So that if demand equals supply for all but one of the markets in an economy, the two must also be equal in the remaining market. The law was formulated by the French economist Marie Walras (1834-1910).

warrant (WT) 1. A receipt that describes goods held in a warehouse, transferable by endorsement. In this sense a warfinger warrant (also known as a warfinger receipt) is a similar receipt describing goods on a warf. 2. A long-dated option. 3. A security of a specific market value that may be exchanged for a certain share at a predetermined price. The warrant's value lies in the difference between the predetermined conversion price and the current market price of the share.

warranted growth rate The rate at which economic growth must occur if it is to be sustained (according to the *Harrod-Domar economic growth model*), equal to the savings ratio (savings as a fraction of national income) divided by the capital/output ratio.

warranty A promise by a manufacturer or seller to correct any defects in goods sold. In some manufacturing companies, an amount is estimated as possible warranty expense and treated as a liability.

wasting asset An asset that has a limited useful life (such as an irreplaceable natural resource that becomes depleted as it is consumed).

Ways and Means Advance An advance paid by the Bank of England to the *consolidated fund.*

weakening of a currency The situation in which a currency's price falls in terms of other currencies, usually because of a fall in the demand for it or because of a strengthening of other currencies.

wealth The total of a person's or a country's assets, both tangible and intangible.

wealth effect The effect that changes in somebody's wealth has on savings and consumption. Because most people's wealth is tied up in property, the wealth effect may be correlated with property values.

wealth tax A tax levied annually on wealth (which is notoriously difficult to define). It is used in some European countries but not in the UK.

wear and tear A popular and legal term for *depreciation.* It is the decrease in value of an item due to deterioration through normal use rather than through accident or negligence.

welfare General well-being; with the resources needed for a satisfying life. *See also* **utility**.

welfare criterion A way of assessing whether or not to make a proposed economic change by considering people's welfare. For example, *see* **Pareto optimality**.

welfare economics A branch of **normative economics** that deals with how economic activity ought to be organized to achieve maximum welfare. Inevitably it involves making **value judgements**.

welfare state A society that aims to provide at least a minimum standard of living for all of its members, including basic income, education, housing and medical care, as well as various benefits such as those for sickness, unemployment and after retirement.

wholesale price The price of goods traded wholesale, often in bulk or large quantities. It includes the price of bulk raw materials used as inputs and large quantities of products (outputs). *See* **wholesaler**.

Wholesale Price Index A measure of inflation that takes into account prices of raw materials and wholesale prices charged by producers.

wholesaler A person who buys goods in bulk from a producer and then sells them in smaller quantities to retailers or other wholesalers, earning a profit either by charging a commission to the retailer or by adding to the manufacturer's price. *See* **mark-up**.

Williamson trade-off model A way of analysing the possible results of a company merger in terms of lower costs (benefits) and higher prices (detriments). The model was devised by Oliver Williamson. *See also* **discretionary competition policy**.

windfall gain or loss A gain or loss resulting from circumstances outside the control of the recipient (such as changes in the net present value of earnings because of changes in discount rates).

windfall tax A once-only tax levied on British privatized companies under the terms of the budget of 1977 (it was 23%, payable in two annual instalments). The term has now been extended to include other such taxes.

winding-up The cessation of a company's business activity and the start-up of its **liquidation**.

window-dressing Another term for creative accounting, in which a favourable account sheet is created (without resort to actual fraud).

WIP Abbreviation of *work in progress.*

withdrawals An alternative term for *leakages from the circular flow of incomes.*

withholding tax A tax on the interest on a deposit or investment deducted at source (the depositor or investor receives net interest).

worker-controlled firm A business (usually labour-intensive) that is owned and controlled by the people who work for it.

worker participation The involvement of employees in the planning and management of an organization.

workers' cooperative An alternative term for *worker-controlled firm.*

working capital The capital available for the day-to-day running of a company, used to pay such expenses as salaries, purchases, and so on.

working population An alternative term for *labour force.*

work in progress (WIP) (The value of) goods currently under manufacture or services being supplied, but not completed at the end of an accounting period.

World Trade Organization (WTO) A free trade organization encompassing more than 100 countries which superseded the *General Agreement on Tariffs and Trade (GATT).*

write down To take the cost of an asset and deduct the amount by which it has depreciated in capital terms. This gives its written-down or book value. *See also depreciation.*

write off To charge the whole of the value of an asset to expenses or loss (ie, assign it zero value on the balance sheet). It is also known as charge off in the USA. *Bad debts* may also be written off.

WT Abbreviation of *warrant.*

WTO Abbreviation of *World Trade Organization.*

X

X-efficiency A type of *efficiency* in which there is no slack in the production process—for any input the maximum technically-possible output is obtained. It is a measure of the management's effectiveness.

X-inefficiency A situation in which there is slack in the production process—a failure to get the maximum possible output from a given input. It is a symptom of ineffective management.

Y

yardstick competition A situation in an industry with monopoly producers where a regulator fixes a maximum permissible price (usually based on the average costs to the producers). A company that can sell at prices below this 'yardstick' stands to make more profit that its rivals.

yield The return on an investment, taking into account the annual income and the capital value of the investment, usually expressed as a percentage. There are also various other methods of calculating yield.

yield curve The usual tendency for a security's yield to rise with increasing maturity.

yield gap The difference in average yield between investments in ordinary shares and in gilt-edged securities.

Z

ZBB Abbreviation of *zero-based budgeting.*

zero-based budget (ZBB) A budget calculated as through it were being prepared for the first time using a zero base (with no initial commitment to spend on any activity).

zero growth The situation in an economy in which there is no expansion. *See also* **stagnation**.

zero-rated goods and services Goods and services that are liable for *value-added tax* **(VAT)** but are currently rated at zero tax.

zero-sum game In *game theory*, a situation in which one player's gain is the same as the other players' losses, no matter what the strategy adopted. Applied to a non-expanding market with two rival companies, it means that one company can increase sales only of the other's sales decrease.

Z